Hoeksche Waard
AIR-ZUIDWAARTS / SOUTHBOUND
New Landscape Frontiers

THOTH Publishers Bussum
AIR Foundation Rotterdam

contents
AIR-ZUIDWAARTS / SOUTHBOUND

4 INTRODUCTION
- 5 WYTZE PATIJN
- 6 ADRIAAN VAN DER STAAY
- 7 MIRJAM SALET

8 PROGRAMME
- 10 ANNE-MIE DEVOLDER

18 RESEARCH
- 20 VISUAL RESEARCH
- 21 JOHN DAVIES
- 24 HET OBSERVATORIUM
- 25 MARK PIMLOTT
- 26 SCHIE 2.0
- 28 HENRIK HÅKANSSON
- 30 AD VAN DENDEREN
- 32 WIJNANDA DEROO
- 34 BERTIEN VAN MANEN
- 36 HANS VAN HOUWELINGEN
- 37 BIRTHE LEEMEIJER
- 38 JOOST GROOTENS
- 40 JAN KONINGS/ESTER VAN DE WIEL
- 42 HONORÉ δ'O
- 44 ANTHROPOLOGICAL RESEARCH
- 46 HENK DE HAAN
- 50 PHYSICAL PLANNING RESEARCH
- 54 SJOERD CUSVELLER

66 DESIGN TASK	**72 DESIGN RESEARCH**	**140 AFTERTHOUGHTS**	**153 APPENDIX**
68 SJOERD CUSVELLER/ ANNE-MIE DEVOLDER	74 FRITS PALMBOOM/JAAP VAN DEN BOUT 84 PETER CALTHORPE/MATTHEW TAECKER 92 STEFANO BOERI 100 FRANÇOIS ROCHE 108 DETTMAR/BEUTER/FRITZ/HASTENPFLUG 114 BINDELS/GIETEMA/HARTZEMA/KLOK 122 MARIEKE TIMMERMANS 132 DIRK SIJMONS/YTTJE FEDDES	142 ARNOLD REIJNDORP 146 BROESI/JANNINK/VELDHUIS 149 ERIC LUITEN	154 CHRONICLE 156 PERSONAL PARTICULARS 158 PERSONS INVOLVED 160 COLOPHON

AIR-ZUIDWAARTS / SOUTHBOUND	INTRODUCTION	PROGRAMME	RESEARCH	DESIGN TASK	DESIGN RESEARCH	AFTERTHOUGHTS	APPENDIX
4	**WYTZE PATIJN** ADRIAAN VAN DER STAAY MIRJAM SALET	ANNE-MIE DEVOLDER	**VISUAL RESEARCH** JOHN DAVIES HET OBSERVATORIUM MARK PIMLOTT SCHIE 2.0 HENRIK HÅKANSSON AD VAN DENDEREN WIJNANDA DEROO BERTIEN VAN MANEN HANS VAN HOUWELINGEN BIRTHE LEEMEIJER JOOST GROOTENS JAN KONINGS/ESTER VAN DE WIEL HONORÉ δ'O **ANTHROPOLOGICAL RESEARCH** HENK DE HAAN **PHYSICAL PLANNING RESEARCH** SJOERD CUSVELLER	SJOERD CUSVELLER/ ANNE-MIE DEVOLDER	FRITS PALMBOOM/JAAP VAN DEN BOUT PETER CALTHORPE/MATTHEW TAECKER STEFANO BOERI FRANÇOIS ROCHE DETTMAR/BEUTER/FRITZ/HASTENPFLUG BINDELS/GIETEMA/HARTZEMA/KLOK MARIEKE TIMMERMANS DIRK SIJMONS/YTTJE FEDDES	ARNOLD REIJNDORP BROESI/JANNINK/VELDHUIS ERIC LUITEN	CHRONICLE PERSONAL PARTICULARS PERSONS INVOLVED COLOPHON

photo: Wijnanda Deroo

INTRODUCTION

WYTZE PATIJN
ADRIAAN VAN DER STAAY
MIRJAM SALET

You can't stop a landscape

The Dutch landscape is pre-eminently a man-made affair. Centuries of water management, processing and polder formation express our control of both city and landscape. Our nature has to a large extent been devised and constructed. One of our country's most striking characteristics is openness and vastness. The horizon is resolutely present and so also the sky and the clouds.

Our countryside has changed a lot this century. It is no longer countryside in a traditional, agrarian sense. Other enterprises, in a finely-woven structure, have for the most part added new economic meaning. These past decades have seen urbanization manifesting itself in earnest. More so than in previous centuries there have been changes, modifications and most especially additions. Often in the most brutal manner, without taking the special character of the landscape into account. Many feel that this process of increasing urbanization is unstoppable and that its progress can scarcely be resisted. I think they are right. Many also feel that this process cannot be brought under control, guided or structured, since economic development needs to be given free rein. I think they are wrong.

The question of whether one can urbanize with circumspection, inspired by landscape values, has been penetratingly asked by the manifestation AIR-Zuidwaarts/Southbound and divergently answered by various designers by means of design research. The result is a magnificent study. I consider it of great importance to bring this study to everyone's attention. It shows that a different approach is indeed possible. That the choice between free economic development with unbridled urbanization, and the conservation and maintenance of a landscape, is a non-choice.

A landscape cannot be brought to a halt. The issue is how this urbanization can take place with the landscape as explicit departure-point. AIR-Zuidwaarts/Southbound shows possible ways of achieving this. These can bring our thinking on urbanization and landscape to another level.

Wytze Patijn
Government Architect

The effects of an enterprise

The effects of an enterprise like AIR-Zuidwaarts/Southbound cannot be assessed with any certainty in the short term. However, towards the end of the project it could be seen to offer inspiration and encouragement in very different directions.

Firstly in the direction of the inhabitants of the researched areas, namely Hoeksche Waard and the delta as a whole. These are exposed to 'inevitable' developments in the shape of road networks, residential areas, industry and commercial sites. Nor do the administrators of the agrarian regions in particular, appear to have much choice. It is understandable that reactions to AIR were somewhat sceptical at first.

AIR-Zuidwaarts/Southbound did not harbour the illusion that it could protect Hoeksche Waard from every external influence. What we did intend, however, was to present a diversity of intelligent solutions. If the administrators and the population have more options than just being for or against, it widens the perspective of an open discussion about the future. It will then be possible to say yes to one issue and no to another. And not just for the sake of saying it, but with conviction and in concert. Unlike the initial fairly widespread belief that it was scarcely possible to debate the future of Hoeksche Waard and the delta constructively, today there is a wider commitment to discussing their future. Many factors have contributed to this improved climate. One of which, if what they say is true, is AIR-Zuidwaarts/Southbound.

Another area in which we hope AIR may have an effect is among the designers of the proposals. The proposals collected and commented upon in this book demonstrate that spatial planning can go beyond developing noncommittal scenarios. Although it was not AIR's intention to elicit immediately workable plans and then execute them, it was hoped that in the long run something of the results would eventually filter through to day-to-day practice.

AIR-Zuidwaarts/Southbound mobilized the creativity of national and international designers to give the most concrete shape to their submissions. They have not chosen the easy way out either. Adopting the long-term perspective explicitly offered by AIR, they have tackled a number of difficult issues which customarily remain beyond the horizon of day-to-day design work. I am not thinking so much of changes in mobility and economy, which are bound to occur, but rather of the less recognized problems of the changing environment in the delta. On the one hand they bring our entire traditional water management under discussion, on the other they raise the question of whether an intelligent environmental management cannot make a virtue of necessity.

A more general effect may perhaps be mentioned, one wider than the impact on population, administrators and experts alone. In a mental climate dominated by market-oriented thinking and globalization, public opinion soon lapses into apathy. The willingness of many to contribute to AIR-Zuidwaarts/Southbound, to take part in the discussions, to take a position on problems and to work hard because they believe in something, not because it may earn good money, is encouraging. At century's end, this is a healthy sign. It shows that early twentieth-century Utopianism and the horrors that followed, have not led to a Fall of the West, to a weary 'Après nous le déluge', but to new ambitions and imaginative powers. May this book stimulate a design for our future that is vibrant, forceful and out of the ordinary, also in those less heeded parts of the Netherlands and so too of the world.

Adriaan van der Staay
Chairman of the Board, AIR Foundation

INTRODUCTION

WYTZE PATIJN
ADRIAAN VAN DER STAAY
MIRJAM SALET

Hoeksche Waard rediscovered

Rotterdam and artists are matters looked upon somewhat askance in Hoeksche Waard. This was also the initial reaction to the arrival there of AIR-Zuidwaarts/Southbound. All those arty types and designers, wasn't this just a presage of the Rotterdam wish to asphalt our region? An artistic wolf in sheep's clothing? The request for financial support for the project by the municipalities of Hoeksche Waard was preceded by plenty of discussion in the committees and councils. Even after conclusion of the design phase, many inhabitants of Hoeksche Waard are still sceptical.

But not all. For something quite unexpected happened along the way: Hoeksche Waard was rediscovered. Not as an empty region where you can only find clods of clay, but as a place with a fully fledged identity of its own and wonderful wide views, water and fields of flowering Bildstar potatoes.

Out of respect for this identity, analyses and designs were made that exhibited a wealth of imagination and creativity. Not all the designs were ultimately considered realistic, but they did inspire. Thus the discussion on what is the most desired development for the region, received a new impulse, but it also increased confidence and an awareness of quality.

A few Hoeksche Waard participants in AIR-Zuidwaarts/Southbound have intimated that they wish to continue the discussion on the quality of the region. This implies that thinking about the value and the future of the region has gained a firm footing. This is a good thing for all its inhabitants and their administrations, especially since recent developments prove how uncertain that future is. The various parties look upon Hoeksche Waard in quite different ways. For that reason alone, it is useful for the region to continue independently, not in a defensive stance but creatively. If they succeed in keeping track of reality yet dare to let imagination take over from time to time, AIR-Zuidwaarts/Southbound will to my mind have made an inspiring and valuable contribution.

Mirjam Salet
Mayor of 's-Gravendeel

AIR-ZUIDWAARTS / SOUTHBOUND

The programme of AIR-Zuidwaarts/Southbound unfolded as a symphony in three parts. The overture THE DISCOVERY OF HOEKSCHE WAARD was mainly a study of the social and cultural history, identity and characteristics, dynamics and resistance of the island by visual artists and scientists for the purpose of sketching a framework for the design commission. The second part THE EXPLORATION OF HOEKSCHE WAARD was the link between visual research and design research. In October 1998 a three days' international conference took place. The conference was concluded with the establishment of the design commission. The finale THE FUTURE OF HOEKSCHE WAARD focused on the results of the design research. The final chord was the symposium on the future of Hoeksche Waard and the agenda of Dutch physical planning on the basis of the design results.

PROGRAMME
ANNE-MIE DEVOLDER

AIR-ZUIDWAARTS/SOUTHBOUND	INTRODUCTION	PROGRAMME	RESEARCH	DESIGN TASK	DESIGN RESEARCH	AFTERTHOUGHTS	APPENDIX
	WYTZE PATIJN ADRIAAN VAN DER STAAY MIRJAM SALET	ANNE-MIE DEVOLDER	**VISUAL RESEARCH** JOHN DAVIES HET OBSERVATORIUM MARK PIMLOTT SCHIE 2.0 HENRIK HÅKANSSON AD VAN DENDEREN WIJNANDA DEROO BERTIEN VAN MANEN HANS VAN HOUWELINGEN BIRTHE LEEMEIJER JOOST GROOTENS JAN KONINGS/ESTER VAN DE WIEL HONORÉ δ'O **ANTHROPOLOGICAL RESEARCH** HENK DE HAAN **PHYSICAL PLANNING RESEARCH** SJOERD CUSVELLER	SJOERD CUSVELLER/ ANNE-MIE DEVOLDER	FRITS PALMBOOM/JAAP VAN DEN BOUT PETER CALTHORPE/MATTHEW TAECKER STEFANO BOERI FRANÇOIS ROCHE DETTMAR/BEUTER/FRITZ/HASTENPFLUG BINDELS/GIETEMA/HARTZEMA/KLOK MARIEKE TIMMERMANS DIRK SIJMONS/YTTJE FEDDES	ARNOLD REIJNDORP BROESI/JANNINK/VELDHUIS ERIC LUITEN	CHRONICLE PERSONAL PARTICULARS PERSONS INVOLVED COLOPHON

AIR-Zuidwaarts/Southbound
Waar het landschap begint/New Landscape Frontiers

From 4 September 1998 to 8 August 1999 the sixth AIR event (Architecture International Rotterdam) took place at various locations in Rotterdam and Hoeksche Waard. The subject of 'AIR Zuidwaarts/Southbound' was the spatial design of the southernmost area of the Randstad and the delta between Rotterdam and Antwerp. The event more especially focused on the cultural-historical landscape of the isle of Hoeksche Waard, south of Rotterdam, an agricultural area feeling the pressure of urbanization. The relationship between the island's dikes, villages, monumental farms and nature runs the risk of being disrupted. Loss of agriculture, new demands on water management and increasing pressure of urbanization on Hoeksche Waard will effect irreversible changes. AIR-Zuidwaarts/Southbound embarked on a search for new concepts for this area primarily aimed at synthesizing new urban functions with the landscape and cultural-historical values of the rural area. This interdisciplinary architecture festival yielded numerous designs, visions and strategies for a new relationship between town and country and the relationship between urbanization, mobility, agriculture, nature and recreation. This is the report of a quest to find the components of the design task, and of AIR-Zuidwaarts/Southbound's cultural impact on the national debate. At an early stage the City of Rotterdam, Hoeksche Waard municipalities and the Province of Zuid-Holland gave their support to the theme and the objectives of AIR-Zuidwaarts/Southbound.

Southbound
Traditionally, the east-west direction has always been the most important for Rotterdam. The port moved westward, but the principal hinterland has, for years, been Germany. In addition, the north-south direction (from Schiphol via Rotterdam and the port of Antwerp to the economic centre of Europe) has been becoming increasingly significant. One of its consequences is the ever greater pressure of urbanization on the delta and the coastal area south of the Randstad: Hoeksche Waard. This build-up of urban and industrial activity has yet to lead to major interventions. However, the map of north-west Europe demonstrates that Hoeksche Waard's position is less marginal than it initially seemed. The island is part of the Rhine-Scheldt delta, and is a crucial north-south link between Rotterdam and Antwerp. The reported developments cannot remain without consequence for Hoeksche Waard.

New landscape frontiers
From the start AIR events have always acted as a catalyst to trigger off and stimulate the debate on new urban development.[1] For that purpose attention is drawn to developments and challenges whose outlines were just visible at that moment. AIR seeks to draw attention to such developments at an early stage to make the issues clearer, sharpen the debate and suggest perspectives for solutions.
AIR Zuidwaarts/Southbound selected the Rhine-Scheldt delta and Hoeksche Waard as a subject. This choice was prompted by the following observations.[2]
1. Spatial design in the Netherlands is applied too much from a limited national perspective. Besides, the idea persists that town and country are polar opposites, and that interventions will inevitably lead to a loss of rural character. These 'certitudes' are very relevant issues for Hoeksche Waard today.
2. One element in the complex task of AIR-Zuidwaarts/Southbound concerns the landscape as a collection of memories. The area's emptiness and openness are, to a certain extent, of relative significance. In reality the topography reflects many cultural-historical layers which are used intensively. For Hoeksche Waard is the outcome of a history of occupation spanning many generations. The old trenches and creeks, the artefacts that recall the struggle against floods and silting, the dikes and polder borders, the division of properties, the churches, mills and ribbons of farms are all elements that tell Hoeksche Waard story. Landscape design is almost always a precarious matter because the population, the users and visitors are fond of places, views and relics. Landscape positions us in space and time.
3. As the city grows and leisure and mobility increase, a significant trend may be discerned: the increasing demand for recreation, quiet and green space in the vicinity of the city.
4. Dissatisfaction with the appearance of current urban expansion, recreational facilities, industrial zones, man-made nature and large

Three AIR-magazines

civil engineering works in the Netherlands is making its presence felt. More consideration should be given to what these users of space have in common before a welter of plans are drawn up for individual areas of attention.

5. It was time to carefully explore the possibility of a planning process for the rural area that would take account of and sustain the typical characteristics of a region.

Hoeksche Waard as a subject of research

Ordnance survey maps including Hoeksche Waard show it to be part of a larger entity in three different ways.

First, Hoeksche Waard is increasingly feeling the effects of the economic force field developing at right angles to the rivers between Rotterdam and Antwerp. The gradual 'overspill' of Rotterdammers to places like Oud-Beijerland, Strijen and Klaaswaal, the arrival of businesses on the outskirts of the villages and the rapidly swelling daily tailbacks at the tunnels and bridges are visible consequences. Construction of the high-speed rail link (HSL) and plans for the A4, both vital components of the so-called north-south corridor are harbingers, on the macro scale, of further activity in the area. The proposed development of a substantial industrial site at the crossroads of two motorways is a further contributory factor.

Second, Hoeksche Waard is part of the conglomerate of Zuid-Holland and Zeeland islands that have gradually been reclaimed from the tidal area of the Rhine and Scheldt rivers and the North Sea. This quality will have a twofold effect on possible changes in water management and spatial use. Its location in the delta may be seized upon and parts of the area made to play a role as a buffer and as a reservoir of potable, industrial, rain and river water. The ecological qualities of salt marshes and mud flats outside the dikes may be improved by enlarging their surface area and connecting them with the lowest-lying land inside the dikes.

Last but certainly not least, there is Hoeksche Waard's significance as an agricultural 'field' in the Dutch delta. Developments in agriculture, horticulture and glasshouse cultivation has increased substantially in the past two decades. With seawater banished from Haringvliet and Volkerak by the Delta Works and land parcels, roads and water courses streamlined in the interests of land consolidation, the conditions for production are good. However, in the light of future European agricultural policy both the organization and the produce of Hoeksche Waard agriculture will change.

Hoeksche Waard is a planning arena that does not so much encourage the question of whether all developments – including glasshouse construction and the arrival of new businesses – may or may not take place, but rather where, in what sequence and at what scale. Even if government should refrain from calling for large-scale changes on the island, Hoeksche Waard will steadily change colour in that the six municipal councils, the district water board and the landowners will at all times continue to respond to the changing conditions inside and outside the region – just as they have always done. Besides, it is conceivable that if the agricultural 'counter-pressure' gradually eases off, the area will rapidly see various other land use forms arrive. This is a development that may even be observed in the protected Green Heart. AIR-Zuidwaarts/Southbound has been seeking possibilities for old and new to go together harmoniously. Options in which the landscape will have a future without loss of its current cultural-historical value; options which offer new economic perspectives.

Local identity and regional design

If policy does not change, current urbanization of the area around the Randstad will continue unhindered, leading to drastic consequences at various levels: for its inhabitants and users, for the much valued open landscapes, for the region's spatial diversity and for the relationship between city and country.

AIR-Zuidwaarts/Southbound has been searching for a response to 'urban pressure' that does more justice to the landscape's value, the social and cultural significance of existing structures and the attendant developments. The findings on physical-spatial developments in Hoeksche Waard and the social and cultural layeredness of the area in relation to that of the Rotterdam region will gain relevance if they are studied in a wider context of urbanization trends and rural developments elsewhere in Europe.

On the one hand, AIR-Zuidwaarts/Southbound seeks to pick up on the international discourse on the significance of the local identity of regions in tomorrow's Europe. On the other, it set out to confront policy-makers, authorities and politicians with ground-breaking visions on regional design issues.

As with previous AIR events, there is little intention of putting directly into practice the results of the design task of AIR-Zuidwaarts/Southbound. AIR instead aimed to trigger off national or international discussion with new issues and tasks. AIR-Zuidwaarts/Southbound sought to boost integrated regional design for the rural area. This was achieved by interpreting and assessing the qualities and significance of Hoeksche Waard. Both the romantic position on rurality (everything remains as it is) and the modernistic position (everything changes) are redefined in the metaposition. AIR looked for the substance of this metaposition, which would transcend the familiar romantic and modernistic views and thus make such concepts as 'urban landscape' and 'urban field' more meaningful for regional design on the scale of the Netherlands and Europe.

From research to design

AIR-Zuidwaarts/Southbound was a symphony in three movements. The first part, *Discovering Hoeksche Waard*, more especially studied the island's social and cultural history, identity and characteristics, and its resistance and dynamics. From this it was possible to draw up a framework for the design task. The spatial and social characteristics, and thus the region's identity, were variously brought into view proceeding from a number of research issues. Visual artists, photographers, designers, anthropologists, authors and new-media designers literally charted the region's qualities.[3]

Part two, *Exploring Hoeksche Waard*, gathered together the different strands of the task. A three-day international conference was held in October 1998 as a link between the visual-arts and design research. Its key topic was Hoeksche Waard in the Rhine-Scheldt delta. The reader[4] published in conjunction with the international conference, contained the results of the visual, anthropological and spatial research and presented and discussed the results of the first phase. The programmes of the various authorities – Hoeksche Waard municipalities, the Province of Zuid-Holland, the City of Rotterdam, Hoeksche Waard pressure groups – were explained and critiqued. As changes in Hoeksche Waard are comparable to processes elsewhere in Europe, the contributions from expert 'key speakers' were most inspiring and informative. The conference ended with a definition of the design task,[5] which concentrated on the need for new combinations of programmes and innovative design methods. What, how much and where is construction possible in Hoeksche Waard without disrupting characteristic landscape values? This approach effectively rules out rampant urbanization.

The second AIR-magazine published a diversity of impressions and reports of the international conference.[6]

The finale, *Hoeksche Waard's Future*, was a major exhibition in the Netherlands Architecture Institute. This focused on the concepts, visions and strategies for the island's future development. The visual artists' research served as a run-up to the presentation of the designs. But there was more. For urban planning is a discipline that does not respect static, aesthetic images, which is why it is difficult to confine to drawings or models. Much more than architecture, it engenders discussion and decision-making. The visual resources act literally as the medium between the various pressure groups engaged in their exchange of views. The result in practice is almost always different from what the drawing once conjured up. Urban planning is the discipline of permanent change. This definition of the profession and the issues referred to by AIR-Zuidwaarts/Southbound established the exhibition design. The exhibition itself became a platform for debate: the visual resources further the dialogue between the visitors and the designs, and the discussion between the various pressure groups and designers. The opening of the exhibition coincided with the appearance of the third AIR-magazine. This used text and visuals to make the designs accessible to the public at large.[7] This last phase concluded with the symposium at which administrators, investors, scientists, trade and industry and pressure groups debated, on the strength of the design results, the future of Hoeksche Waard and the agenda of Dutch spatial planning.[8]

Excursions, exhibitions, picnics, meetings with artists, and Architecture Day in and around Hoeksche Waard had been organized simultaneously with the exhibition. This way the public could themselves experience the characteristic landscapes and regional architecture in the crossover between city, port and rural area through the eyes of the photographers, artists, architects and planners, archaeologists and architectural historians.

The yield

The designers of AIR-Zuidwaarts/Southbound presented the large regional scale as an integrated design task. They looked upon globalization, mobility changes, agriculture, water management, nature and the environment as forces that have an effect on spatial issues. Surveying the results, all the designs illustrate this new attitude towards unavoidable change. The fear of impending urbanization and the call for renewal of rural areas have been taken seriously. Without questioning the spatial characteristics of the region, all the designers submitted proposals that encouraged vitality into the region and the delta. They introduced such issues as ecological development of agriculture, nature and water, increased space for water reservation, tourism, natural conservation, and dwelling. Inspired by rural qualities, region-specific concepts were worked up to solve the spatial problems. Together with the development strategies and concrete proposals they are valuable contributions to the debate on designing the Netherlands.

Other than in the often abstract planning discussions on the alleged contrast between town and country, the present designers not only made the decisions more sharply focused, they also gave new impetus to the contents. All designs were communicative and accessible to a wide public.

The debates on the schemes brought essential matters to light. Practically all the designers were guided by water management and the design of rural areas and its potential. These are aspects which play a minor role in current spatial planning and in the debates. Therefore it is not a choice on the basis of existing administrative structures, sectoral or institutionalized, but one rooted in an integrated, socio-cultural approach. The design teams pointed out the

The international conference at Lantaren/Venster, October 1998

photo: Tineke de Lange

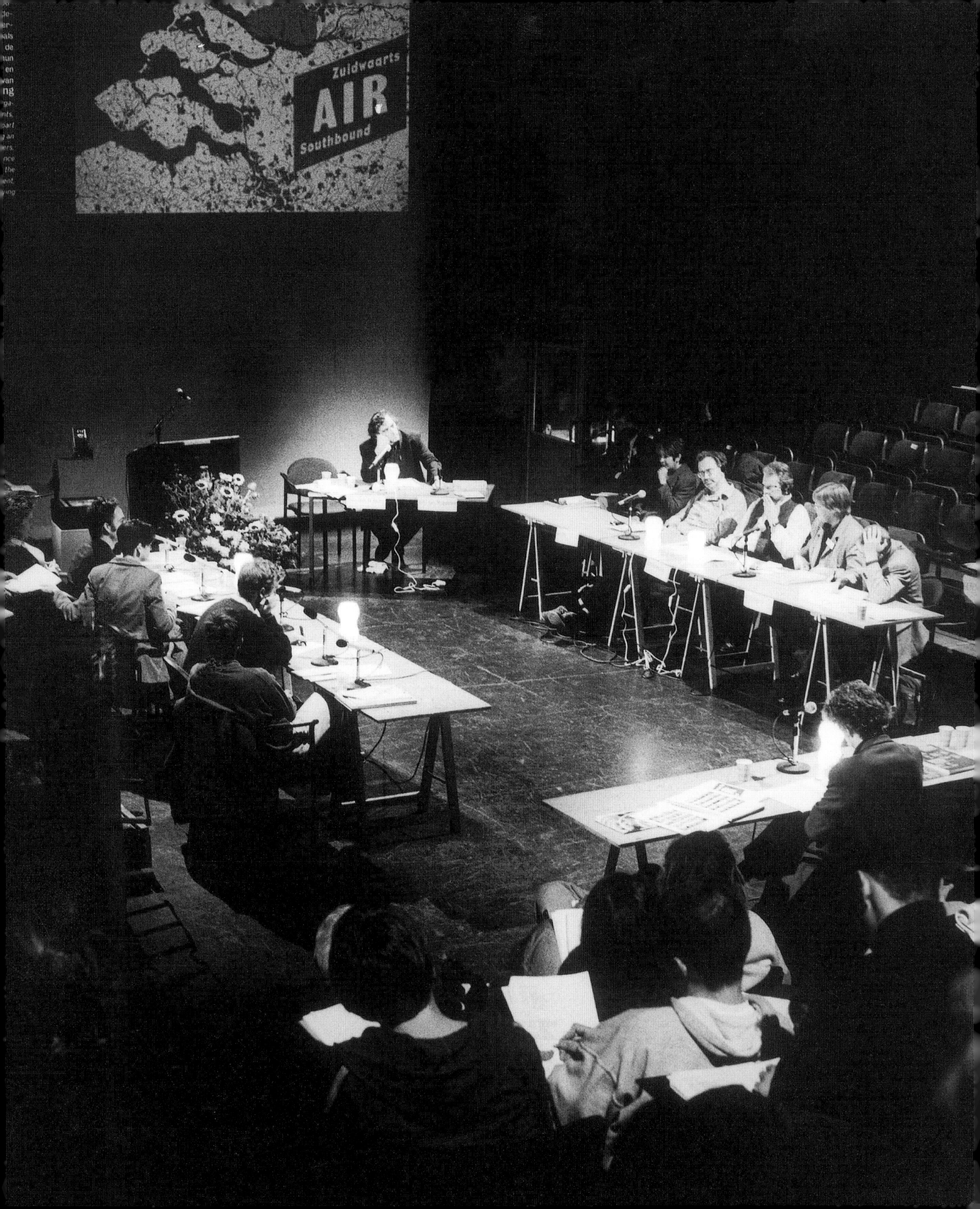
Zuidwaarts
AIR
Southbound

AIR-ZUIDWAARTS / SOUTHBOUND

PROGRAMME

ANNE-MIE DEVOLDER

Exhibition 'Waar het landschap begint/New Landscape Frontiers', Netherlands Architecture Institute, May-August 1999
photos: Thijs Wolzak

15

PROGRAMME
ANNE-MIE DEVOLDER

importance of spatial design focused on exploiting specific opportunities and supporting agricultural developments which capitalize on the close proximity of urban amenities and the market. There must also be support for the regional, touristic product based on the qualities of the Rhine-Scheldt delta and the vicinity of the Randstad. Moreover, effectuation of a new water-management system must be promoted, one predicated upon a new balance between salt-water movements and freshwater needs. Finally, there were calls to support an intelligent mode of reapplying traditional architecture and construction.

It gradually became clear that the spatial quality of steadily urbanizing regions like Hoeksche Waard has increasingly become subject to processes of differing scope. There are designers who want to place each of these scale upheavals in its own territory, there are others who accept and visualize them, and others still who want to harmonize them by adopting a mediating role and introducing an intermediate scale. On the subject of spatial design as a reconnaissance of the future, there were schemes made that proceeded from thinking in scenarios, schemes that explicitly chose between the urban and rural frontiers, and others that aimed for a concrete development programme. All the designers without exception were critical of the equal status customarily accorded to the various spatial targets. They expressly looked for a meaningful distinction between dominant and derivative spatial processes or they explicitly proposed an ideal sequence of enacting.

Art as a means for reinterpretation and for attracting a wider audience

AIR-Zuidwaarts/Southbound's interdisciplinary programming has resulted in a different way of researching, defining and imaging Hoeksche Waard, bringing a firmer grasp of the dynamics and resistance of one area in the changing urban field.

Exploring and exceeding the boundaries between the various disciplines was one of the ways to encourage a dialogue on the cultural-historical identity and the area's local qualities.[9] Moreover, the interdisciplinary formula enabled other cultural organizations to join in from their own field of activity. Witte de With (centre for contemporary art), Rotterdam Arts Centre (CBK), six Rotterdam galleries, the Rotterdam Theatre, the Rotterdam Foundation for Education through the Arts (SKVR), 'Kunstgebouw Rijswijk', the Rotterdam Academy of Architecture, ArchiCenter Rotterdam, V2_Organisatie and the Boijmans Van Beuningen Museum all organized their own activities. The upshot is that the theme of AIR-Zuidwaarts/Southbound penetrated further than the Rotterdam area and people outside the disciplines involved became interested in the position and problematics of the rural area of Hoeksche Waard.

The effect

Interestingly, the media regularly devoted their energies to AIR throughout the year. Newspapers, professional journals, radio and TV gave a great deal of time to the event. AIR has turned Hoeksche Waard into a cultural issue by placing it in the spotlight. The public at large has been able to get acquainted with it. As AIR-Zuidwaarts/Southbound progressed, support grew for the landscape as a framework for integrating design and policy. Not only were local chauvinism and local pride in the island's identity boosted, initial scepticism changed into enthusiasm for the designers' contributions to the discussion on the future of Hoeksche Waard.

In September 1999 AIR-Zuidwaarts/Southbound was presented at the third Urban Planning Biennial in Herne (Germany), whose subject was sustainable development of urban regions. On the initiative of a group of Hoeksche Waard dwellers, the exhibition of the designs 'AIR Hoeksche Waard: Where do we go from here?' was shown in Hoeksche Waard from 7 October to mid November 1999. At the same time discussions on the island's future were held with groups from the community, regional politicians and administrators. The visions and concepts for the future of Hoeksche Waard by the eight design teams served as the basis and inspiration for these meetings.

A not insignificant spin-off of the event's design research is the effect it has had on national politics. On 26 August 1999 the Government decided that there is to be no extra space for glasshouses and a mere 100 hectares are to be reserved for a new industrial site on the north side. On 6 October 1999 a motion was passed in the Dutch Parliament to 'draw up in deliberation with the municipalities concerned a development plan, "Hoeksche Waard National Landscape", with an attendant investment programme' with the purpose of conserving and protecting the landscape's open character.

For well over a year, the area-specific character of Hoeksche Waard landscape was the subject of an intelligent and inspiring confrontation between artists, scientists, designers, administrators and the local population. Everyone was able to picture in their own way the concepts and visions because these were so strong. The outcome of AIR-Zuidwaarts/Southbound now turn out to be just as significant for other areas faced with the same task. All the more so since the changing rural area around large conurbations under pressure of urbanization is a very real theme today.

Now that the Central Government is preparing its Fifth Report on Spatial Planning, it is not just an all-in vision from the landscape-quality perspective on the future design of rural areas that needs debating, but also how this is to be guided and brought to fruition.

Thanks are due to Bart Lootsma, Eric Luiten, Olof Koekebakker, Bernard Colenbrander and Arnold Reijndorp for the use I have made of their contributions.

1. See AIR Chronicle, pp. 154-155
2. The event was an initiative of the Rotterdam Arts Council. The Architecture section, chaired by Prof. Willem Frijhoff, selected the subject for this sixth edition of AIR. The initial notes for the event were prepared by a study group of the Architecture section. The Rotterdam Arts Council set up a foundation, stichting AIR, to organize the event. The foundation's director and board were advised by a programming committee chaired by Christine de Baan
3. 'De Ontdekking van de Hoeksche Waard' (Discovering Hoeksche Waard), a stichting AIR publication
4. 'Waar het landschap begint/New Landscape Frontiers'. Conference reader 29-31 October, a stichting AIR publication
5. See 'The design task', Sjoerd Cusveller and Anne-Mie Devolder, pp. 68-71
6. 'De Verkenning van de Hoeksche Waard' (Exploring Hoeksche Waard), a stichting AIR publication
7. 'De Toekomst van de Hoeksche Waard' (Hoeksche Waard's Future), a stichting AIR publication
8. See the essays by Broesi/Jannink/Veldhuis and Eric Luiten, pp. 146-151
9. On this procedure and its impact on other fields of art and culture, see the essay by Arnold Reijndorp, pp. 142-145

AIR-ZUIDWAARTS / SOUTHBOUND

At the invitation of the AIR Foundation a number of visual artists, photographers and designers from the Netherlands and from abroad stayed two weeks in Hoeksche Waard. They were asked to investigate the regional identity and authenticity, the atmosphere, the stories and myths, the social and cultural stratification, and the physical-spatial character of Hoeksche Waard. The photographers were asked to focus primarily on visible transformations of the countryside, like the memories stored in the landscape, the artificial and the natural features of the Dutch landscape, the changes noticeable both at the level of the landscape and the street, the culture of the youth, the asylum seekers, the native population and immigrants, those living and working in Hoeksche Waard. The designers were commissioned to explore 'unknown' aspects and hidden information in the area for the 'mental map' of Hoeksche Waard. Their task was to trace other kinds of spatial patterns and densifications, which either increase the quality of the location or 'catalogue' the typical features of Hoeksche Waard. The results of this exploration should inspire the designing of programmes on a small scale. The visual artists were presented with the following key questions:

1. The changing relation between Hoeksche Waard and Rotterdam and the south wing of the Randstad in a European perspective: how is the function of the agricultural and horticultural region in Hoeksche Waard changing in light of the growing interest in ecological restoration, recreational tourism or European agricultural and horticultural policy?

2. What defines the social and cultural identity of Hoeksche Waard? How are the various environmental and historical structures experienced? What are the norms and values among the various villages and hamlets? Does something like a social and cultural identity characteristic of Hoeksche Waard exist and, if so, what determines it?

3. Myth and reality: In what way is the myth of the so-called 'virginal' condition of Hoeksche Waard landscape cultivated and activated? How is it refuted? What changes did the landscape undergo and is it still undergoing? How is this visible in the landscape?

4. Exchange and interrelationship between town and countryside: the change from agricultural to recreational landscape, the change from the migration of Hoeksche Waard dwellers to Rotterdam, to Rotterdammers migrating to Hoeksche Waard. What is urban in Hoeksche Waard, what is rural in Rotterdam? Where does urbanization end, where does the rural begin? How is the (cultural) landscape and the urban palpable and visible in the countryside?

5. Globalization: How contemporary is Hoeksche Waard? How internationally oriented is Hoeksche Waard? How and in what way is Hoeksche Waard interwoven with global economy?

6. The island feeling: Due to the construction of tunnels and roads, but also to the prevailing physical and visual inaccessibility of the riverbanks, environmentally Hoeksche Waard is no longer to be recognized as an island. What is it that defines the island feeling or the island mentality? Is Hoeksche Waard an indivisible entity? Can one say 'I am from Hoeksche Waard'? How is this something defined, what aspects of the regional characteristics and environmental features of the island play a part in it?

RESEARCH

VISUAL RESEARCH
JOHN DAVIES
HET OBSERVATORIUM
MARK PIMLOTT
SCHIE 2.0
HENRIK HÅKANSSON
AD VAN DENDEREN
WIJNANDA DEROO
BERTIEN VAN MANEN
HANS VAN HOUWELINGEN
BIRTHE LEEMEIJER
JOOST GROOTENS
JAN KONINGS/ESTER VAN DE WIEL
HONORÉ δ'O

AIR-ZUIDWAARTS / SOUTHBOUND

Visual Research

JOHN DAVIES In the series 'Signs of Nature' Davies was looking for traces of tradition and renewal in the landscape. He photographed all the windmills of Hoeksche Waard; windmills surrounded by terraced houses, in expanding industrial complexes; but also the archetype of the isolated mill in the landscape where time seems to have stopped. He also recorded the parcelling out of the land. In the new districts canals straight as arrows are dug and houses built in rigid order. One day, these human interventions will be experienced as 'natural' and 'authentic'. (pag. 21-23)

HET OBSERVATORIUM The artists Andre Dekker, Ruud Reutelingsperger and Geert van de Camp built an observatory in Hoeksche Waard. On a platform were three spaces serving as a kitchen, toilet, shelter and sleeping-place. You could, if you wished, spend 24 consecutive hours there and give your thoughts free rein. The isolation and the fact that you were thrown back upon your own resources were enough to stimulate the participants' experiences and perceptions of the place. Reports of those thoughts, experiences and perceptions are presented by the artists in images, text, film and sound. (pag. 24)

MARK PIMLOTT The Canadian-British artist Mark Pimlott made two films. 'One' and 'The other'. They were shot in Hoeksche Waard and show the landscape in all its facets: island waterways, roads, houses, building sites, factories, trees, boats, cars. The montage stresses the general rather than the specific: the film is about Hoeksche Waard, but could just have well been taken elsewhere in the Netherlands or even in another part of the world. This moving up and down between the local and the general puts the problems of Hoeksche Waard in a universal perspective. (pag. 25)

SCHIE 2.0 (Lucas Verweij en Ton Matton) Verweij and Matton recorded sheds, houses, roads and cars from Hoeksche Waard. This material, supplemented with data on Hoeksche Waard and Rotterdam from the Central Statistics Office, was published in the form of picture postcards under the title 'Hoeksche Lines'. The surface areas of Rotterdam and Hoeksche Waard are nearly equal in size. Their findings exhibit a surprising contrast. They also developed 'the autarkic dwelling'. With this house, based on ecological principles, they seek to contribute to building forms characteristic of the region. (pag. 26-27)

HENRIK HÅKANSSON During his stay in Hoeksche Waard the Swedish artist Henrik Håkansson spotted and mapped many kinds of birds. Representatives of nature organizations were interviewed at his request. Their visions on the future nature development in Hoeksche Waard have been recorded on video. One of his proposals is to install cameras in nesting boxes so as to be able to follow the flying and breeding movements of birds. (pag. 28-29)

AD VAN DENDEREN Ad van Denderen kept returning to Hoeksche Waard to photograph everyday life: playing children, people laying wreathes on May 4, a summer day near Haringvliet bridge, an African woman by herself on a road leading towards the 'Watchman'. A Croatian, a Serb and a Bosnian good-humouredly drinking beer together at a concrete picnic table on the river dike. (pag. 30-31)

WIJNANDA DEROO She explored the natural and artificial in Hoeksche Waard landscape. The photographs show the vastness of the landscape where human traces are all too visible. A gate obstructing the view of the horizon, a cozy garden with furniture from the local hosehold store, from where the surrounding landscape can be enjoyed, a hedge of cultivated fruit trees or pieces of glistening foil as tombstones in the meadow. By arranging the photographs in series, the viewer's awareness is aroused of the beauty of the artificial in every form of repetition, rhythm and parallel. (pag. 32-33)

BERTIEN VAN MANEN Bertien van Manen met a lot of people during her stay, cycling through Hoeksche Waard. There were talks and laughter; Bertien was allowed to take a few photographs. Thirteen portraits give an impression of the population of Hoeksche Waard in their own environment. The farmer, the clergyman and his wife, mother and daughter, a young couple on a motorbike, a councillor and his wife, the proprietress of a pub. (pag. 34-35)

HANS VAN HOUWELINGEN Change and tolerance are the subjects of discussion between the clergymen Russcher, Maas and Groenenberg of the Reformed Congregation in Oud-Beijerland in the film 'The Village Church'. They discuss the possible consequences of 'foreigners' living in Hoeksche Waard. 'Foreigner' here means anyone not from Hoeksche Waard. It is not always possible to admit other religious communities. The images were alternated with others of a village celebration in Hoeksche Waard. (pag. 36)

BIRTHE LEEMEIJER In the first magazine, Birthe Leemeijer placed an advertisement for balloon rides over Hoeksche Waard. The artist spoke to balloonists about their experiences, observations and impressions, and noted down their statements and views. The ballooning route, the names of the passengers and their observations were recorded on a map. Afterwards, each of the participants received one such map and a ballooning badge. (pag. 37)

JOOST GROOTENS A lot of methods can be used to map an unknown place. Joost Grootens used birthmarks constituting a person's unexchangeable identity. In order to record the identity of Hoeksche Waard he projected 26 birthmarks on the map: these dots were the locations to be visited; the alphabet of Hoeksche Waard. In these places he looked for traces telling different stories. For each place he collected four traces, of which photographs were then taken. His interest was in small signs of human presence: chewing-gum stains, a forgotten eyeliner, a faded arrow on the road surface. (pag. 38-39)

JAN KONINGS/ESTER VAN DE WIEL The designers Jan Konings and Ester van de Wiel present an 'Agroguide' for a revival of the countryside in Hoeksche Waard. It alternates recreation facilities, tourist tips, practical information and educational recommendations. "Recreation park 'The Haystack'. A piece of land with 64 haystacks, very simple accommodation, a toilet shed, your own sleeping bag and cooking equipment desirable; report to the farmer and pay him." (pag. 40-41)

HONORÉ δ'O The Belgian artist Honoré δ'O looked for forms of 'speeding down' in Hoeksche Waard. According to him Hoeksche Waard is fine as it is and there is no need for urbanization. His proposal for a series of pivoting lampposts can be seen as both a warning and an appeal to people to remain aware and adopt a critical attitude towards the coming changes. During the exhibition 'Waar het landschap begint/New Landscape Frontiers' a protomodel could be seen of the pivoting lamppost 'Fan Light' sited opposite the Netherlands Architecture Institute (NAi). (pag. 42-43)

The exhibition period at the NAi in the months of May and June 1999 was marked by special excursions to Hoeksche Waard. All the excursions were based on ideas and/or under the guidance of Ad van Denderen, Wijnanda Deroo, Honoré δ'O, Joost Grootens, Henrik Håkansson, Bertien van Manen, Mark Pimlott and Jan Konings/Ester van de Wiel.

RESEARCH

VISUAL RESEARCH
JOHN DAVIES
HET OBSERVATORIUM
MARK PIMLOTT
SCHIE 2.0
HENRIK HÅKANSSON
AD VAN DENDEREN
WIJNANDA DEROO
BERTIEN VAN MANEN
HANS VAN HOUWELINGEN
BIRTHE LEEMEIJER
JOOST GROOTENS
JAN KONINGS/ESTER VAN DE WIEL
HONORÉ δ'O
ANTHROPOLOGICAL RESEARCH
HENK DE HAAN
PHYSICAL PLANNING RESEARCH
SJOERD CUSVELLER

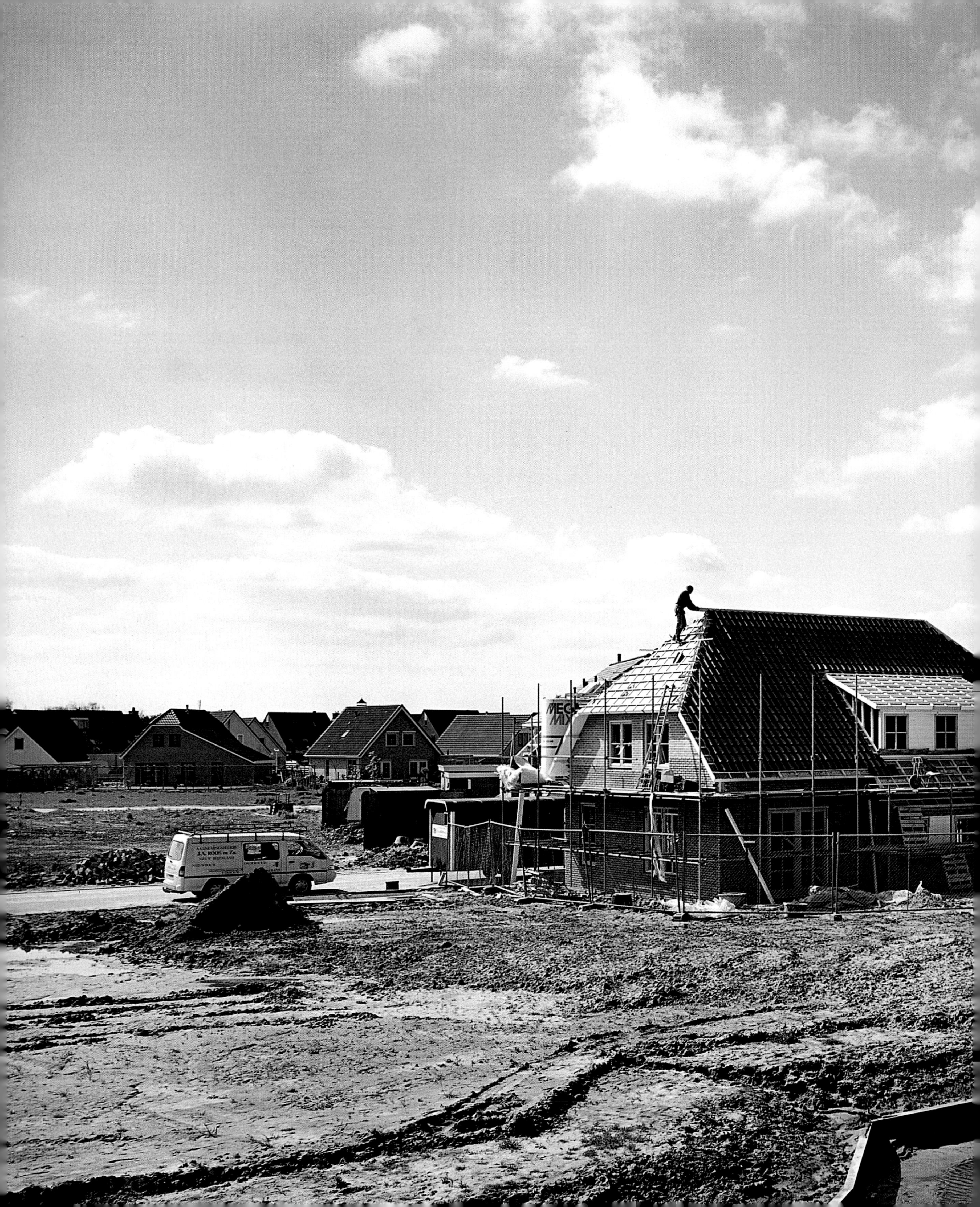

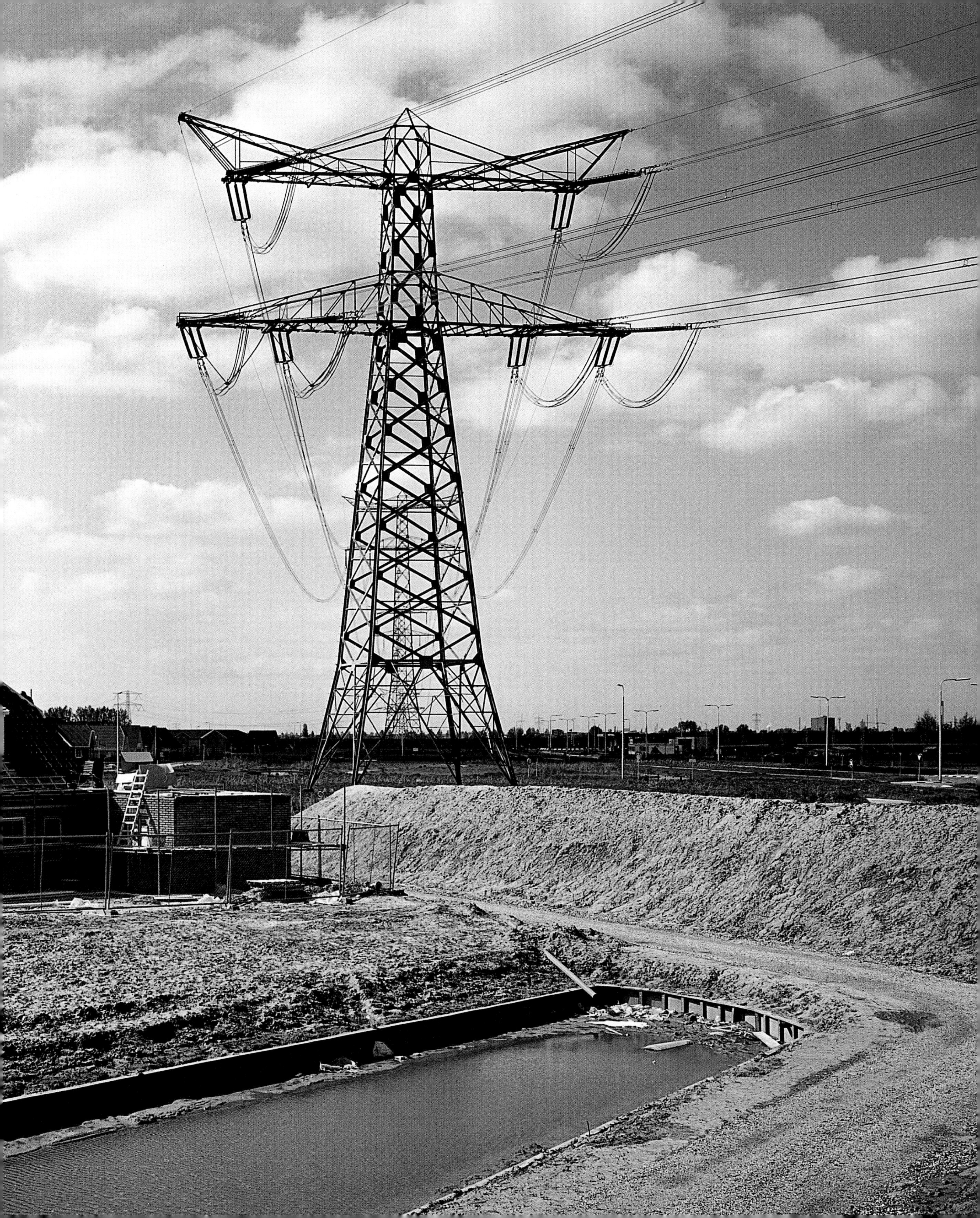

AIR-ZUIDWAARTS / SOUTHBOUND

RESEARCH

VISUAL RESEARCH
JOHN DAVIES
HET OBSERVATORIUM
MARK PIMLOTT
SCHIE 2.0
HENRIK HÅKANSSON
AD VAN DENDEREN
WIJNANDA DEROO
BERTIEN VAN MANEN
HANS VAN HOUWELINGEN
BIRTHE LEEMEIJER
JOOST GROOTENS
JAN KONINGS/ESTER VAN DE WIEL
HONORÉ δ'0
ANTHROPOLOGICAL RESEARCH
HENK DE HAAN
PHYSICAL PLANNING RESEARCH
SJOERD CUSVELLER

photos: Geert van de Camp

Two films

Despite the specific character of Hoeksche Waard and the region around it, its future is not so much associated with its own past as the pasts and presents of other places which have already come to be. The conditions which surround it at this time are similar to those that have surrounded other places before.

When I visited Hoeksche Waard for an extended period earlier this year, I was struck by the parallels between its places and the place where I was raised – a modest suburb on a rural island outside a mid-sized Canadian city (Montreal). These parallels were not restricted to physical appearance – they existed in the relationships between the cities and their regions, and the use that those cities make of their regions. They were about the positions people were put in, how they were expected to live and work and how they were encouraged to desire things for themselves that conformed to limited patterns that were not of their own making.

For several years, I have studied the phenomenon of the urbanisation of North America, noting in particular how the imperatives of capital have been associated with certain myths of occupation of the world a fear of the Other and of death. To that story of urbanisation has been tied the story of suburbanisation. The suburb carries the burden of the 'American Dream'. In the story of the suburb, which has been repeated and repeats itself ad infinitum, in America and now in Europe, basic relationships are inscribed: those that exist between the individual and the city, the individual and nature and between the individual and society. In the suburb, these relationships are a complex of contradictions held in tension.

In the suburb, one can live both in the city and outside the city the same time. One can convince oneself of living in nature. One can feel at the edge of the World and yet in the full embrace of society, and furthermore a society of fundamental composition: of families with children and animals and houses and vehicles that guarantee independence and groupings of dwellings that connote communality. It is a contradictory mixture that works to affect an atmosphere of contentedness.

In such an environment, which seems ideal and at times idyllic, one is susceptible to everything that is on offer. The suburb is an Eden that is full of innocuous and enticing fruit. The suburb is a place designed for and dedicated to the mechanics of consumption. It is vital that it is kept a nearly-satiated outpost of the city, that its citizens are happy out on the edges of the world. They must be allowed to indulge in fantasy.

As it has become is clear that large urban centres are problematic yet the work that they do is absolutely necessary, new urban models have had to be invented. Quite apart from the case of the urbanisation of America, which has its own particular circumstances and qualities, ideas have been developed in Europe which have attempted to find an ideal urban complex. Historically, the most influential of these has consisted of interdependent utopian elements distributed over an increasingly redundant rural landscape, connected by infrastructure. In the nineteenth century, Ebenezer Howard's 'Garden City' model proposed 'perfect' centrally planned town units, highly idealised and hierarchical in their design. Many of these were to be evenly distributed over the countryside, connected by a rail network. The infrastructure was intended to be used solely for the movement of goods. The interdependency between towns was economic, with each component of the matrix aware only of its own idealised 'nature'. By maintaining the innocence of the urban populations of each through isolation, the workings of the economic complex could be guaranteed. This kind of economic model is, of course, political.

The blatancy of Howard's model would be found intolerable if proposed openly today. There are, however, echoes of that model in the workings of our urban centres and their environs, their regions. The working of the city, its nature, has been masked by the extreme mobility offered by the automobile, which clothes its users in the mantle of democracy, individualism and freedom.

The situation of Hoeksche Waard in relation to Rotterdam and the delta region between it and Antwerpen seems specific at close scrutiny, yet is rather typical when places in the context of international patterns of regional suburbanization. These tend to follow American precedents. There, we see a continuing investment in the building of image-based suburbs, fantasy-based leisure and retail facilities and even the transformation of inner cities into museums of themselves for the purpose of entertaining visitors and inhabitants alike. All are part of a bourgeois revolution in the reclamation of lifestyle. Despite the specificity of the historical, social and geographic conditions of Hoeksche Waard, the character of contemporary internationalised regional urbanisation will determine its features and fortunes. That specificity will be absorbed into the generic urbanised territory, affecting only differences in land value and the social hierarchies that come with incidents of 'specialness'.

I have made two films. One is placed in the context of discussions surrounding 'Increases and decreases in scale', while the other is in the context of 'Generations and commitment'. The structure of the two films is simple: over static images of places in Hoeksche Waard is a monologue, which moves in one film from a discourse on regional urbanisation to the social effects – reflected in the individual – of that urbanisation in the next. The images presented in the films are those of places which are at the threshold of development: places which can be seen as at the moment of beginning; places poised between what is known and what is not yet known; places which may be seen as sites of human imagination. The narration spoken over that which is seen is generic and is intended to illuminate aspects of that imagination.

My own experience of the suburb, which can be described as a degraded urban experience, revealed the compromised significance of the suburb. In Hoeksche Waard, one already sees not only physical modifications, but shifts in the hopes and ill-defined desires of people who live there, particularly the young. Mixed with wishes to be part of the compelling life of the city are contacts with fundamental things. In Hoeksche Waard, nature is manipulated but is still real. The presence of the city there intensifies nature's significance. This place, as it is and as it will be, locates its inhabitants: they are at the edge of the world, in an idyll where they can project their imagination and fear; yet they are held back by the embrace of culture. They are between-people. That very between-ness is the problem of the suburb and of Hoeksche Waard in the present and the future. It stands between a possible unknown and the call of a cynical culture that understands the power of the mythification of that unknown, that uses it to perpetuate its own fictions, its mirages of freedom.

AIR-ZUIDWAARTS / SOUTHBOUND

RESEARCH

VISUAL RESEARCH
JOHN DAVIES
HET OBSERVATORIUM
MARK PIMLOTT
SCHIE 2.0
HENRIK HÅKANSSON
AD VAN DENDEREN
WIJNANDA DEROO
BERTIEN VAN MANEN
HANS VAN HOUWELINGEN
BIRTHE LEEMEIJER
JOOST GROOTENS
JAN KONINGS/ESTER VAN DE WIEL
HONORÉ δ'O
ANTHROPOLOGICAL RESEARCH
HENK DE HAAN
PHYSICAL PLANNING RESEARCH
SJOERD CUSVELLER

Hoekse lijnen

Hoekers vernielen evenveel als Rotterdammers maar plegen 5 maal minder vaak een geweldsmisdrijf

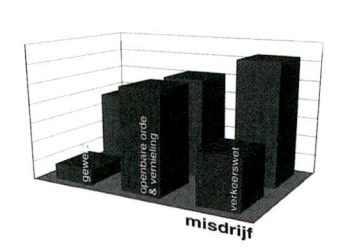

De Hoeksche Waard telde in 1996 132 geweldsmisdrijven en 842 vernielingen en verstoringen van de openbare orde. Er zijn 81.032 inwoners. Dit is 1,04 vernieling per 100 inwoners tegenover 1,02 in Rotterdam. (6.055 vernielingen / 4.553 geweldsmisdrijven / 592.754 inwoners). Bron: CBS
© 1998 *Hoekse Lijnen* is een subjectieve analyse van de Hoeksche Waard door
Schie 2.0 Rotterdam tel 010 4772535

Hoekse lijnen

Op het eiland woont per 2 hectare één ongetrouwde vrouw
Op hetzelfde oppervlakte rijden twee auto's
Op het eiland is ruimte voor 63.465 kippen

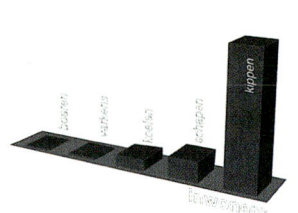

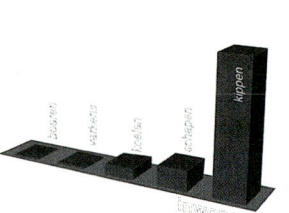

De Hoeksche Waard telde in 1996 op 29.901 hectare 14.804 ongehuwde vrouwen en 33.145 personenauto's. Er is een hokkappaciteit voor 63.465 kippen. Bron: CBS
© 1998 *Hoekse Lijnen* is een subjectieve analyse van de Hoeksche Waard door
Schie 2.0 Rotterdam tel 010 4772535

Hoekse lijnen

Het inkomen is hier 13% hoger dan in Rotterdam
Er staat 50% meer hypotheek uit

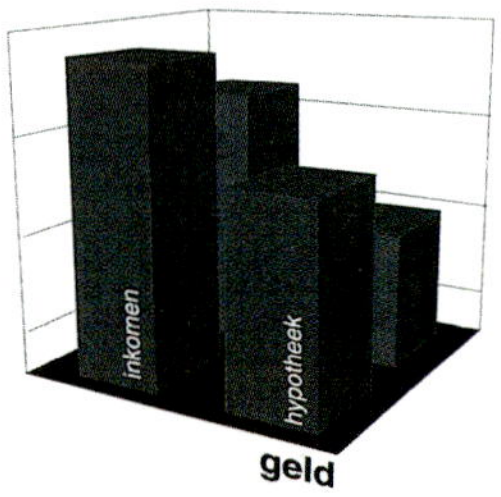

Het gemiddelde bruto jaarinkomen (1995) in Hoeksche Waard is ƒ 32.667 per persoon. Er staat gemiddeld ƒ 21.845 aan hypotheek uit.
In Rotterdam is het inkomen ƒ 27.350 en de hypotheek ƒ 14.353. Bron: CBS.
© 1998 *Hoekse Lijnen* is een subjectieve analyse van de Hoeksche Waard door
Schie 2.0 Rotterdam tel 010 4772535

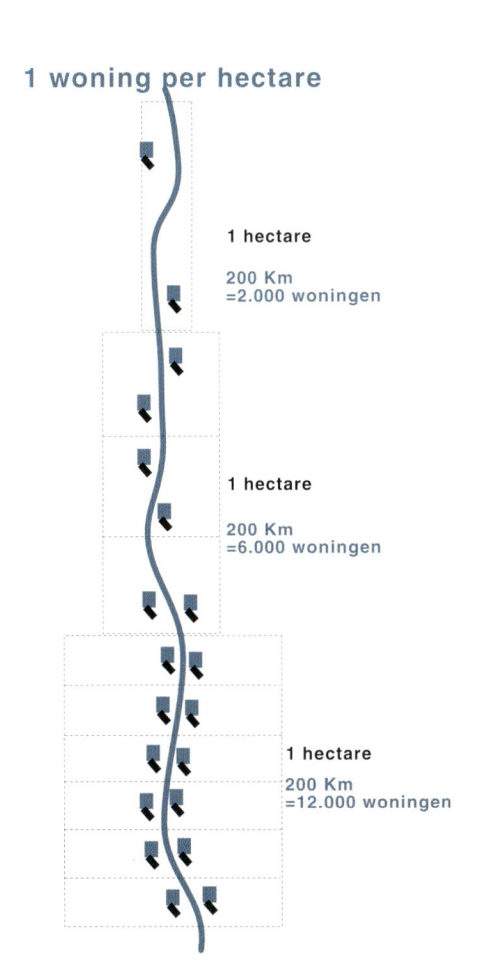

1 woning per hectare

1 hectare
200 Km
= 2.000 woningen

1 hectare
200 Km
= 6.000 woningen

1 hectare
200 Km
= 12.000 woningen

1

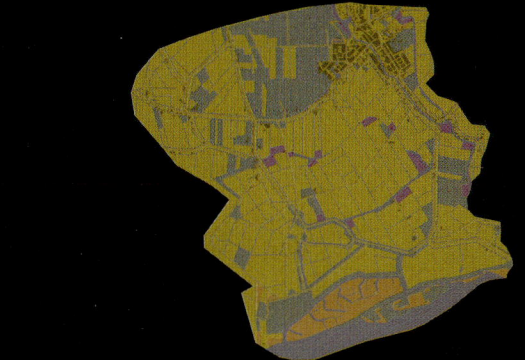

Farmers in Hoeksche Waard are permitted to build houses on their fields bordering creeks, provided they convert the field into a nature area.

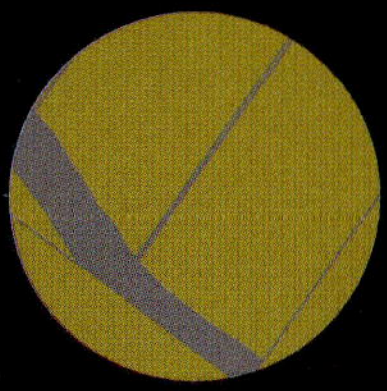

2

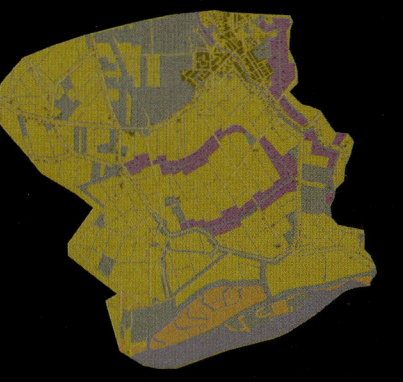

Housing must meet the following conditions:
1 At most 1 dwelling per hectare.
2 No infrastructure permitted; houses must be completely autarkic, solar cells, water collection and purification ensure comfortable living.
3 The hectares of 'nature plots' are to be lodged with an Owners' Association and maintained as a whole by an authorized local nature manager.

3

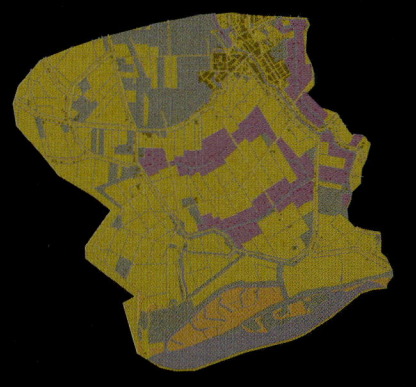

In this way the entire bank length of the Hoek creeks — 200 kilometres in all — can be turned into a nature area. One single 'stepping-stone' will ultimately generate the main ecological fabric. Ten-thousand 'green' homes are proposed; final numbers will depend on the project's success. The more homes, the more nature.

The creeks in Hoeksche Waard have been designated as the framework for the main ecological fabric.

Land reallocation and wide-scale farming have caused the meandering paths of the creeks to be straightened.

Farmer A releases one hectare of farm land for a 'nature plot' and builds a self-sufficient house on it.

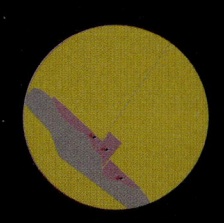

If that sells well, Farmer B will follow suit. If not, the process will come to a halt.

If several farmers create 'nature plots' with self-sufficient buildings on them, a series of stepping-stones will be formed. Gradually this will expand into an uninterrupted green bank.

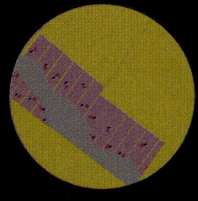

The creation of long, narrow plots will make it possible to build larger numbers of dwellings. The green bank will increase in density.

AIR-ZUIDWAARTS / SOUTHBOUND

28

RESEARCH

VISUAL RESEARCH
JOHN DAVIES
HET OBSERVATORIUM
MARK PIMLOTT
SCHIE 2.0
HENRIK HÅKANSSON
AD VAN DENDEREN
WIJNANDA DEROO
BERTIEN VAN MANEN
HANS VAN HOUWELINGEN
BIRTHE LEEMEIJER
JOOST GROOTENS
JAN KONINGS/ESTER VAN DE WIEL
HONORÉ δ'O
ANTHROPOLOGICAL RESEARCH
HENK DE HAAN
PHYSICAL PLANNING RESEARCH
SJOERD CUSVELLER

1.	Great Crested Grebe	Skäggdopping	Podiceps cristatus	Fuut	56.	Stock Dove	Skogsduva	Columba oenas	Holeduif
2.	Great Cormorant	Storskarv	Phalacrocorax carbo	Aalscholver	57.	Wood Pigeon	Ringduva	Columba palumbus	Houtduif
3.	Grey Heron	Häger	Ardea cinerea	Blauwe Reiger	58.	Collared Dove	Turkduva	Streptopelia decaocto	Turkse Tortel
4.	Spoonbill	Skedstork	Platalea leucorodia	Lepelaar	59.	Turtle Dove	Turturduva	Streptopelia turtur	Zomertortel
5.	Greater Flamingo	Flamingo	Phoenicopterus ruber	Flamingo	60.	Cuckoo	Gök	Cuculus canorus	Koekoek
6.	Mute Swan	Knölsvan	Cygnus olor	Knobbelzwaan	61.	Little Owl	Minerva uggla	Athene noctua	Steenuil
7.	Black Swan	Svart Svan	Cygnus atratus	Zwarte Zwaan	62.	Long-eared Owl	Hornuggla	Asio otus	Ransuil
8.	Greylag Goose	Grågås	Anser anser	Grauwe Gans	63.	Tawny Owl	Kattuggla	Strix aluco	Bosuil
9.	Barnacle Goose	Vitkindadgås	Branta leucopsis	Brandgans	64.	Swift	Tornseglare	Apus apus	Gierzwaluw
10.	Canada Goose	Kanadagås	Branta canadensis	Canadese Gans	65.	Great Spotted Woodpecker	Större hackspett	Dendrocopos major	Grote Bonte Specht
11.	Shelduck	Gravand	Tadorna tadorna	Bergeend	66.	Skylark	Sånglärka	Alauda†arvensis	Veldleeuwerik
12.	Egyptian Goose	Nilgås	Alopochen aegyptiacus	Nijlgans	67.	House Martin	Hussvala	Delichon urbica	Huiszwaluw
13.	Mallard	Gräsand	Anas platyrhynchos	Wilde Eend	68.	Swallow	Ladusvala	Hirundo rustica	Boerenzwaluw
14.	Gadwall	Snatterand	Anas strepera	Krakeend	69.	Meadow Pipit	A¨ngspiplärka	Anthus pratensis	Graspieper
15.	Wigeon	Bläsand	Anas penelope	Smient	70.	Pied Wagtail	Sädesärlsa,	Motacilla alba	Witte Kwikstaart
16.	Teal	Kricka	Anas crecca	Wintertaling	71.	Yellow Wagtail	Gulärla,	Motacilla flava	Gele Kwikstaar
17.	Garganey	Årta	Anas querquedula	Zomertaling	72.	Dunnock	Järnsparv	Prunella modularis	Heggemus
18.	Pintail	Stjärtand	Anas acuta	Pijlstaar	73.	Nightingale	SydNäktergal	Luscinia megarhynchos	Nachtegaal
19.	Shoveler	Skedand	Anas clypeata	Slobeend	74.	Robin	Rödhake	Erithachus rubecula	Roodborst
20.	Tufted Duck	Vigg	Aythya fuligula	Kuifeend	75.	Bluethroat	Blåhake	Luscinia svecica	Blauwborst
21.	Pochard	Brunand	Aythya ferina	Tafeleend	76.	Stonechat	Svarthuvad buskskvätta Saxicola torquata		Roodborsttapuit
22.	Goldeneye	Knipa	Bucephala clangula	Brilduiker	77.	Whinchat	Buskskvätta	Saxicola rubetra	Paapje
23.	Marsh Harrier	Brun Kärrhök	Circus aeruginosus	Bruine Kiekendief	78.	Black Redstart	Svartrödstjärt	Phoenicurus ochruros	Zwarte Roodstraat
24.	Goshawk	Duvhök	Accipiter gentilis	Havik	79.	Redstart	Rödstjärt	Phoenicurus phoenicurus	Gekraagde Roodstaart
25.	Buzzard	Ormvråk	Buteo buteo	Buizerd	80.	Wheater	Stenskvätta	Oenanthe oenanthe	Tapuit
26.	Hobby	Lärkfalk	Falco subbuteo	Boomvalk	81.	Blackbird	Koltrast	Turdus merula	Mere
27.	Kestrel	Tornfalk	Falco tinnunculus	Torenvalk	82.	Song Thrush	Taltrast	Turdus philomelos	Zanglijster
28.	Pheasant	Fasan	Phasianus colchicus	Fazant	83.	Mistle Thrush	Dubbeltrast	Turdus viscivorus	Grote Lijster
29.	Grey Partridge	Rapphöna	Perdix perdix	Patrijs	84.	Reed Warbler	Sävsångare	Acrocephalus scirpaceus	Kleine Karakiet
30.	Moorhen	Rörhöna	Gallinula chloropus	Waterhoen	85.	Sedge Warbler	Rörsångare	Acrocephalus schoenobaenus	Rietzanger
31.	Coot	Sothöna	Fulica atra	Meerkoet	86.	Icterine Warbler	Härmsångare	Hippolais icterina	Spotvogel
32.	Avocet	Skärfläcka	Recuvirostra avosetta	Kluut	87.	Garden Warbler	Trädgårdsångre	Sylvia borin	Tuinfluiter
33.	Oystercatcher	Strandskata	Haematopus ostralegus	Scholekster	88.	Whitethroat	Törnsångare	Sylvia communis	Grasmus
34.	Great Ringed Plover	Strandpipare	Charadrius hiaticula	Bontbekplevier	89.	Lesser Whitethroat	A¨rtsångare	Sylvia curruca	Braamsluiper
35.	Grey Plover	Kustpipare	Pluvialis squatarola	Zilverplevier	90.	Blackcap	Svarthätta	Sylvia atricapilla	Zwartkop
36.	Golden Plover	Ljungpipare	Pluvialis apricaria	Goudplevier	91.	Chiffchaff	Gransångare	Phylloscopus collybita	Tjiftjaf
37.	Lapwing	Tofsvipa	Vanellus vanellus	Kievit	92.	Willow Warbler	Lövsångare	Phylloscopus trochilus	Fitis

43 B MIDDELHARNIS
Bernisse
Groot-
Zuidoord
Polder Zuidoord
Beningerwaard
Leenheeren
Goudswaard
Noordpolder
Polder
Oude
Korendijk
Gemeente Korendijk
Oudendijk
Eendragtspolder
Lange Eendragtsweg
Korendijk
Slikken
Hitsertsche- of Vuile Gat
Polder
Blanken
Slikken
Stad aan 't Haringvliet

AIR-ZUIDWAARTS / SOUTHBOUND

RESEARCH

VISUAL RESEARCH
JOHN DAVIES
HET OBSERVATORIUM
MARK PIMLOTT
SCHIE 2.0
HENRIK HÅKANSSON
AD VAN DENDEREN
WIJNANDA DEROO
BERTIEN VAN MANEN
HANS VAN HOUWELINGEN
BIRTHE LEEMEIJER
JOOST GROOTENS
JAN KONINGS/ESTER VAN DE WIEL
HONORÉ δ'O
ANTHROPOLOGICAL RESEARCH
HENK DE HAAN
PHYSICAL PLANNING RESEARCH
SJOERD CUSVELLER

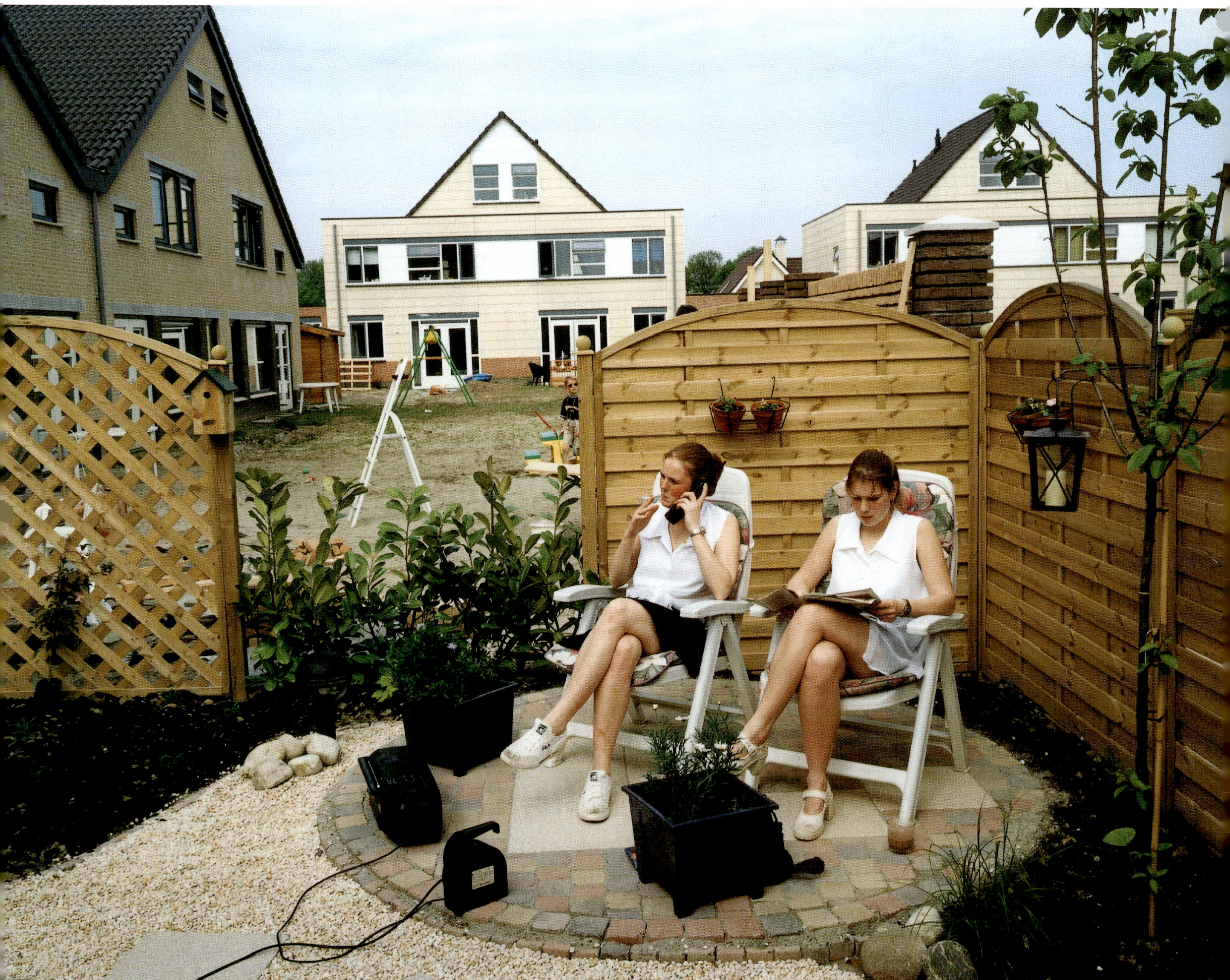

AIR-ZUIDWAARTS / SOUTHBOUND

RESEARCH

VISUAL RESEARCH
JOHN DAVIES
HET OBSERVATORIUM
MARK PIMLOTT
SCHIE 2.0
HENRIK HÅKANSSON
AD VAN DENDEREN
WIJNANDA DEROO
BERTIEN VAN MANEN
HANS VAN HOUWELINGEN
BIRTHE LEEMEIJER
JOOST GROOTENS
JAN KONINGS/ESTER VAN DE WIEL
HONORÉ δ'O
ANTHROPOLOGICAL RESEARCH
HENK DE HAAN
PHYSICAL PLANNING RESEARCH
SJOERD CUSVELLER

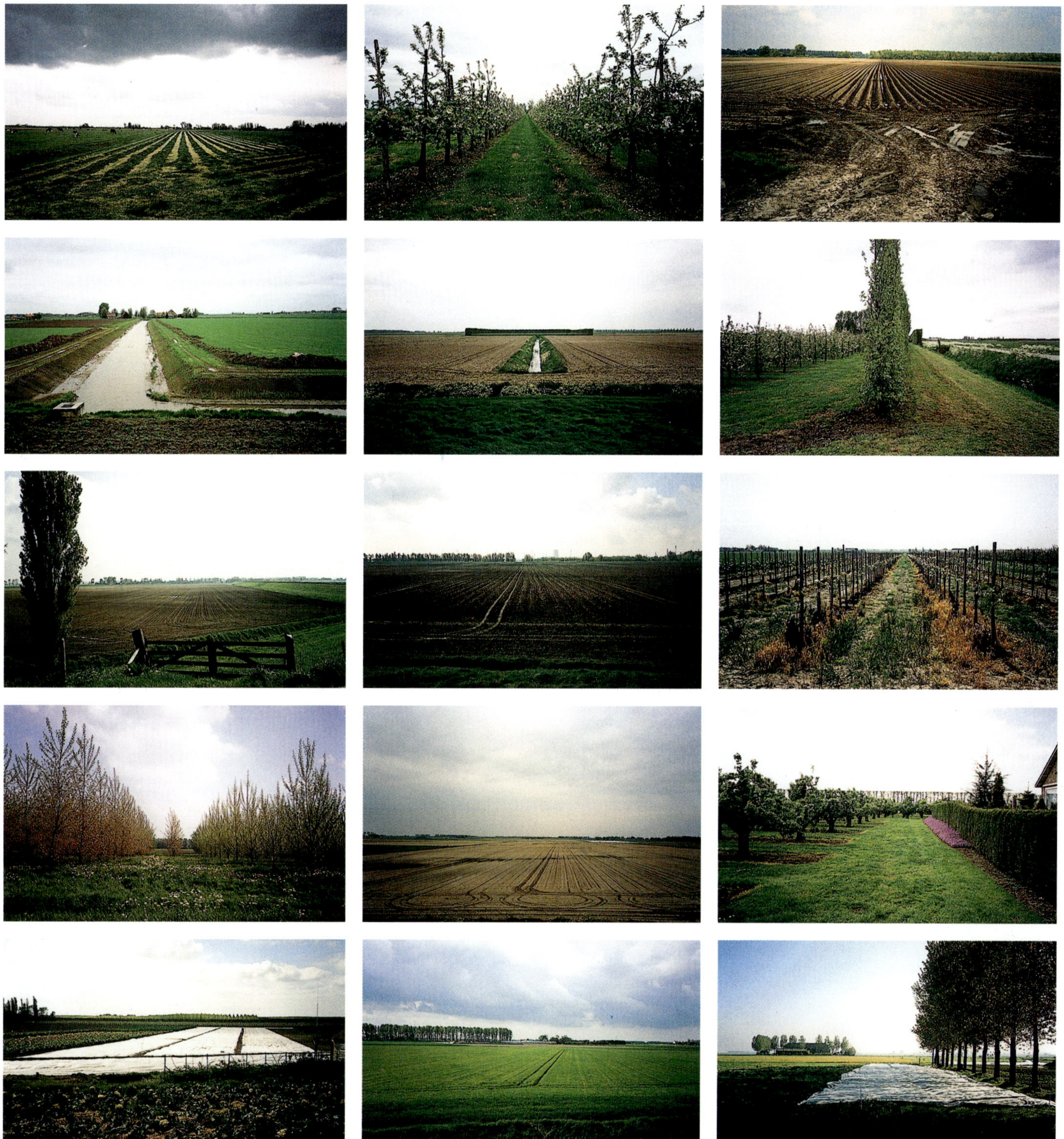

AIR-ZUIDWAARTS / SOUTHBOUND

34

RESEARCH
VISUAL RESEARCH
JOHN DAVIES
HET OBSERVATORIUM
MARK PIMLOTT
SCHIE 2.0
HENRIK HÅKANSSON
AD VAN DENDEREN
WIJNANDA DEROO
BERTIEN VAN MANEN
HANS VAN HOUWELINGEN
BIRTHE LEEMEIJER
JOOST GROOTENS
JAN KONINGS/ESTER VAN DE WIEL
HONORÉ δ'O
ANTHROPOLOGICAL RESEARCH
HENK DE HAAN
PHYSICAL PLANNING RESEARCH
SJOERD CUSVELLER

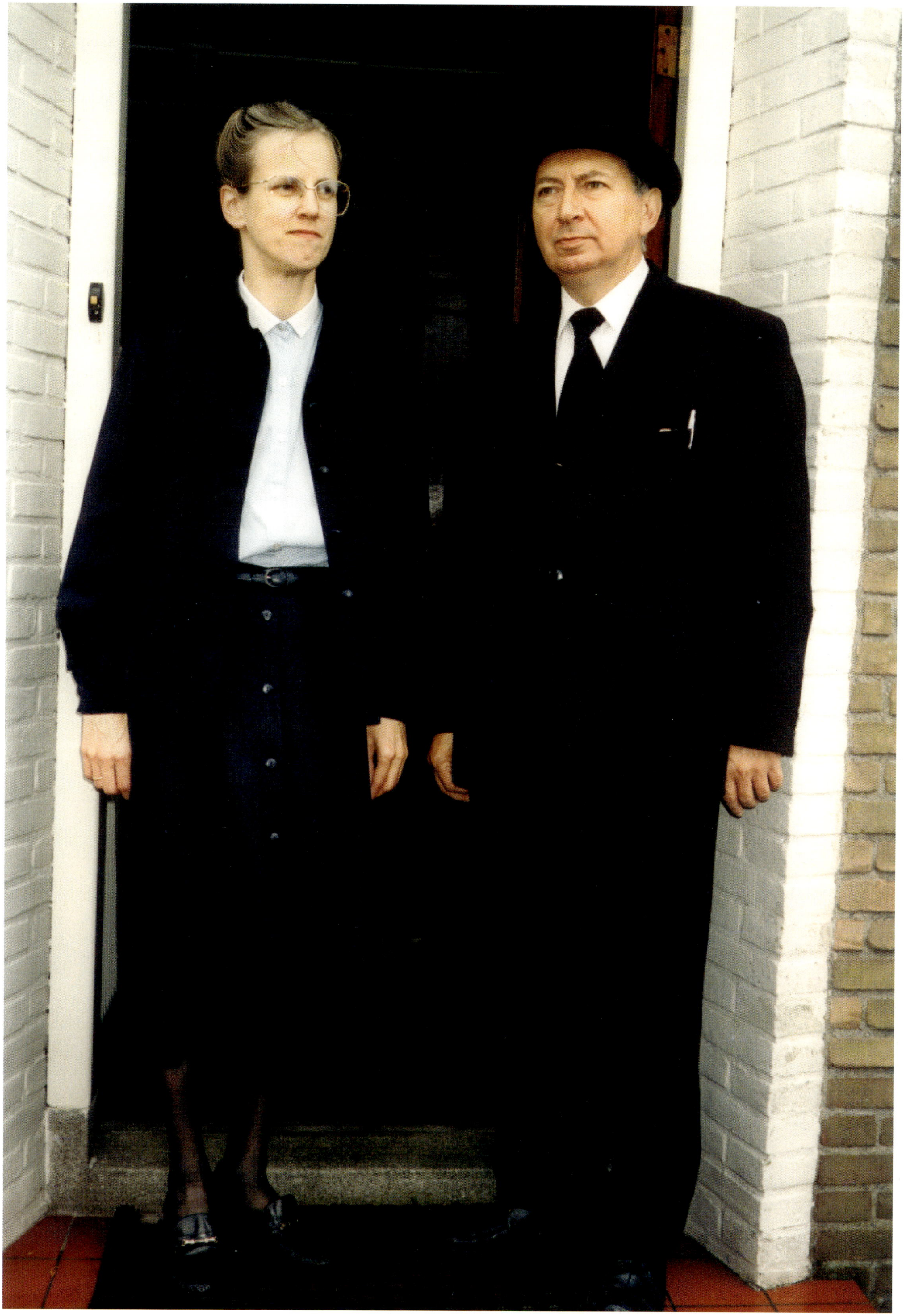

AIR-ZUIDWAARTS / SOUTHBOUND

RESEARCH

VISUAL RESEARCH
JOHN DAVIES
HET OBSERVATORIUM
MARK PIMLOTT
SCHIE 2.0
HENRIK HÅKANSSON
AD VAN DENDEREN
WIJNANDA DEROO
BERTIEN VAN MANEN
HANS VAN HOUWELINGEN
BIRTHE LEEMEIJER
JOOST GROOTENS
JAN KONINGS/ESTER VAN DE WIEL
HONORÉ δ'O
ANTHROPOLOGICAL RESEARCH
HENK DE HAAN
PHYSICAL PLANNING RESEARCH
SJOERD CUSVELLER

RESEARCH
VISUAL RESEARCH
JOHN DAVIES
HET OBSERVATORIUM
MARK PIMLOTT
SCHIE 2.0
HENRIK HÅKANSSON
AD VAN DENDEREN
WIJNANDA DEROO
BERTIEN VAN MANEN
HANS VAN HOUWELINGEN
BIRTHE LEEMEIJER
JOOST GROOTENS
JAN KONINGS/ESTER VAN DE WIEL
HONORÉ δ'O
ANTHROPOLOGICAL RESEARCH
HENK DE HAAN
PHYSICAL PLANNING RESEARCH
SJOERD CUSVELLER

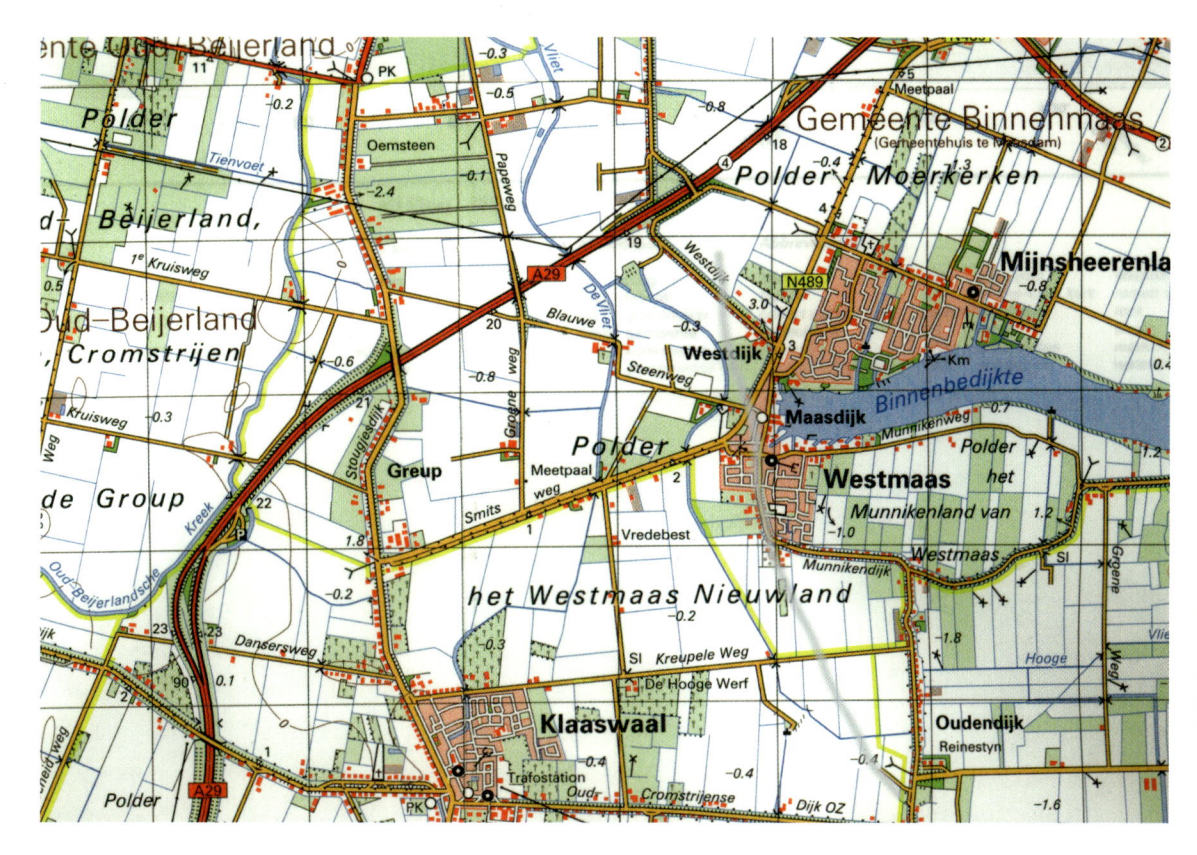

Dhr. G. Bijl from Puttershoek
'I saw parcels of land in various colours and sizes. Westmaas was decorated with flags, and ended the ribbon of the Binnenmaas. The shape of the parcels, the Brussels sprouts, I think everything should be preserved as much as possible.'

Mw. A. Mesker from Mookhoek
'I'm from Austria, and I feel more affinity for the mountain landscape. In general I find Hoeksche Waard landscape pretty boring. As we were approaching everything from the air, I saw a lot more mess. For instance, there was a huge, brown manure heap. What people usually keep hidden behind the front of their houses, could now be seen very easily.'

Dhr. P. Berkelaar from Rotterdam
'A lot of green, a lot of cows and sheep running away. The landscape is very bare and flat. Westmaas had decked itself out beautifully with flags for a big party.'

Mw. Van Dijk from Spijkenisse
'It was splendid. Especially from the air.'

Mw. M.A. Rijsdijk-Blinde from Strijen
'It was foggy, but I love the flat land. The flight was short and there were so many impressions. The straight fields and farmlands and the winding ribbon of the Binnenmaas. I saw my own Brussels sprouts. Your own food, your own professional know-how.'

Dhr. De la Fontaine from Rotterdam
'It was flat, patterned, a bit hazy and still.'

Mw. N. Faber from Strijen
'There was beautiful flat countryside. It was quiet between the towns.'

AIR-ZUIDWAARTS / SOUTHBOUND

RESEARCH

VISUAL RESEARCH
JOHN DAVIES
HET OBSERVATORIUM
MARK PIMLOTT
SCHIE 2.0
HENRIK HÅKANSSON
AD VAN DENDEREN
WIJNANDA DEROO
BERTIEN VAN MANEN
HANS VAN HOUWELINGEN
BIRTHE LEEMEIJER
JOOST GROOTENS
JAN KONINGS/ESTER VAN DE WIEL
HONORÉ δ'0
ANTHROPOLOGICAL RESEARCH
HENK DE HAAN
PHYSICAL PLANNING RESEARCH
SJOERD CUSVELLER

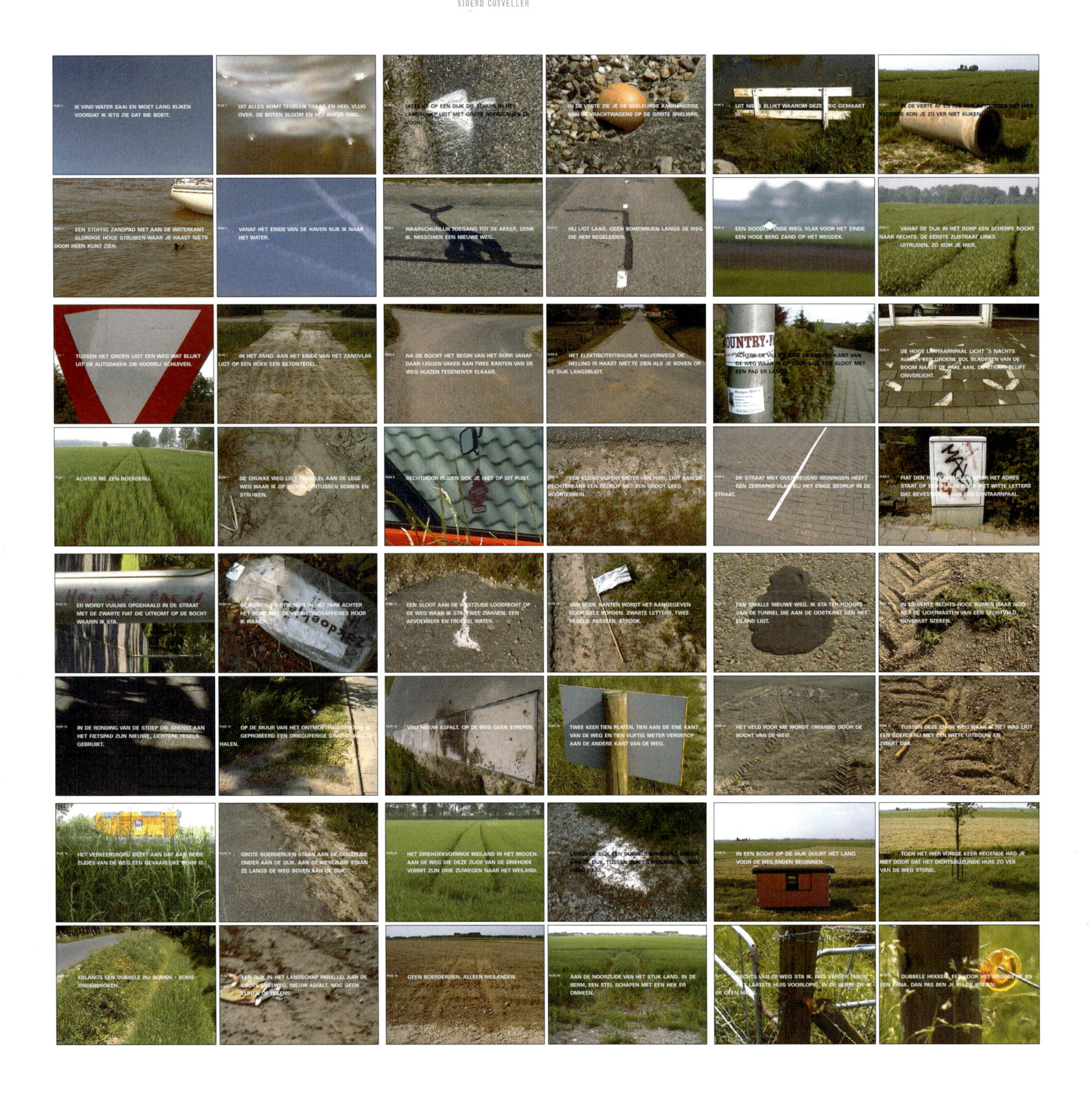

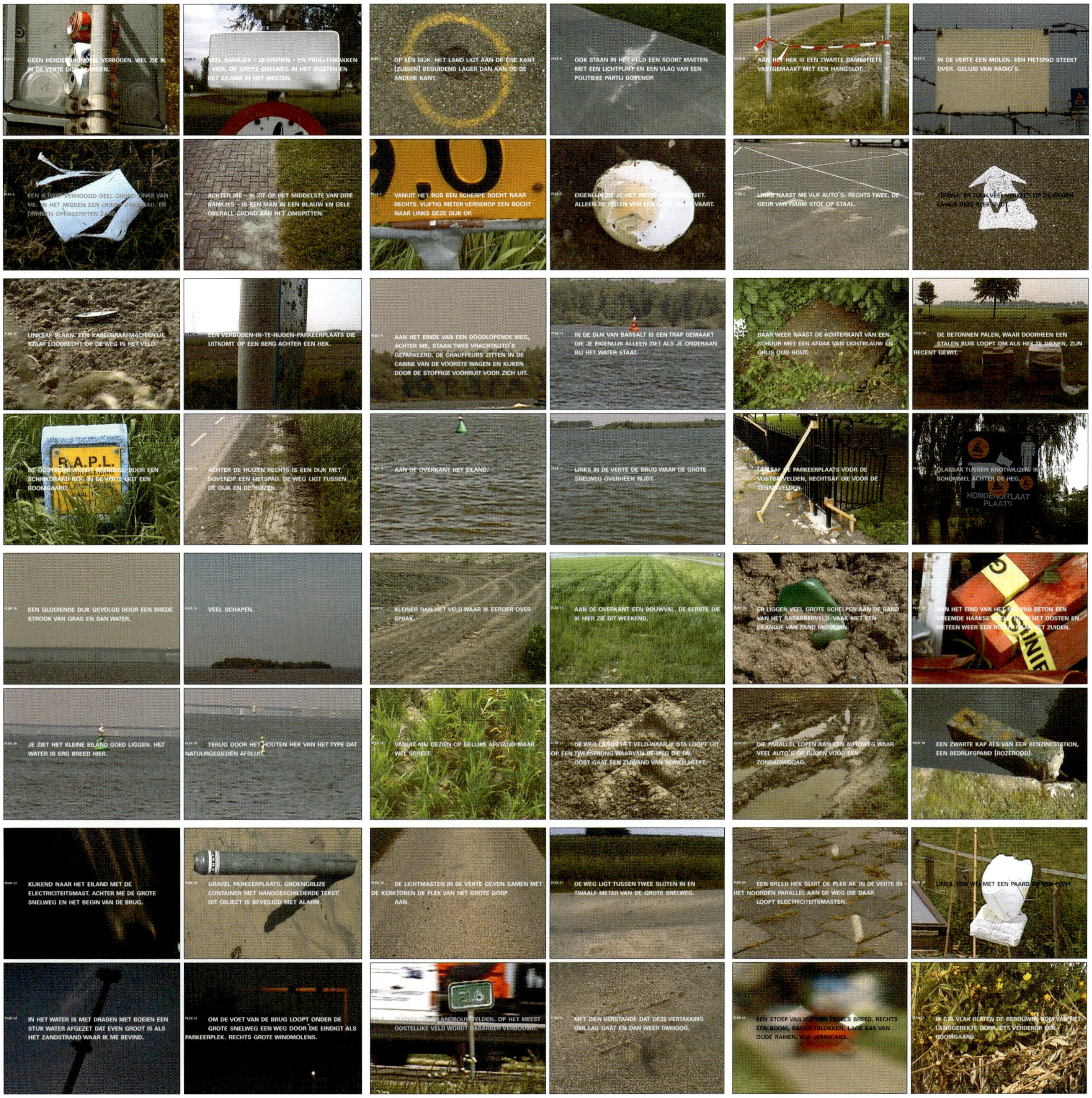
GEEN HERDERSHONDEN VERBODEN. WEL ZIE IK IN DE VERTE DRIE PAARDEN.
VEEL BANKJES - ZEVENTIEN - EN PRULLENBAKKEN - VIER. DE GROTE SNELWEG IN HET OOSTEN EN HET EILAND IN HET WESTEN.
OP EEN DIJK. HET LAND LIGT AAN DE ENE KANT (ZUIDEN) BEDUIDEND LAGER DAN AAN DE DE ANDERE KANT.
OOK STAAN IN HET VELD EEN SOORT MASTEN MET EEN LICHTPUNT EN EEN VLAG VAN EEN POLITIEKE PARTIJ BOVENOP.
AAN HET HEK IS EEN ZWARTE DAMESFIETS VASTGEMAAKT MET EEN HANGSLOT.
IN DE VERTE EEN MOLEN. EEN FIETSPAD STEEKT OVER. GELUID VAN RADIO'S.
EEN IETWAT VERHOOGD DEEL GROND LINKS VAN ME. IN HET MIDDEN EEN ONDIEP ZWEMBAD. ER OMHEEN OPENGERETEN ZAND.
ACHTER ME - IK ZIT OP HET MIDDELSTE VAN DRIE BANKJES - IS EEN MAN IN EEN BLAUW EN GELE OVERALL GROND AAN HET OMSPITTEN.
VANUIT HET BOS EEN SCHERPE BOCHT NAAR RECHTS. VIJFTIG METER VERDEROP EEN BOCHT NAAR LINKS DEZE DIJK OP.
EIGENLIJK ZIE JE HET WATER NIET. ALLEEN DE ZEILEN VAN EEN BOOT DIE VAART.
LINKS NAAST ME VIJF AUTO'S. RECHTS TWEE. DE GEUR VAN WARM STOF OP STAAL.
TERWIJL ER TOCH VEEL VERKEER OP DE WEGEN LANGS DEZE PLEK RIJDT.
LINKSAF SLAAN. EEN KABELGRAAFMACHIENTJE STAAT LOODRECHT OP DE WEG IN HET VELD.
EEN VERBODEN-IN-TE-RIJDEN-PARKEERPLAATS DIE UITKOMT OP EEN BERG ACHTER EEN HEK.
AAN HET EINDE VAN EEN DOODLOPENDE WEG, ACHTER ME, STAAN TWEE VRACHTAUTO'S GEPARKEERD. DE CHAUFFEURS ZITTEN IN DE CABINE VAN DE VOORSTE WAGEN EN KIJKEN DOOR DE STOFFIGE VOORRUIT VOOR ZICH UIT.
IN DE DIJK VAN BASSALT IS EEN TRAP GEMAAKT DIE JE EIGENLIJK ALLEEN ZIET ALS JE ONDERAAN BIJ HET WATER STAAT.
DAAR WEER NAAST DE ACHTERKANT VAN EEN SCHUUR MET EEN AFDAK VAN LICHTBLAUW EN GRIJS OUD HOUT.
DE BETONNEN PALEN, WAAR DOORHEEN EEN STALEN BUIS LOOPT OM ALS HEK TE DIENEN, ZIJN RECENT GEWIT.
DE OOSTBERM WORDT BEËINDIGD DOOR EEN SCHRIKDRAAD HEK. IN DE VERTE LIGT EEN BOOMGAARD.
R.A.P.L.
ACHTER DE HUIZEN RECHTS IS EEN DIJK MET BOVENOP EEN FIETSPAD. DE WEG LIGT TUSSEN DE DIJK EN DE HUIZEN.
AAN DE OVERKANT HET EILAND.
LINKS IN DE VERTE DE BRUG WAAR DE GROTE SNELWEG OVERHEEN RIJDT.
LINKSAF DE PARKEERPLAATS VOOR DE VOETBALVELDEN, RECHTSAF DIE VOOR DE TENNISVELDEN.
GLASBAK TUSSEN KNOTWILGEN. SCHOMMEL ACHTER DE HEG.
HONDENUITLAAT PLAATS
EEN GLOOIENDE DIJK GEVOLGD DOOR EEN BREDE STROOK VAN GRAS EN DAN WATER.
VEEL SCHAPEN.
KLEINER DAN HET VELD WAAR IK EERDER OVER SPRAK.
AAN DE OVERKANT EEN BOUWVAL. DE EERSTE DIE IK HIER ZIE DIT WEEKEND.
ER LIGGEN VEEL GROTE SCHELPEN AAN DE RAND VAN HET RABARBERVELD. VAAK MET EEN EILANDJE VAN ZAND MIDDENIN.
AAN HET EIND VAN HET PAD VAN BETON EEN VREEMDE HAAKSE BOCHT NAAR HET OOSTEN EN METEEN WEER EEN BOCHT NAAR HET ZUIDEN.
JE ZIET HET KLEINE EILAND GOED LIGGEN. HET WATER IS ERG BREED HIER.
TERUG DOOR HET HOUTEN HEK VAN HET TYPE DAT NATUURGEBIEDEN AFSLUIT.
VANUIT MIJ GEZIEN OP GELIJKE AFSTAND MAAR WEL SCHEEF.
DE WEG LANGS HET VELD WAAR IK STA LOOPT UIT OP EEN TWEESPRONG WAARVAN DE WEG DIE PAL OOST GAAT EEN ZIJWAND VAN BOMEN HEEFT.
DIE PARALLEL LOPEN AAN EEN AUTOWEG WAAR VEEL AUTO'S OP RIJDEN VOOR EEN ZONDAGMIDDAG.
EEN ZWARTE KAP ALS VAN EEN BENZINESTATION, EEN BEDRIJFSPAND (ROZEROOD).
KIJKEND NAAR HET EILAND MET DE ELECTRICITEITSMAST. ACHTER ME DE GROTE SNELWEG EN HET BEGIN VAN DE BRUG.
GRAVEL PARKEERPLAATS. GROENGRIJZE CONTAINER MET HANDGESCHILDERDE TEKST: DIT OBJECT IS BEVEILIGD MET ALARM.
DE LICHTMASTEN IN DE VERTE GEVEN SAMEN MET DE KERKTOREN DE PLEK VAN HET GROTE DORP AAN.
DE WEG LIGT TUSSEN TWEE SLOTEN IN EN TWAALF METER VAN DE GROTE SNELWEG.
EEN BREED HEK SLUIT DE PLEK AF. IN DE VERTE IN HET NOORDEN PARALLEL AAN DE WEG DIE DAAR LOOPT ELECTRICITEITSMASTEN.
LINKS EEN WEI MET EEN PAARD EN EEN PONY.
IN HET WATER IS MET DRADEN MET BOEIEN EEN STUK WATER AFGEZET DAT EVEN GROOT IS ALS HET ZANDSTRAND WAAR IK ME BEVIND.
OM DE VOET VAN DE BRUG LOOPT ONDER DE GROTE SNELWEG EEN WEG DOOR DIE EINDIGT ALS PARKEERPLEK. RECHTS GROTE WINDMOLENS.
21.6
TUSSEN TWEE LANDBOUWVELDEN. OP HET MEEST OOSTELIJKE VELD WORDT RABARBER VERBOUWD.
MET DIEN VERSTANDE DAT DEZE VERTAKKING OMLAAG GAAT EN DAN WEER OMHOOG.
EEN STOEP VAN VIJFTIEN TEGELS BREED. RECHTS ÉÉN BOOM, BASSALTBLOKKEN, LAGE KAS VAN OUDE RAMEN, VIJF JERRYCANS.
IK STA VLAK BUITEN DE BEBOUWDE KOM VAN HET LANGGEREKTE DORP. IETS VERDEROP EEN BOOMGAARD.

AIR-ZUIDWAARTS / SOUTHBOUND

RESEARCH
VISUAL RESEARCH
JOHN DAVIES
HET OBSERVATORIUM
MARK PIMLOTT
SCHIE 2.0
HENRIK HÅKANSSON
AD VAN DENDEREN
WIJNANDA DEROO
BERTIEN VAN MANEN
HANS VAN HOUWELINGEN
BIRTHE LEEMEIJER
JOOST GROOTENS
JAN KONINGS/ESTER VAN DE WIEL
HONORÉ δ'O
ANTHROPOLOGICAL RESEARCH
HENK DE HAAN
PHYSICAL PLANNING RESEARCH
SJOERD CUSVELLER

Leisure Park 'De Hooiberg'

The countryside is changing, partly because of increased demand for leisure opportunities. Hoeksche Waard is a 'blind spot' on the tourism map of the Netherlands, but that too is about to change. Some agricultural land is to become new nature and farmers are proving to be innovative entrepreneurs, who see tourism as a new source of income. Various aspects of agro-tourism are highlighted in the four scenarios, under which Leisure Park 'De Hooiberg'.

The Oudeland van Strijen polder is an old cultural landscape with distinctive farms. Here you can experience real country life. Sleep in a haystack, help the farmer work the land or milk a goat. A number of farmers have joined forces and receive visitors in a theme park.

Jan Vervoort: "We first heard about 'De Hooiberg' [the haystack] from one of Nel's yoga friends. And we got onto it right away. Well, we were just in time booking. I was rather sceptical to start with, but I decided to go with the flow. I envisaged myself with my nose in my books whilst the others had their activity holiday. But before I realized it, I was just as active as they were.

It's very well arranged: the overall set-up at 'De Hooiberg' is a kind of farmer's cooperative. Our part was called 'De Hooiberg', and that's where it all began. We lived in a straw bungalow: a house made entirely of straw. And it's an odd experience! Just the smell, but the actual house too – it's a kind of straw igloo. At 'De Silo', another farm in the group, you could either stay in ultramodern sheds on the farmer's land or at what they call a 'Bed and Bread'. A bit more luxury, but I much preferred the straw. What about the other farm? People there were in farm labourers' huts. That farmer kept sheep. Ours had cows and the owner of 'De Silo' was an arable farmer. But the set-up's pretty smart – they don't farm to sell, but for (and with) their guests. So we just joined in, but actually we were farming for ourselves. Even our toilets were used for compost. Not that you could smell them; they were proper toilets.

The farmer's wife at 'De Hooiberg' had her own small-scale cheese plant, where all the girls could make their own cheeses. But all the home-made cheeses, including hers, were sold there. In fact, everything was: 'De Silo' had potatoes, which we ate there. Our boy was fascinated. Peter was determined to go into the fields, to hoe. So there he was, in a field of potatoes (learning about it from one of the farm-hands and now he knows more about potato weeds than the entire family put together), and his were served up at dinner-time! He thought it was almost a miracle!

So there's a shop where they sell things from the premises. It's next to the restaurant 'De Fruitgaard' [the orchard]. It serves home-grown produce and you can order all kinds of local dishes. They call that local mess 'spelt'. It wasn't fit to eat, I thought – and they scrapped it in the Middle Ages. But the others loved it. Plus: potatoes with buttermilk, scrapple, gruel with raisins and spices, salted beans. And then it's time for dessert, ice-cream with fruit: Go and pick your own, and write down what you've picked. So you get it out of the orchard or the kitchen garden.

Sarah's going through the terrible teens. She drives us mad. But fortunately she spent all her time organizing fun parties at 'Hoekland'. It's a disco in a barn. There's one of those sixteen-year-old moped types that all the girls are mad about. I was worried she'd end up in the hay with one of the local worthies, because there's this haystack (a.k.a. youth hostel) where the kids get together. When your own daughter's involved, you're a bit older and stuffier, you know. So I went to check it out. Well, it's just a decent youth hostel: separate rooms; lights off at ten-thirty; not too much messing around at night... And if you want to stay up and have a drink, you can, beside the campfire. All very exciting and romantic around the fire.

And I wasn't any trouble either! I got on really well with Farmer Velthuijs. He showed me round the property and told me a lot about the area. He even got me milking cows in the end, and then I was hooked. Soon I was pollarding willows, from which we built embankments; and there were trips in the tractor bus and down streams. Sarah was absolutely dreadful; she refused to go canoeing because there was a cow too close to the water. We had to argue for an hour, even though that's the nice part – the cows half across the boat as you canoe past. And the goats, they're nosy too. Herons, ducks, reeds in your hair. Great! But we did take part in the polder sports contests because of her, and she made sure we won the polder sports cheese slice! I haven't laughed so much in years. She uprooted almost half the camping site in the pitchfork-catching contest.

We'll be going again next year, but we'll be trying 'De Silo', because another couple told us that it was great. And now Peter has serious farming ambitions, because he wants to be as close as possible to that farmer. And I'll leave my books at home."

DISCOTHEEK HOEKLAND

(Code:g177)
Groepsaccommodatie voor 40-75 pers.

Omschrijving: grote recreatiezaal; ruime keuken met kookeiland, 7 grote gaspitten, koelkasten; slaapzaal met zowel stapelbedden als 1 persoonsbedden; 5 toiletten & wasgelegenheden; 5 douches.

(Code:b345)
BoerenBed & Brood voor 2

Omschrijving: gastenkam haard en open keuken; sla sauna; telefoon, computer, luxe boerderijontbijt word lunch en diner buitenshuis;

)
che boerderij voor 6-24 pers.

ng: wonen, werken, eten in de
l. prehistorische kleding, cursus
ken, manden vlechten en koe

(Code:b148)
BoerenBed & Brood voor 3 pers.

Omschrijving: gastenkamers met eigen sanitair; woonkamer en keuken van de familie; douche; strijkijzer aanwezig; wasmachine te gebruiken; telefoon in noodgevallen; boerderijontbijt, lunchpakket en avondeten inbegrepen.

)
oor 2-8 pers.

ng: vrijstaand; zeer eenvoudig
en; composteringstoilet; evt.
kookgerei zelf meenemen; aan-
afrekenen bij de boer.

jeugdherberg 'de Hooiberg'

(Code:r517)
Strohut voor 2-4 pers.

Omschrijving: vrijstaand; slaapgelegenheid; compos slaapzak en kookgerei zelf melden en afrekenen bij de

BLOEMKOOL

AIR-ZUIDWAARTS / SOUTHBOUND

42

RESEARCH

VISUAL RESEARCH
JOHN DAVIES
HET OBSERVATORIUM
MARK PIMLOTT
SCHIE 2.0
HENRIK HÅKANSSON
AD VAN DENDEREN
WIJNANDA DEROO
BERTIEN VAN MANEN
HANS VAN HOUWELINGEN
BIRTHE LEEMEIJER
JOOST GROOTENS
JAN KONINGS/ESTER VAN DE WIEL
HONORÉ δ'O
ANTHROPOLOGICAL RESEARCH
HENK DE HAAN
PHYSICAL PLANNING RESEARCH
SJOERD CUSVELLER

photos: Roy Bijhouwer

Proposal Honoré δ'O

43

AIR-ZUIDWAARTS / SOUTHBOUND

The cultural anthropologist Henk de Haan, attached to the WURC in Wageningen as rural sociologist, supervised students during two research projects in Hoeksche Waard. The first one is about youth cultures in Hoeksche Waard. This research was aimed at describing various youth cultures in Hoeksche Waard. It was carried out in a number of village nuclei and focused on young males and females aged between 16 and 21. The central question was the degree of diversity and the extent to which this diversity consists of variations on a collective rural culture. The research has resulted in an essay describing, on the basis of a series of portraits, what it is like to be young in Hoeksche Waard. The results of this research are important for the future. Considering the requirements that are imposed on the quality of life, the attitude of young people is very important. The second research was about the history of occupation and identity of the farm. The vast polder land of Hoeksche Waard accommodates many monumental farms. They are often located far away from the road, making an impression of impregnable fortresses. However, there is a history hidden behind the walls of these jewels of rural architecture. Generations of farmers and their families lived and worked there. They planted the farmyard, worked in the fields and maintained the farmhouse. For the inhabitants of Hoeksche Waard the farmhouses are more than just industrial buildings or monuments. The farm is linked with the name of a family, its reputation in the village, and the ups and downs of the residents. The farm symbolizes the unchanging, the constant. While the organization of the work and the management were undergoing continuous drastic changes and the residents came and went, the farm was like a beacon in rough seas. The history of the occupation and ownership of several farms has been reconstructed on the basis of archive documents. The second research should be seen in the context of the current perception of monumental farmhouses. A third research project, 'New forms of agrarian entrepreneurship and innovation in Hoeksche Waard', has yet to be carried out. The countryside is often depicted as a stronghold of conservatism, where they distrust modernizing and prefer to rely on the fixed, familiar patterns. Particularly the rural population is thought to adjust only with great difficulty to the new requirements that are imposed on farming. This research will attempt to correct this view. The starting point of the research is the fact that the agrarian company is faced with all kinds of new challenges. Many farmers consider such developments not as a threat but as a stimulus for creating a new basis for employment and thus the continued existence of the business. This research will focus on listing these initiatives. What is the potential of Hoeksche Waard, in light of the proximity of the urban area? It will offer an insight into the creative ways in which farming anticipates the social and economic integration of the countryside with urban surroundings.

RESEARCH

ANTHROPOLOGICAL RESEARCH
HENK DE HAAN

AIR-ZUIDWAARTS / SOUTHBOUND	INTRODUCTION	PROGRAMME	RESEARCH	DESIGN TASK	DESIGN RESEARCH	AFTERTHOUGHTS	APPENDIX
46	WYTZE PATIJN ADRIAAN VAN DER STAAY MIRJAM SALET	ANNE-MIE DEVOLDER	**VISUAL RESEARCH** JOHN DAVIES HET OBSERVATORIUM MARK PIMLOTT SCHIE 2.0 HENRIK HÅKANSSON AD VAN DENDEREN WIJNANDA DEROO BERTIEN VAN MANEN HANS VAN HOUWELINGEN BIRTHE LEEMEIJER JOOST GROOTENS JAN KONINGS/ESTER VAN DE WIEL HONORÉ δ'O **ANTHROPOLOGICAL RESEARCH** HENK DE HAAN PHYSICAL PLANNING RESEARCH SJOERD CUSVELLER	SJOERD CUSVELLER/ ANNE-MIE DEVOLDER	FRITS PALMBOOM/JAAP VAN DEN BOUT PETER CALTHORPE/MATTHEW TAECKER STEFANO BOERI FRANÇOIS ROCHE DETTMAR/BEUTER/FRITZ/HASTENPFLUG BINDELS/GIETEMA/HARTZEMA/KLOK MARIEKE TIMMERMANS DIRK SIJMONS/YTTJE FEDDES	ARNOLD REIJNDORP BROESI/JANNINK/VELDHUIS ERIC LUITEN	CHRONICLE PERSONAL PARTICULARS PERSONS INVOLVED COLOPHON

photo: Ad van Denderen

Rural youth between town and country: rural realities and urban myths

The process of urbanization has not erased a sense of 'otherness' among rural residents. On the contrary, it has provoked discourses and practices that are very much framed into classical notions of rurality and locality. This process is particularly explicit among rural young people. From a survey among secondary school children, it was possible to identify a variety of positions on urbanization and regional development. Young people of course lack the experience of age to put current developments into perspective. For them, urbanization is a self-evident characteristic of their life-world. This explains a certain indifference and an insufficiency of knowledge. And yet there is a clear tendency among young people to frame their views of their region into contrasting images. They have no doubts about the character of Hoeksche Waard: it is rural through and through. The 'rural' is overwhelmingly conceptualized in terms of agriculture on the one hand and the predominantly localized character of social and cultural life on the other. If young people express their attitudes towards current developments in Hoeksche Waard, they in fact mainly ventilate value judgements on this real or imagined rural society.

Two perspectives may be distinguished on local rural life and urbanization. On the one hand there is a rural perspective, which highly values small-scale society and interconnaissance. The urban is portrayed as a threat to this idealized community. Moreover, there is a general scepticism towards metropolitan lifestyles in general. On the other hand, there is an urban perspective which welcomes urban influences as positive. Urban life is associated with more freedom, less social control and more possibilities for entertainment. Rotterdam, and city life in general, is highly valued and contrasted with the backward and boring life in the country. Attitudes are thus constructed in terms of desires and myths, based on different conceptualizations of urban and rural realities. These diverging ideas about rural and urban life are more than abstract constructions, however. They are based on real experiences, preferences and, more importantly, are embedded in everyday practice. It is especially through networks of friendship and shared forms of entertainment that young people express their urban or rural identity. Local rural identity is particularly expressed by visiting pubs, clubs and parties in nearby villages in a simple, uncommercialized atmosphere where most people know each other. By organizing their famous schuurfeesten (parties in a shed) rural youth has contributed to reinvigorating rural culture by expressively contesting the urban-style disco. A schuurfeest is the manifestation par excellence of a new self-confidence among rural youth. They are proud of themselves and don't feel ashamed of their local attachment, unrefined manners and dialect. All these attributes are presented as symbols of identity and otherness vis-à-vis urban-oriented youth and lifestyles. Instead of being colonized or marginalized by urbanization, the 'new' rural youth has provided a strong symbolic answer. The urban-oriented youth is generally marked by a preference for urban forms of entertainment. They look down upon 'de boeren' (the peasants) and how they enjoy themselves, seeking instead the anonymous thrill of city life.

The urbanization of the countryside: retreat and revival of rurality

Hoeksche Waard has experienced an intense process of urbanization during the past decades. Most villages have built extensive new housing estates and large areas are now used for the expanding service and industry sectors. Over the past ten years the number of people living in Hoeksche Waard has increased by more than 30 per cent. Hoeksche Waard is not only an attractive site for industrial investment, but also increasingly a favourable place to live for commuters. The predominantly rural local population has thus experienced considerable social, economic and visual change in its environment. In terms of access to services, employment structure and other objective indicators of urban–rural differences, Hoeksche Waard shares many of the characteristics of an urban area. The only significant difference is that residential areas are more dispersed and surrounded by agricultural land. The 'open' countryside with its farms, dikes and fields still very much conforms to the rural image.

But the process of urbanization has not erased the sense of 'otherness' among the majority of residents. On the contrary, it has provoked a local discourse on rurality and locality framed by traditional notions of rural–urban differences. While new concepts of rurality emanating from urban desires are increasingly gaining in importance among the new residents (recreation, nature conservation, and a quiet place to live) the locals tend to stress the disruption of 'community life'. 'Urbanity' is symbolized by 'Rotterdam' and urbanization depicted as a process by which Rotterdam's problems are exported to Hoeksche Waard. Thus, the local population feels threatened by growing crime, loss of identity, individualism, mass society and moral values. 'Rotterdam' has actually brought about a change in thinking. While urban life used to be an abstract, irrelevant notion in the past, it is now an everyday reality that encourages reacting to and rethinking one's own condition. In a context characterized by a plurality of lifestyles and practices, an awareness of distinction obviously raises the question of identity.

RESEARCH
VISUAL RESEARCH
JOHN DAVIES
HET OBSERVATORIUM
MARK PIMLOTT
SCHIE 2.0
HENRIK HÅKANSSON
AD VAN DENDEREN
WIJNANDA DEROO
BERTIEN VAN MANEN
HANS VAN HOUWELINGEN
BIRTHE LEEMEIJER
JOOST GROOTENS
JAN KONINGS/ESTER VAN DE WIEL
HONORÉ δ'O
ANTHROPOLOGICAL RESEARCH
HENK DE HAAN
PHYSICAL PLANNING RESEARCH
SJOERD CUSVELLER

Signs in the landscape: the construction of identities in Hoeksche Waard

The landscape of Hoeksche Waard is characterized by regular agricultural fields, scattered farmhouses, a diversity of settlement forms, dikes, polders, riverbanks and seashores. Each characteristic contributes to the perception of a landscape with a specific identity. Identity and identities are however not based on natural, objective or functional characteristics alone. Identities are also shaped in the process of attributing values, meanings and symbols to the material and natural world. The formation of identities is a social, cultural, political and personal process, and depends on knowledge, life experience and value judgements. So nothing has an unvarying, pre-established identity but instead has multiple identities and different layers of meaning. A farmhouse, for instance, may represent a model of vernacular architecture for one observer, a unit of production for another, or fond memories of family events from a third perspective. The vernacular formation of identity rests upon comparative knowledge of rural building styles, functional representation on economic consideration, and the association with family events on personal experience and emotions. Currently, Hoeksche Waard is experiencing a process whereby local social identities are confronted with political, scientific and urban constructions of identity. In general, a distinction can be made between different levels of identity formation.

First, at the local level the material, natural world constitutes the actual living and working spaces. In a rural context much effort gets put into creating a productive environment, basically resulting in a variety of forms to control and manipulate nature. Each field, farm, windmill, waterway or dike represents a chain in a complex agrarian production system. The identity of things is closely associated with use-value. But this is only one version of how people attribute identities to elements in a landscape. The landscape is also a collection of signs, reflecting personal histories, social stratification, forms of attachment and memorable events. People are not only able to draw a physical map of their environment, but also a cognitive map, i.e., each field, farm, house or street is a place where the social meets the material. A farmhouse is known through its inhabitants, a field through the people who own and use it, and so on. The more people are able to compose such a cognitive map of their environment, the more they are able to develop a sense of belonging and a sense of place. And, more importantly, if they can impress their own identity on the environment, they have a local identity. Local ways of identity formation are thus very much bound to intimate knowledge of people and places and it is basically an internal process.

Research in Hoeksche Waard has shown that the internal process of identity formation consists of numerous narratives that bring to life objects that have no meaning for outsiders. With the loosening relationship with the land as a result of a declining agricultural population, growing numbers of newcomers and spatial transformations, the capacity of people to perceive the landscape in social terms and to impress their identity on places has gradually declined. Thus, people find it less easy to develop a sense of belonging. Especially the farming population has suffered from a loss of identity. In the past their imprint on the landscape was omnipresent. As employers and holders of key positions in water management boards, the municipal council and the church, they formed a local elite with a highly visible presence. Over the past decades farmers have lost these positions. Many farm families have, moreover, abandoned farming altogether and thus became anonymous subjects with no reference to visible elements in the landscape. The declining significance of the landscape as the visual representation of personal identities, memories and events is well illustrated by the attitude of young farmers. Although they farm patrimonial land, they seem to distance themselves from any emotional link to the land and the ancestral farm. They derive their identity not from place or family of origin, but from professional attributes shaped within a delocalized culture.

The second way in which landscape identities are shaped differs fundamentally from the first. The context within which meanings are attributed is not the local community and its territory but a collection of ideas and preferences that are projected upon a region. This decontextualization of identity formation is associated with the integration of Hoeksche Waard in wider social and regional projects. Urban demands for space and broader social and political concerns for nature conservation have redefined the landscape in political and scientific concepts. Landscape values are assigned in terms of needs, interests and uniqueness by policy makers and scientific researchers, and sensual satisfaction by newcomers and visitors.

This multiplication of identities obviously may result in conflicts over rural practices. How the landscape is transformed or conserved touches upon questions of identity. A village is not just a collection of houses and streets; for the people who have lived there most of their lives, it is a social universe, a place with a social identity where they have developed a sense of belonging. Newcomers and visitors cannot recognize this social identity because it is attached to personal experience and memories. As the built environment changes and new residents arrive, the vision of the environment is increasingly structured by neo-rural concepts, which accelerates the process of deterritorialized and depersonalized identities. New trends in urban development and architecture may attempt to build upon endogenous identities, but in reality such design practice is based on urban ideals and constructions of regional authenticity. This is not surprising, because endogenous local perceptions of the landscape are constructed socially, not by design or planning. New concepts of regional development may thus only satisfy those people who identify with urban definitions of rurality.

The results of this investigation are published in 'Waar het landschap begint/New Landscape Frontiers', reader international conference 29/30/31 October 1998 (Rotterdam, AIR). The complete text is available with the author Henk de Haan, WURC, Department Social Science, Hollandseweg 1, 6706 KN Wageningen, e-mail: henk.dehaan@alg.swg.wau.nl

AIR-ZUIDWAARTS / SOUTHBOUND

This chapter presents a selected survey of the present plans and planning initiatives for Hoeksche Waard and its context. The survey is also intended as an illustration of the various standpoints on the future development of Hoeksche Waard, exemplifying at the same time the (spatial) dynamics of the region. It is striking that the plans are no longer exclusively made by the public authorities. Social groups, such as the World Wildlife Fund and the District Water Boards, are active in shaping the spatial planning.

RESEARCH

PHYSICAL PLANNING RESEARCH
SJOERD CUSVELLER

AIR-ZUIDWAARTS / SOUTHBOUND

INTRODUCTION	PROGRAMME	RESEARCH	DESIGN TASK	DESIGN RESEARCH	AFTERTHOUGHTS	APPENDIX
WYTZE PATIJN	ANNE-MIE DEVOLDER	**VISUAL RESEARCH**	SJOERD CUSVELLER/	FRITS PALMBOOM/JAAP VAN DEN BOUT	ARNOLD REIJNDORP	CHRONICLE
ADRIAAN VAN DER STAAY		JOHN DAVIES	ANNE-MIE DEVOLDER	PETER CALTHORPE/MATTHEW TAECKER	BROESI/JANNINK/VELDHUIS	PERSONAL PARTICULARS
MIRJAM SALET		HET OBSERVATORIUM		STEFANO BOERI	ERIC LUITEN	PERSONS INVOLVED
		MARK PIMLOTT		FRANÇOIS ROCHE		COLOPHON
		SCHIE 2.0		DETTMAR/BEUTER/FRITZ/HASTENPFLUG		
		HENRIK HÅKANSSON		BINDELS/GIETEMA/HARTZEMA/KLOK		
		AD VAN DENDEREN		MARIEKE TIMMERMANS		
		WIJNANDA DEROO		DIRK SIJMONS/YTTJE FEDDES		
		BERTIEN VAN MANEN				
		HANS VAN HOUWELINGEN				
		BIRTHE LEEMEIJER				
		JOOST GROOTENS				
		JAN KONINGS/ESTER VAN DE WIEL				
		HONORÉ δ'O				
		ANTHROPOLOGICAL RESEARCH				
		HENK DE HAAN				
		PHYSICAL PLANNING RESEARCH				
		SJOERD CUSVELLER				

Development of 'Groote of Zuidhollandsche Waard'

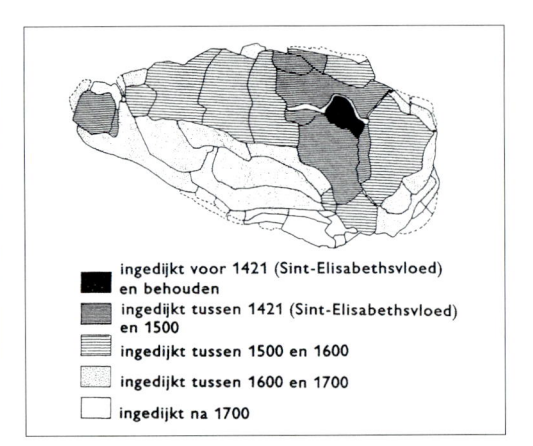

Schematic reproduction of Hoeksche Waard dykes

Topographic map of the Delta from 1573

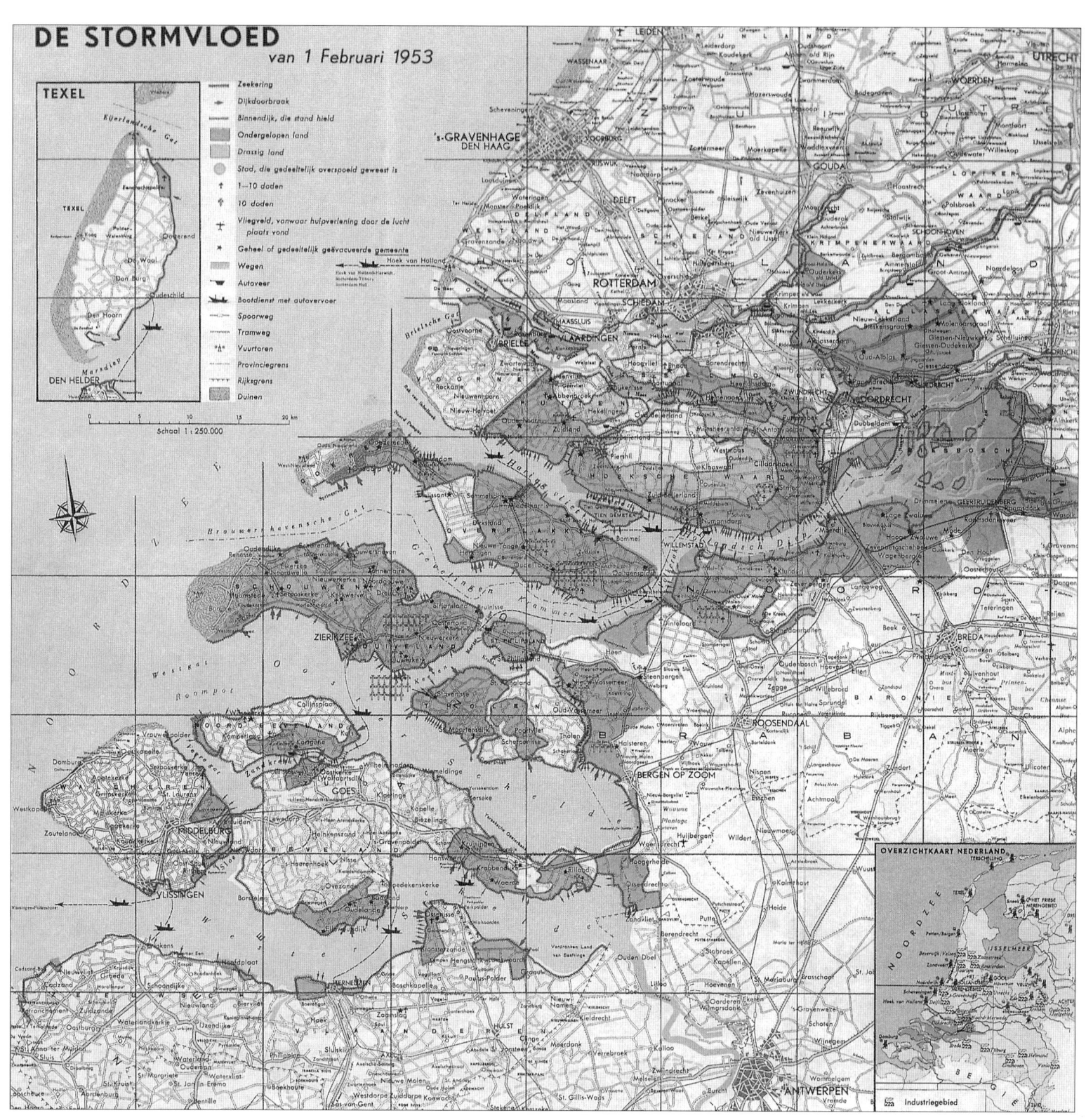

Flooded area after the Great Flood of 1953

AIR-ZUIDWAARTS / SOUTHBOUND

RESEARCH
VISUAL RESEARCH
JOHN DAVIES
HET OBSERVATORIUM
MARK PIMLOTT
SCHIE 2.0
HENRIK HÅKANSSON
AD VAN DENDEREN
WIJNANDA DEROO
BERTIEN VAN MANEN
HANS VAN HOUWELINGEN
BIRTHE LEEMEIJER
JOOST GROOTENS
JAN KONINGS/ESTER VAN DE WIEL
HONORÉ δ'O
ANTHROPOLOGICAL RESEARCH
HENK DE HAAN
PHYSICAL PLANNING RESEARCH
SJOERD CUSVELLER

Present planning documents

In the nineties, after years of relative silence, ideas on the possibilities of developing the south wing of the Randstad and Hoeksche Waard with it, began to take shape in earnest. Following a decade of maintenance or stagnation, this is a sign of optimism resulting from the general economic revival. Once again there is room for investment in the future of the country. The introduction of thinking in models and scenarios stimulates debate on this issue, without leading to definitive and widely supported views.

The planning documents express a general acknowledgement of the special situation of Hoeksche Waard, on the one hand as part of the south wing of the Randstad, on the other as situated between the major ports of Rotterdam and Antwerp or alternatively between the Randstad and the 'Flemish Diamond'. Finally, the region is part of the Rhine-Scheldt delta, where river estuaries, water management, agricultural use and nature conservation seem to dominate the agenda of the future. The starting-point of the plans is highly divergent, depending on where emphasis is laid. Municipalities in Hoeksche Waard greatly value the preservation of their identity. This is a standard against which spatial planning developments for the future are measured. At government level, only abstract concepts for the entire country have been issued so far, such as 'Stedenland' (country of cities) and 'Stromenland' (country of flows). At an interregional level the authorities concerned stress the special geographical location and dynamics of the region. These dynamics exist in the provinces of economy and ecology alike.

The possible coherence between conservation and development has scarcely been investigated as yet in the plans. This complicated force field offers sufficient opportunity for accurately establishing the significance of Hoeksche Waard so as to develop proposals for a perspective of the future. From the collection of plans, three themes for such a perspective emerge. First, transformations resulting from the required change in water management and from the switch in the agricultural sector. Second, transformations resulting from the transit function of the North-South corridor of Rotterdam-Antwerp and the possibilities of establishing in combination logistics, transportation and distribution facilities. And finally, transformations resulting from the role of catchment area for the needs of, among other things, an expanding Randstad: housing, business domiciles, glasshouse cultivation, recreation and green space.

Second Benelux Structural Concept, Benelux Economic Union, 1996

The Second Benelux Structural Concept interprets the Benelux as three overlapping components: North Benelux, South Benelux and Delta Benelux. Three distinct basic structures define how the components hang together: the natural structure, defining to a great extent the ecological functioning of the areas; the urban networks, important for cultural and economic development and the diversity of facilities; and the main infrastructure, which by and large forms the basis of economic performance.

The desired spatial structure is based on five starting-points:

1. A selective concentration of urban and economic activities. The urban junctions and networks primarily qualify as bearers of specific urban activities.

2. A wider development of rural areas. The social, cultural and economic quality of life in large parts of the area are under pressure from trends towards an upscaling in agriculture and the services industry. New methods of cultivation and new products may offer a solution. The quality of space, water and environment are limiting conditions in this respect.

3. Establishing specific concentrations of economic activities. The two principal ports, Rotterdam and Antwerp, and a number of smaller harbours together form one single complex, the largest port in the world with a key distribution function. Cooperation will have to focus in particular on a more efficient functioning of the complex, for instance by complementing the links with the hinterland.

4. Sustained mobility through multimodality. Good functioning of the network of the main infrastructure is crucial to the economic position of the Benelux. Here, each means of transport will have to acquire a place and task of its own, while special attention is to be paid to reinforcing multimodality in the transport of goods and to the role of public passenger transport at a regional level.

5. Development of nature and improvement of the ecological conditions. The spatial concept consists of a series of maps. The character of the Benelux Delta is heavily determined by the valleys of the rivers Rhine, Maas and Scheldt and their tributaries. The north-south chain of urban networks, consisting of the Randstad and the so-called

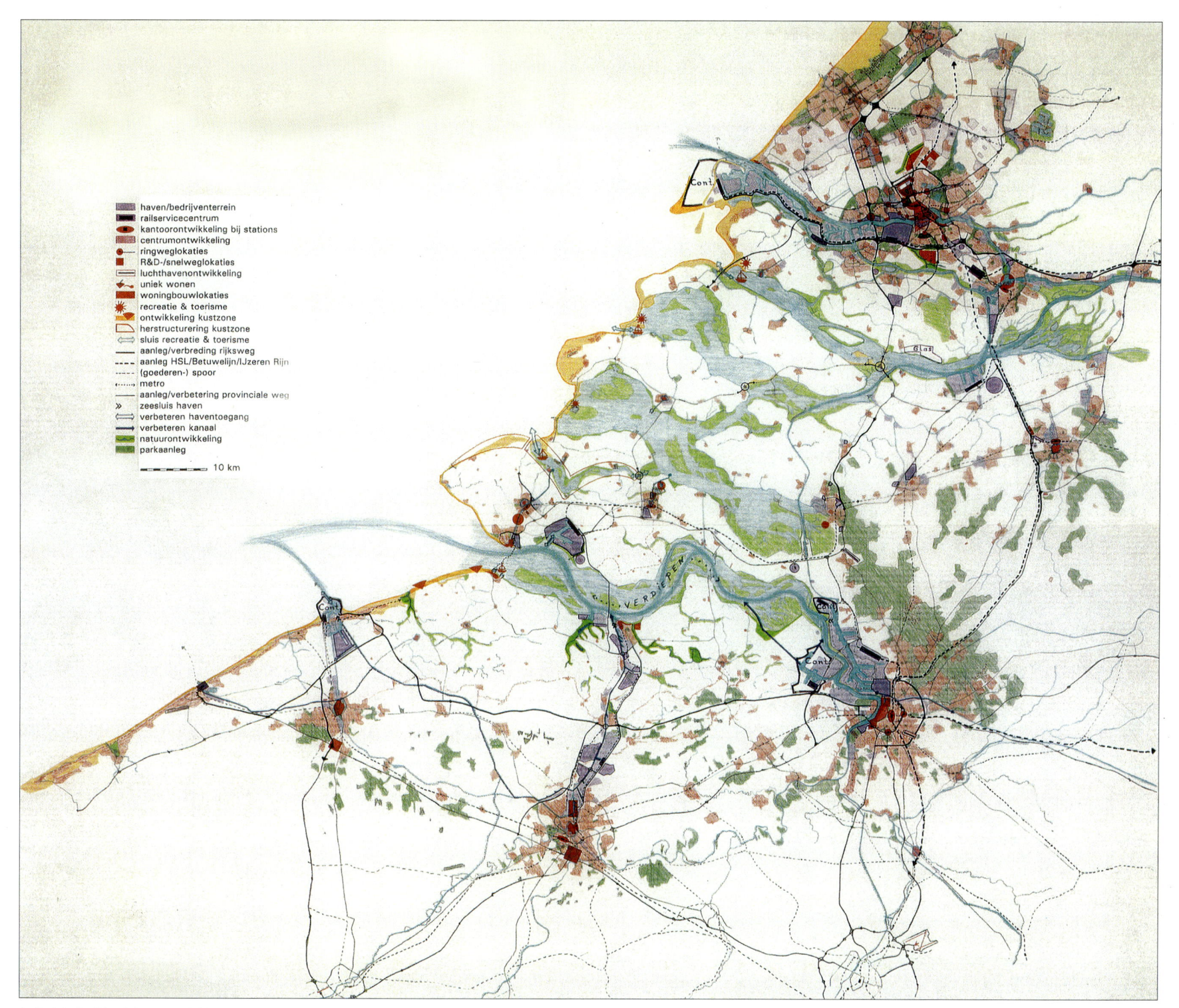

	haven/bedrijventerrein
	railservicecentrum
●	kantoorontwikkeling bij stations
	centrumontwikkeling
●	ringweglokaties
■	R&D-/snelweglokaties
	luchthavenontwikkeling
	uniek wonen
	woningbouwlokaties
✳	recreatie & toerisme
	ontwikkeling kustzone
	herstructurering kustzone
⇦	sluis recreatie & toerisme
	aanleg/verbreding rijksweg
	aanleg HSL/Betuwelijn/IJzeren Rijn
	(goederen-) spoor
	metro
	aanleg/verbetering provinciale weg
»	zeesluis haven
⇨	verbeteren haventoegang
	verbeteren kanaal
	natuurontwikkeling
	parkaanleg

10 km

Projects in the Rhine-Scheldt delta 1998

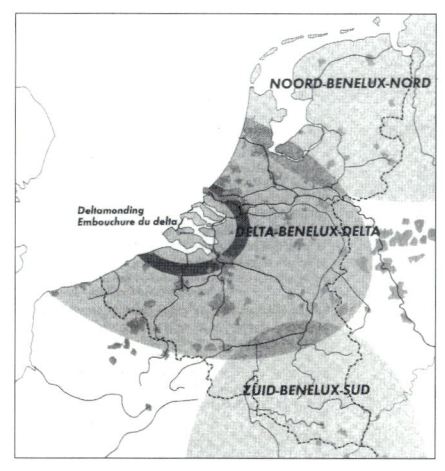

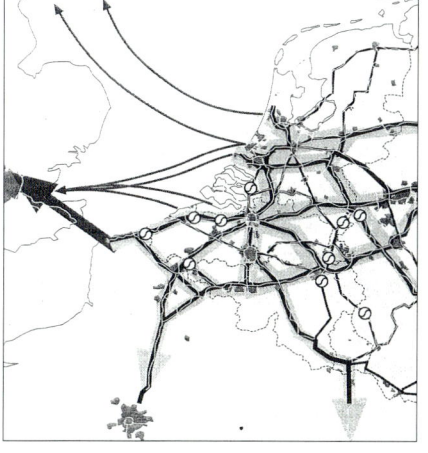

Second Benelux Structural Concept 1996

Three spatial units

Road transport

Benelux Mainport

RESEARCH
VISUAL RESEARCH
JOHN DAVIES
HET OBSERVATORIUM
MARK PIMLOTT
SCHIE 2.0
HENRIK HÅKANSSON
AD VAN DENDEREN
WIJNANDA DEROO
BERTIEN VAN MANEN
HANS VAN HOUWELINGEN
BIRTHE LEEMEIJER
JOOST GROOTENS
JAN KONINGS/ESTER VAN DE WIEL
HONORÉ δ'O
ANTHROPOLOGICAL RESEARCH
HENK DE HAAN
PHYSICAL PLANNING RESEARCH
SJOERD CUSVELLER

Flemish Diamond, offers an environment for establishing high-quality cultural and economic activities. There are many harbours in the delta, which from a spatial point of view are to be regarded as a single port: Benelux Mainport. This is supported by the combined principal connections between the urban networks (north-south) and between the harbours and their hinterland (west-east). The draft is nearly completed, bar a few missing links and problem points.

Delta Perspective, Rhine-Scheldt Delta Cooperation Project, June 1998

The Rhine-Scheldt Delta Cooperation Project focuses on cooperation between all the parties involved with planning in the delta area. The Delta Perspective analyses the area as a contact zone between sea and land, between cities and networks and between two differing cultures with a common language. Its situation on the boundary between sea and land determines the economic strength and ecological resources of the region. As the estuary of a number of large European rivers, the delta presents a natural gateway to the European continent. In economic respect this is expressed in the harbour activities, but also in the logistic-industrial complex. The Rotterdam and Antwerp ports form the major junctions of a harbour network that is among the most important in the world. The ecological resources are closely related to the quality of the region as an estuary. The effect of the tides and the transition from fresh to salt water bring with them special ecological values. The combination of water, beach, dunes and wooded areas also renders the region attractive to daytrippers and tourists.

The Rhine-Scheldt delta is situated between the urban networks of the Randstad, the Flemish Diamond and the North-Brabant chain of towns, with their numerous high-quality facilities in every conceivable field. The degree of urbanization of the delta, on the other hand, is quite limited. This relative openness is a special quality of the delta.

The history of the Rhine-Scheldt delta is marked by the separation into the Southern and Northern Netherlands. The delta is the place where the Catholic south and the Calvinist north meet and interact. The presence of different cultures linked by a single language is a source of wealth.

In this variegated contact zone the Rhine-Scheldt Perspective distinguishes four structures: logistic-industrial system, ecosystem, tourist-recreational system and urban system. The vision of the future of the delta consists of networks based on these systems. The water network is a combination of the great river estuaries and the North Sea, bearers of both ecological and economic developments. Expanding and optimizing the delta-port network requires cooperation

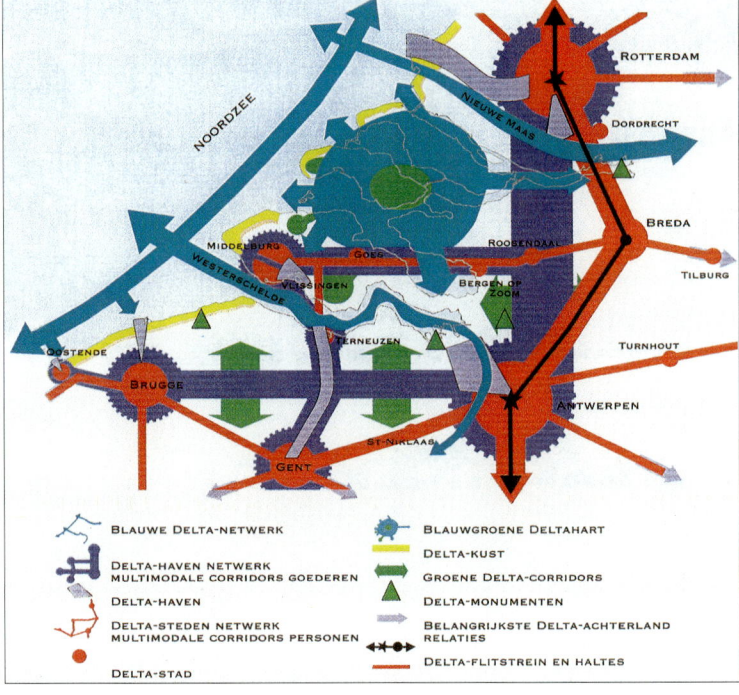

Delta-perspectief, Rijn-Schelde Delta Samenwerkingsproject 1998

and complementation, with the joint input of a high-quality port scenario, new sites of innovation, environmental protection and durable business parks. A multimodal transportation corridor from Rotterdam via Antwerp to Ostend serves as the logistic basis of the harbour network. Rotterdam, Breda, Antwerp and Ghent are the contact points of the delta with the urban networks. And the future HSL (High Speed Line) has an important part to play in the Antwerp-Rotterdam network.

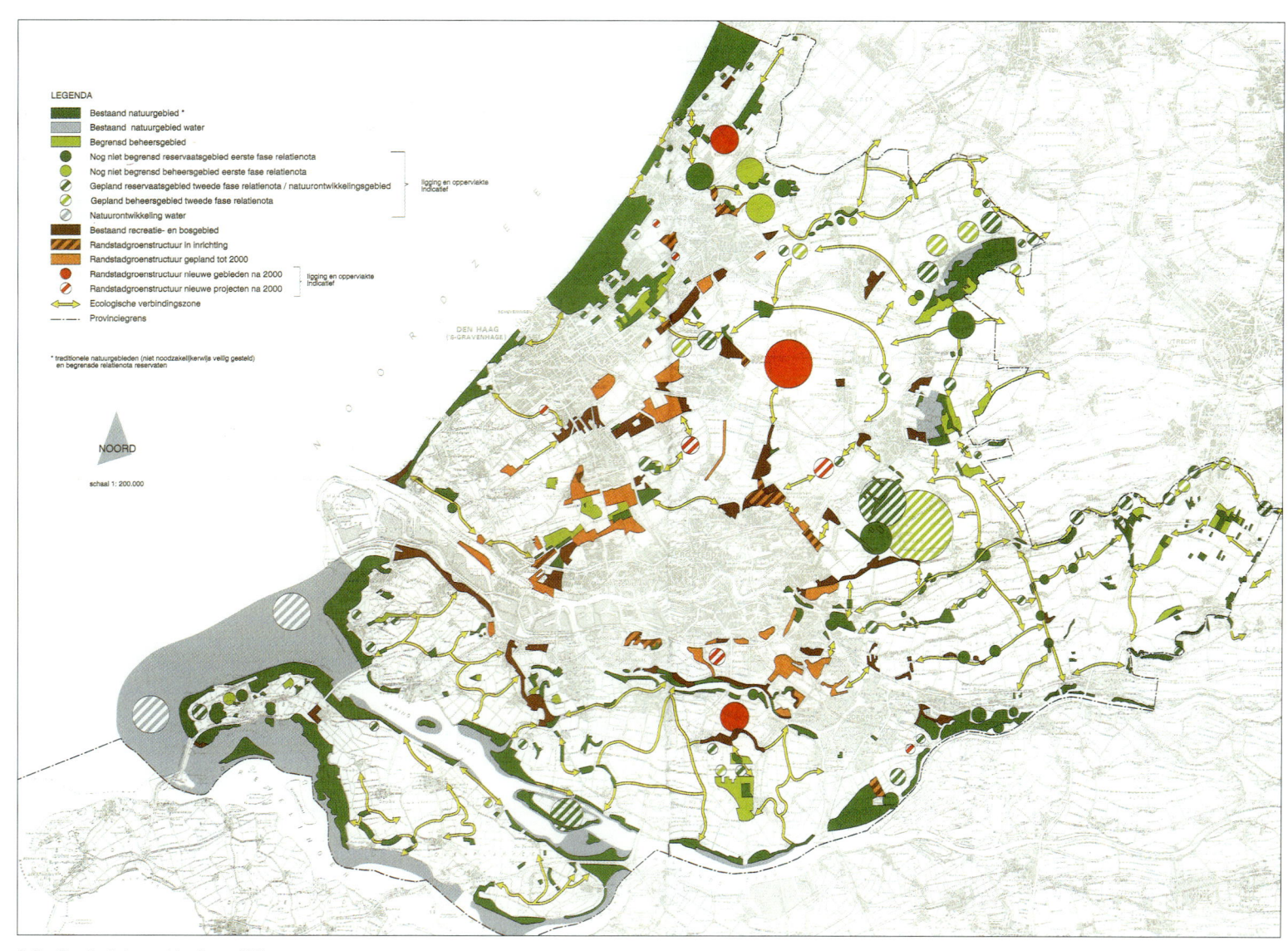

Policy Plan for Nature and Landscape 1991

Policy Plan for Nature and Landscape, Province of Zuid-Holland, 1991

This somewhat older Policy Plan is important because it is actually the first plan to emphasize the development of nature and landscape. Starting-points of the plan are preserving ecological values and realizing a high-quality residential environment in the Randstad's environs. In order to achieve this, the Policy Plan focuses on three related fields. In defining the ecological main structure, ecological values of national and international significance can be preserved. In the south of the province this main structure is determined by the coast, the river banks and the connecting zones. On the Zuid-Holland islands, the connecting zones largely follow the course of the (former) creeks. Landscape renewal is the second focus of attention. Renewal of the landscape in and around the south wing of the Randstad – frequently disrupted by urbanization – is essential to the quality of city-dwelling. The plan proposes a number of new, large green spaces in connection with the urbanization planning process and the establishing of glasshouses, one of them being a green area in the north of Hoeksche Waard. The third point in the Policy Plan is the preservation and active management of outstanding landscape values. To this end, all structuring elements and components of the area having valuable landscape and/or cultural-historical qualities have been recorded on a map.

AIR-ZUIDWAARTS / SOUTHBOUND

RESEARCH
VISUAL RESEARCH
JOHN DAVIES
HET OBSERVATORIUM
MARK PIMLOTT
SCHIE 2.0
HENRIK HÅKANSSON
AD VAN DENDEREN
WIJNANDA DEROO
BERTIEN VAN MANEN
HANS VAN HOUWELINGEN
BIRTHE LEEMEIJER
JOOST GROOTENS
JAN KONINGS/ESTER VAN DE WIEL
HONORÉ δ'O
ANTHROPOLOGICAL RESEARCH
HENK DE HAAN
PHYSICAL PLANNING RESEARCH
SJOERD CUSVELLER

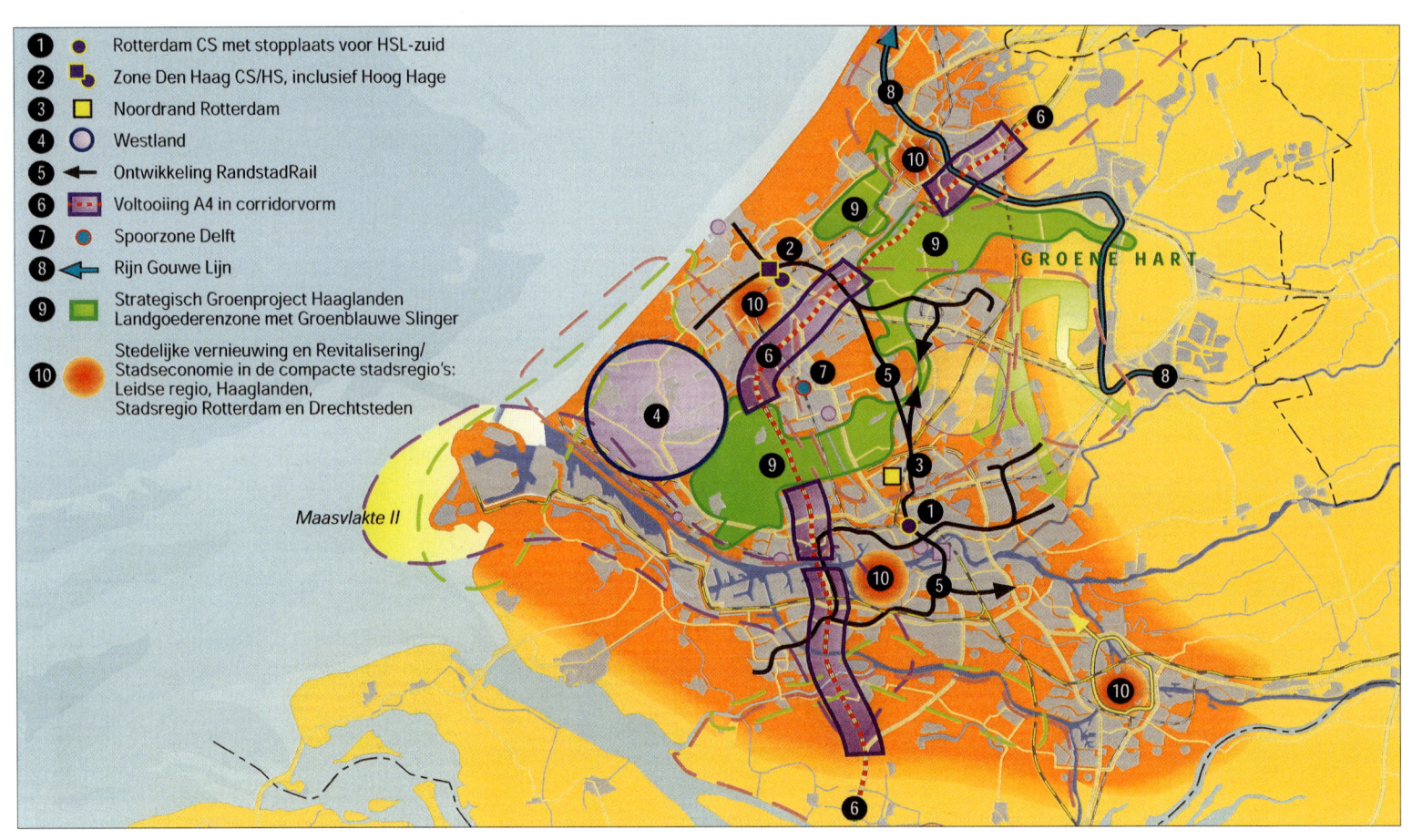

Discussion Report on the Spatial Future of the south wing 1994

Discussion Report on the Spatial Future of the south wing, Province of Zuid-Holland, 1994

The discussion report concludes that development of the south wing of the Randstad is lagging behind that of the rest of the Netherlands. Particularly the absence of high-quality regional public transport, of sufficient transportation capacity and of large green areas around and between the cities, threatens both the future quality of urban life and the position on the international platform. The limits to the possibilities of urbanization in the south wing are coming into view. This calls for an efficient use of space and entry into alliances with adjoining regions.

The solutions are evident from this analysis. These are found in links with the strong spatial aspects of the south wing, in the great diversity of area types and landscapes, the good connections between economic centres in and around the south wing and the European hinterland, and the rich variety of urban environments and facilities.

For the period after 2005 the Discussion Report names several tasks: A permanent restructuring of the city will maintain the required quality of the built environment, further improve the residential environment and stimulate the urban economy. Enduring, high-quality green zones will safeguard the variety of urban and rural areas. Creating a green framework will weld together valuable green spaces and desired ecological connections into one coherent system. Reinforcing a public transport network functioning on a regional scale will link up the various cities and regions (such a regional railway network can be effected by joining the Rotterdam metro, the express tramline in The Hague and a few lines of the Dutch mainline railway, supplemented with a number of missing links). The cities, the green framework and the regional rail network jointly will form the framework for a specific, urban and green layout complementing the city, thus taking the step from 'compact city' to regional urban network. The Discussion Report further elaborates the tasks by establishing a number of spearhead projects: the Blue-Green Serpentine as a green section in the heart of the south wing; the A4 corridor as new economic support; the creating of spatial conditions that generate more work; the peripheral zone of the Green Heart as a buffer area; the restructuring of the Westland; a regional railway network for high-quality public transport in connection with inner-city development and further urbanization.

'Een Haalbare Kaart', metropolitan district of Rotterdam, 1996

'Een Haalbare Kaart' (A Viable Option, a play of words on 'viable proposition' and 'practicable map') presents a survey of the planning policy of the metropolitan district of Rotterdam, resulting in seven strategic tasks. These concern the problematic of the lag in economic development, the insufficient quality of the residential environment and the problems of a metropolis in general. The tasks are aimed at making better use of a number of 'trump cards'. The Mainport, the infrastructure and the favourable situation within the network of European cities offer opportunities for the economy and for employment. Large urban facilities could be utilized more efficiently as generators of work. Finally, it is much more effective to exploit the varied landscape in the direct vicinity of the Rotterdam region as a place for setting up enterprises.

'Een Haalbare Kaart' focuses on three aspects. First, stimulating regional economic activities by making better use of the position of the region in a wider context. Second, combining investments, so that 'weak' sectors can benefit from 'strong' sectors, and third, achieving quality and diversity in spatial environments as key conditions for enterprises and inhabitants alike. Seven dynamic area types are distinguished to this end, amongst which 'highway zones', 'junction locations', 'waterfronts' and 'green urban peripheries'. Developing (the northern part of) Hoeksche Waard is seen as a planning task at an interregional level, where various demands from the regional-quality and European Mainport perspectives converge. Finally, there are great advantages in tying together the various sectoral claims, such as the large infrastructural works of the HSL and A4, a harbour-related business park and river-bank projects, and regional requirements.

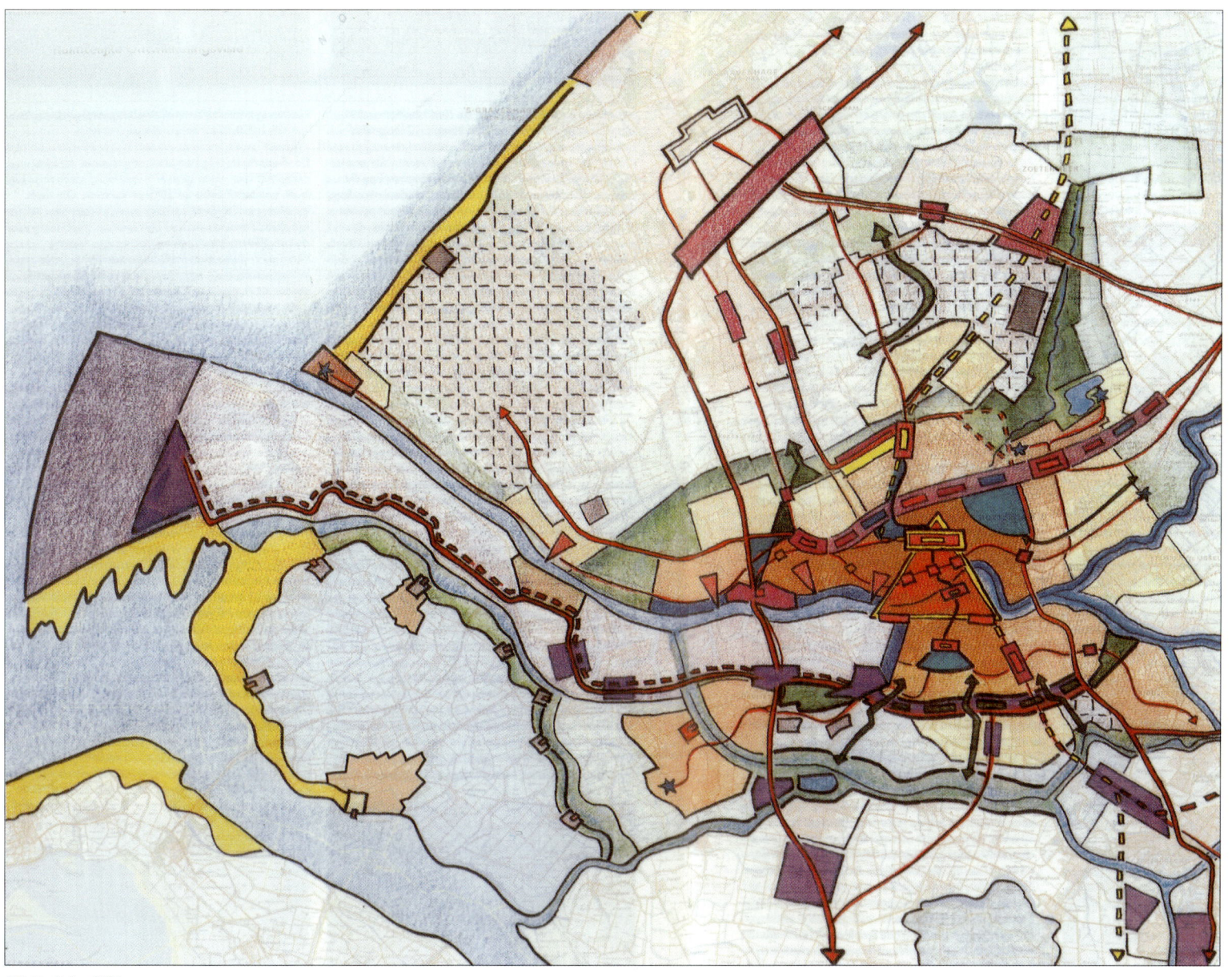

A Viable Option 1996

AIR-ZUIDWAARTS / SOUTHBOUND

RESEARCH
VISUAL RESEARCH
JOHN DAVIES
HET OBSERVATORIUM
MARK PIMLOTT
SCHIE 2.0
HENRIK HÅKANSSON
AD VAN DENDEREN
WIJNANDA DEROO
BERTIEN VAN MANEN
HANS VAN HOUWELINGEN
BIRTHE LEEMEIJER
JOOST GROOTENS
JAN KONINGS/ESTER VAN DE WIEL
HONORÉ δ'O
ANTHROPOLOGICAL RESEARCH
HENK DE HAAN
PHYSICAL PLANNING RESEARCH
SJOERD CUSVELLER

Foaming Water 1998

'Bruisend Water', Zuid-Holland Province and Zuid-Holland Water Board, 1998

'Bruisend Water' (Foaming Water) analyses the developments in water management and their consequences up to the year 2050. Two developments are distinguished here: physical, more or less natural processes, and development in the use of soil and water, depending on social needs and potentials. One of the major natural processes is the expected change in climate. Due to the rise in temperature, strongly varying air currents and an increase in rainfall, the Rhine is acquiring the character of a rain-fed river. Another result of global warming is the rising sea level. The change in climate will have its effect on one of the main functions of rivers: the drainage of water, ice and sediment. In the future this drainage function will become more problematic because of two combined effects. The fall of the rivers will decrease due to the higher sea level, while the drainage peaks will increase in winter because of the changing rain pattern. Apart from this, there is the process of permanent soil subsidence. This is chiefly caused by the settling of clay and peat, and by oxidation of peat layers, in which the groundwater level plays an important part. In deep peat bogs, the rate of subsidence is between 40 and 100 cm per century.

The quality of the water is strongly influenced by social developments. It is expected that river water will get cleaner and that emissions from agriculture, urban areas and industry will lessen. The creation of large green spaces also has a positive effect on the quality of the water. However, in the coming decades it will not be possible to keep the quality of the water up to the required standards without taking extra measures.

In order to cope with these consequences, there are two fundamentally different strategies for the future. The traditional strategy is that water management is a derivative of spatial planning. The other is that spatial planning is directed by water management. The starting-points in both cases are maintaining the present safety level, safeguarding the freshwater supply and exploiting of the dynamics of the delta. A crucial point is the change in 'opening scenario' for the Haringvliet lock sluices. Two variants are suggested. In one variant the lock sluices operate as flood barriers, in the other their opening times are much more limited ('tamed tide'). According to the 'water directs' strategy, the first variant offers the most favourable prospects for firmly restoring to the region the values of the estuary. Due to the fact that the lock sluices are almost permanently open, sediment from the rivers is drained away to the sea. That this also causes the heavily polluted, deeper-lying sediments in the Haringvliet to come to the surface again, is an additional, negative effect. In this 'opening scenario' the boundary between fresh and salt water will be much farther inland. This requires a freshwater supply by way of an intake farther upstream, besides considerable water gauging, temporary storage of rain surplus in (new) nature reserves and more open water. Just as before 1970, agricultural use will have to adapt to the changed circumstances: a shift towards crops that are less susceptible to salt.

A better flow for the drainage of river water towards the sea can be achieved by broadening the river bed through freeing the river forelands. In places where there are no forelands, the dike can be replaced. The obvious move is to combine this with nature development. Extreme peaks in drainage could be diverted to Volkerak, Grevelingenmeer and Oosterschelde.

'Nieuw Rotterdams Peil', World Wildlife Fund, 1997

'Nieuw Rotterdams Peil' (New Rotterdam Watermark) assesses the economic and ecological potential of the Rotterdam region at the level of the entire Rhine-Maas estuary. It views the development of the entire estuary against the background of a rising sea level and out of awareness of the fact that urbanization will increasingly leave its mark on this region. Within this context, it reconsiders the supply of sediments, the tides and the rain surplus as physical factors underpinning the delta. In its proposals 'Nieuw Rotterdams Peil' goes one step further than 'Bruisend Water'.

Sand and silt are the natural materials of which the delta is composed. Sedimentation contributes to a seaward shift of the estuaries, the silting-up of lower-lying banks and growth at the Front delta. It forms the long-term insurance of the estuary against a rise in the sea level. By enlarging the overflow area, a larger sedimentation area grows along with the sea. Consequently, water storage is also increased; this is conducive to safety in the estuary.

In achieving the desired distribution of the sediment, man has a natural ally in the tide, which keeps channels at the right depth and deposits the received matter on the banks. The tide can return to large parts of the area by partially reopening the sea gates.

The Rhine-Maas delta has a fragile freshwater system. Penetration of salt water via open sea arms firstly requires an eastward shift in the points of intake. The rain surplus has to be retained in the polders in a more capacious 'boezem' system of polder outlets, connected with new wetland nature reserves as suppliers of clean water. In addition, soil subsidence and silting-up are combatted by locating these water buffers in the deepest-lying polders.

As a counterpart to the industrial and urbanized estuary of the Nieuwe Maas/Nieuwe Waterweg, 'Nieuw Rotterdams Peil' proposes an open, natural estuary to its south, extending along Haringvliet from Biesbos to the front delta. This vast nature reserve at a mere 20 km from the metropolis, can burgeon into an important walking, cycling and sailing area. Via Spui, Oude Maas, Noord and the concomitant water system, the tidal landscape, with its creeks, woods and grassy mud flats, can percolate into the city and be a guideline for further urbanization.

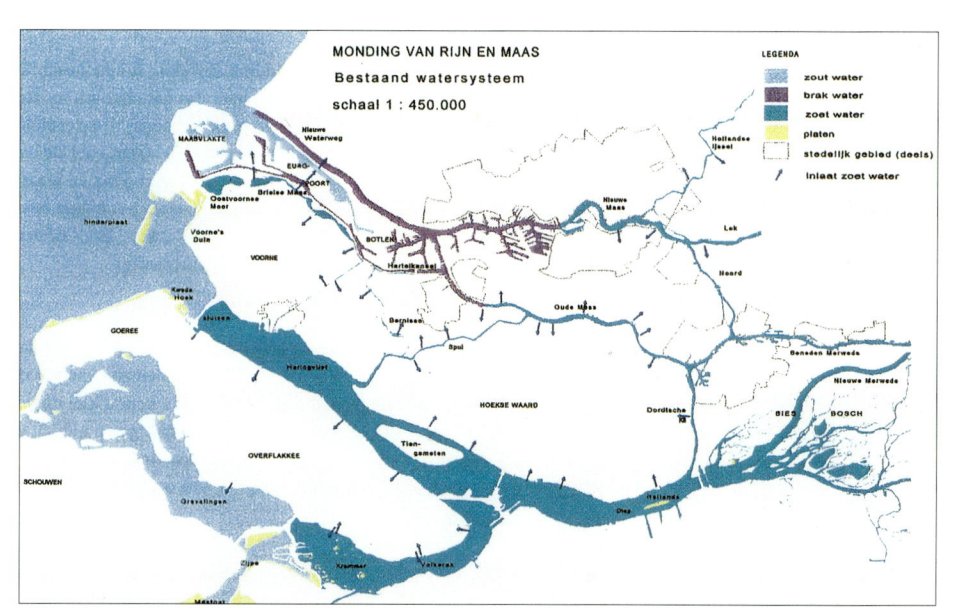

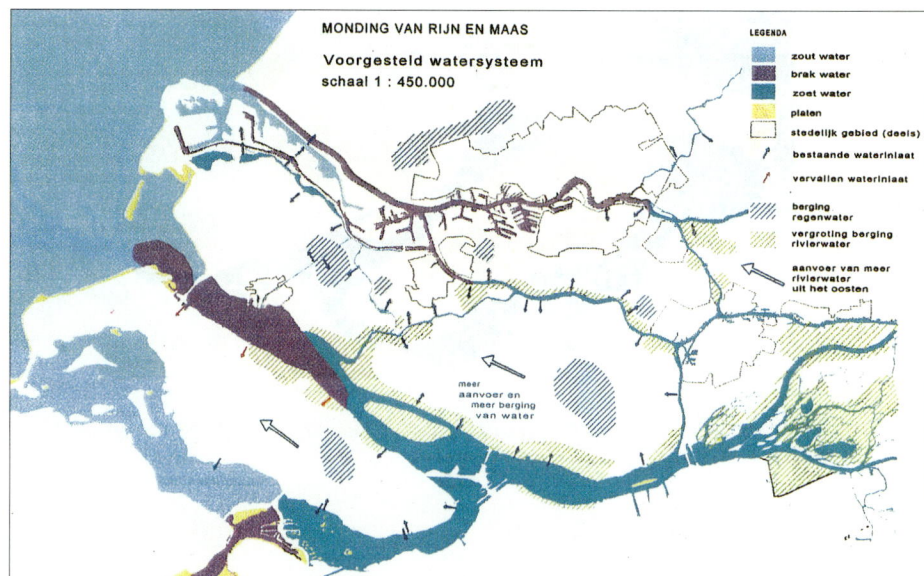

New Rotterdam Watermark 1997

AIR-ZUIDWAARTS / SOUTHBOUND

RESEARCH

VISUAL RESEARCH
JOHN DAVIES
HET OBSERVATORIUM
MARK PIMLOTT
SCHIE 2.0
HENRIK HÅKANSSON
AD VAN DENDEREN
WIJNANDA DEROO
BERTIEN VAN MANEN
HANS VAN HOUWELINGEN
BIRTHE LEEMEIJER
JOOST GROOTENS
JAN KONINGS/ESTER VAN DE WIEL
HONORÉ δ'O
ANTHROPOLOGICAL RESEARCH
HENK DE HAAN
PHYSICAL PLANNING RESEARCH
SJOERD CUSVELLER

Regional Plan for Zuid-Holland South (draft), Zuid-Holland Province, 1998

Operating on a North-West European scale, the Regional Plan for the South region of Zuid-Holland focuses on both the south wing of the Randstad and the northern boundary of the Rhine-Scheldt delta. The Randstad is increasingly becoming an economic network together with nearby urban agglomerations such as the Ruhr, the Flemish Diamond and the Channel Zone. Consequently, the South region is steadily growing as a transit area for international transport, and has little further functional relations with the region itself. At the same time the delta waters and the Biesbos constitute a sizeable wetland area in the ecological main structure of North-West Europe. Its twofold position places the region in a stress field characteristic of the task. The input of the Regional Plan is aimed at making optimum use of the special situation on the southern edge of the Randstad, on the connective axes of the Randstad towards the south, and between the Randstad and the delta area. Because of the close proximity of the Randstad, the 'mainport' of Rotterdam and a relatively large acreage of rural space, the South region offers potential as an overspill and alleviation area for sundry urban functions, in particular the activities connected with transport, glasshouse cultivation, recreation and tourism. However, the region is also part of the delta area. The Regional Plan regards the characteristic waters and creeks as important green supports for further development of the adjacent south wing. Functions of nature, water structures and systems are to be better utilized for the benefit of water storage and drainage, and nature development in combination with water, river-bank and coast management. Three polders, Munnikenland, Oudeland van Strijen and St. Anthony, are to be protected because of their cultural-historical, landscape and natural values. The High Speed Line, the Betuwe Line and the A4 form the 'arteries' of the economy of the south wing of the Randstad. For this purpose, the missing link in the A4 between the Benelux Star and the A29 will have to be realized soon. The A4 is equally important for the South region as an economic corridor. It offers opportunities for distribution activities and Value-Added Logistics for the North-West European market. Besides sites for harbour-related activities the Regional Plan also provides space for the supra-regional need for glasshouses.

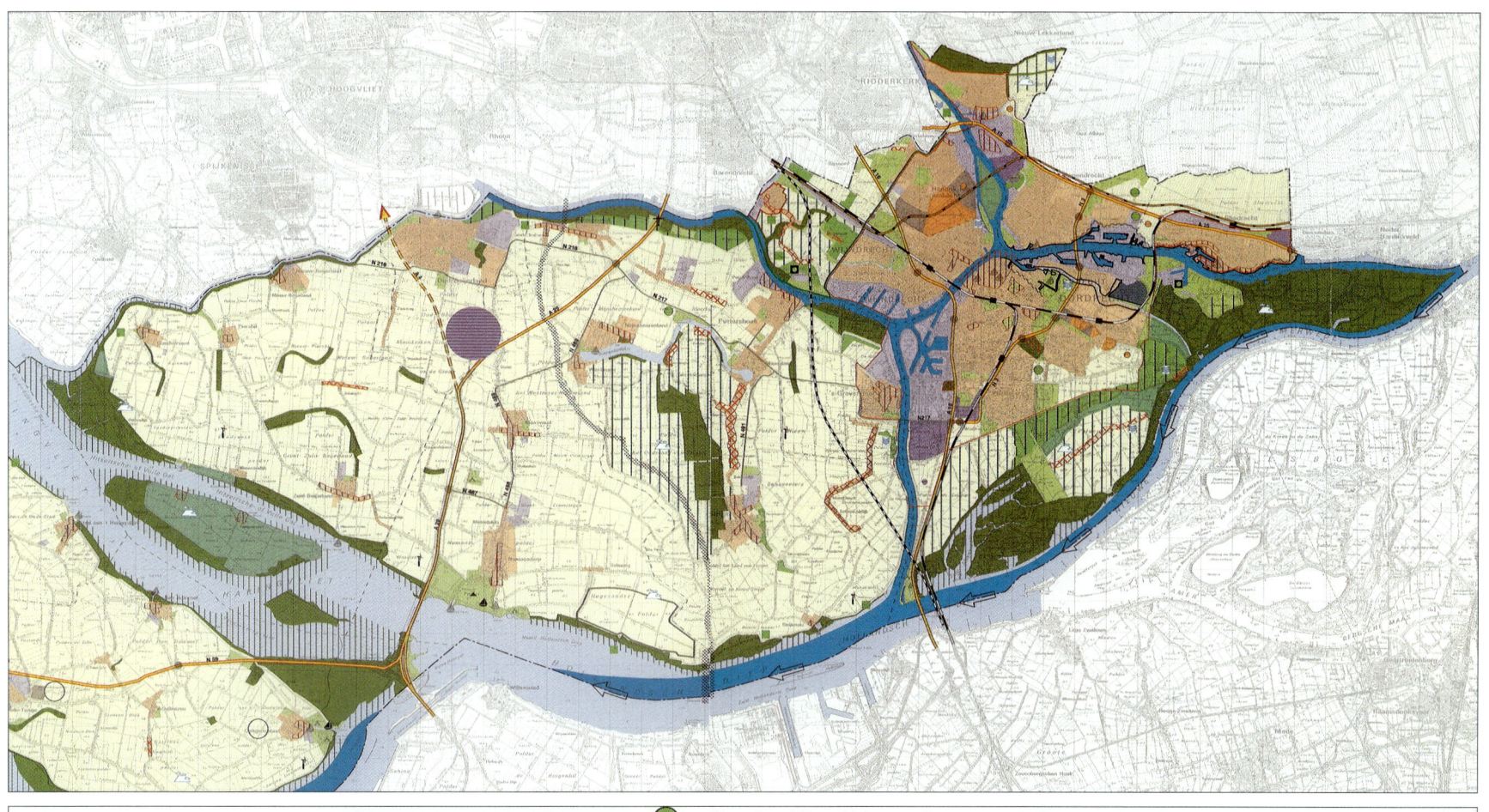

LEGENDA

ALGEMEEN
- Plangrens, tevens provincie- en/of gemeentegrens
- Gemeentegrens
- Grens bufferzone Oost - IJsselmonde

STADS- EN DORPSGEBIED
- Stads- en dorpsgebied - bestaand of in uitvoering
- Stads- en dorpsgebied - nieuw
- Stads- en dorpsgebied - gewenst
- Stads- en dorpsgebied met grote cultuurhistorische waarden
- Bebouwingslinten met grote cultuurhistorische en/of landschappelijke waarden
- Verstedelijkingscontour Drechtsteden
- Verstedelijkingscontour Drechtsteden, nader te bepalen
- Maximale bebouwingscontour Heerjansdam

BEDRIJFSTERREIN
- Bedrijfsterrein - bestaand of in ontwikkeling
- Bedrijfsterrein - nieuw
- Bedrijfsterrein - gewenst

LANDELIJK GEBIED
- Agrarisch gebied
- Agrarisch gebied met natuur- en landschapswaarden (ANL)
- Glastuinbouwgebied
- Voorkeurslocatie glastuinbouw
- Studielocatie gemengde tuinbouw
- Natuurgebied - bestaand
- Natuurgebied - nieuw
- Duinnatuurgebied
- Natuurontwikkelingsgebied
- Recreatie- en/of bosgebied - bestaand
- Recreatie- en/of bosgebied - nieuw
- Recreatie- en/of bosgebied - gewenst
- Recreatie- en/of bosgebied met natuur- en/of landschapswaarden - bestaand
- Recreatie- en/of bosgebied met natuur- en/of landschapswaarden - nieuw
- Jachthaven
- Jachthaven - nieuw
- Verblijfsrecreatie - bestaand
- Verblijfsrecreatie - nieuw
- Zoeklocatie zweefvliegveld

WATER
- Vaarwegen; havens; waterstaatsdoeleinden
- Overig water
- Waternatuurgebied
- Water met nutsfunctie en recreatief gebruik
- Top-afvoer water
- Riviercontour

VERBINDINGEN
- Bestaande spoorweg
- Tracé HSL
- Tracé goederenspoorweg - nieuw (Betuweroute)
- NS - Station
- Verbinding van het rijkshoofdwegennet
- Verbinding van het rijkshoofdwegennet - studietracé
- Regionale weg
- Aansluitpunt wegverbinding

MILIEUBEHEER EN NUTSVOORZIENINGEN
- Te verzwaren of aan te leggen primaire waterkering
- Locatie windenergie
- Leidingenstraat
- Stortplaats met recreatieve eindbestemming
- Milieubeschermingsgebied voor grondwater
- Milieubeschermingsgebied voor stilte

NOORD

Schaal 1 : 100.000

Gedeputeerde Staten van Zuid-Holland, 14 juli 1998

Regional Plan for Zuid-Holland South (draft) 1998

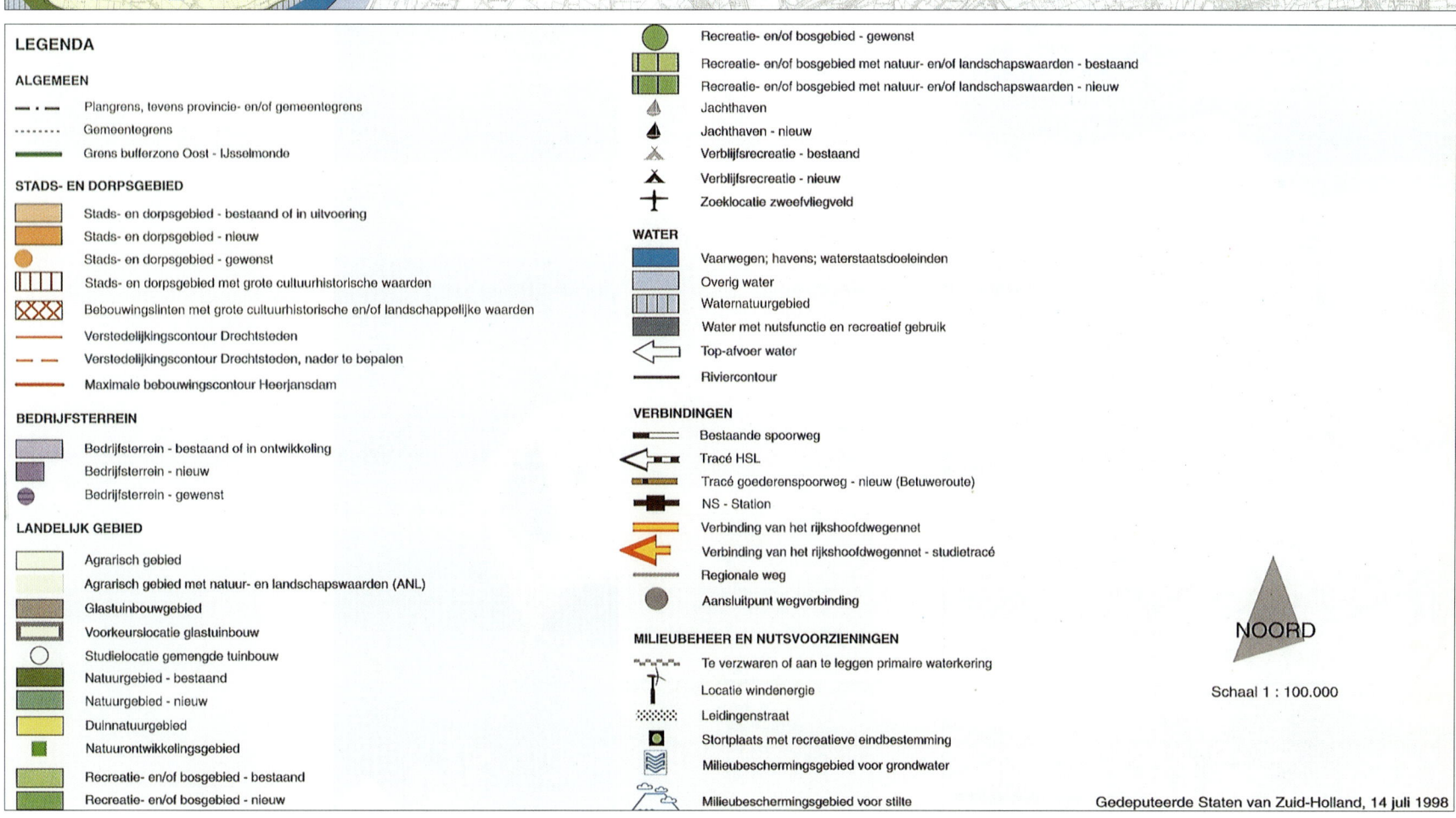

AIR-ZUIDWAARTS / SOUTHBOUND

64

RESEARCH
VISUAL RESEARCH
JOHN DAVIES
HET OBSERVATORIUM
MARK PIMLOTT
SCHIE 2.0
HENRIK HÅKANSSON
AD VAN DENDEREN
WIJNANDA DEROO
BERTIEN VAN MANEN
HANS VAN HOUWELINGEN
BIRTHE LEEMEIJER
JOOST GROOTENS
JAN KONINGS/ESTER VAN DE WIEL
HONORÉ δ'O
ANTHROPOLOGICAL RESEARCH
HENK DE HAAN
PHYSICAL PLANNING RESEARCH
SJOERD CUSVELLER

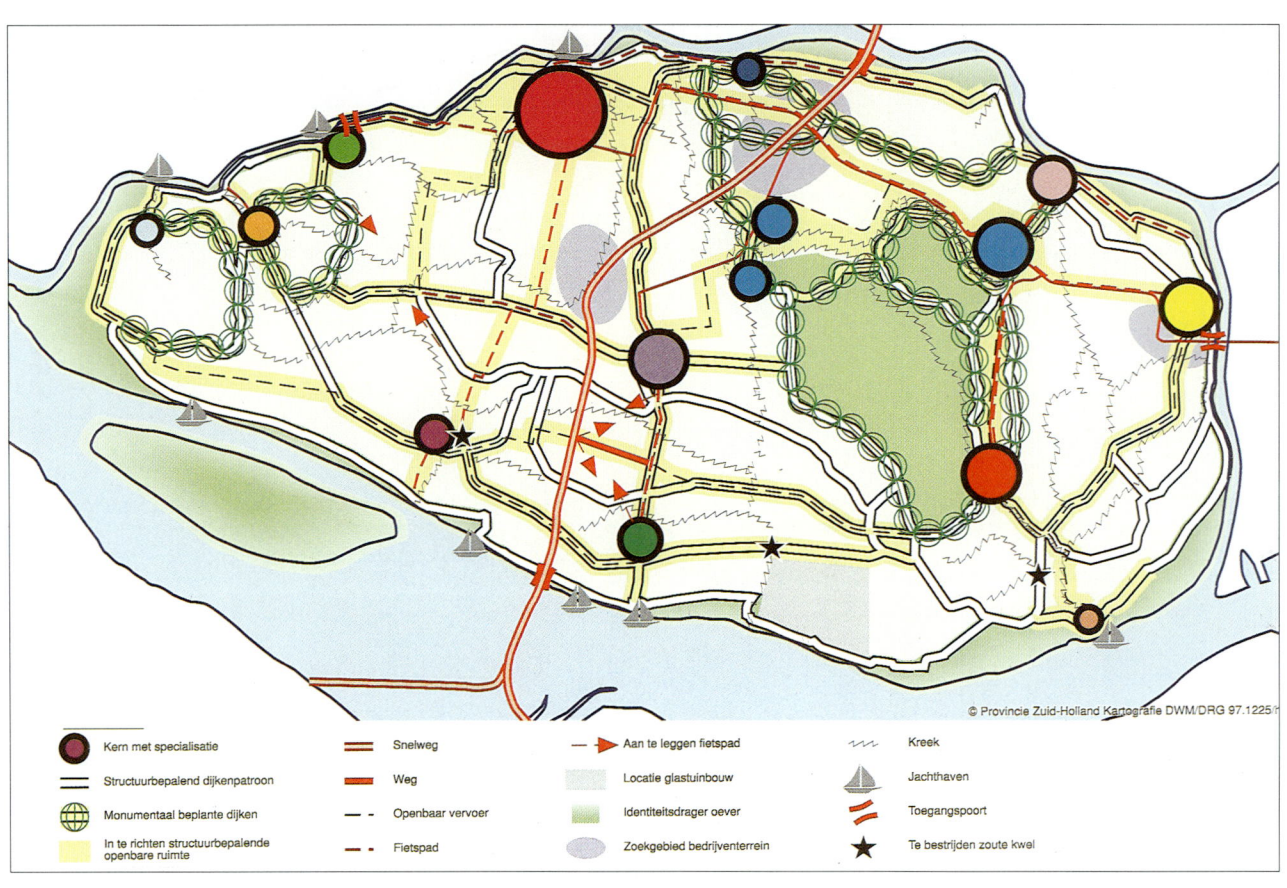

Hoeksche Waard Environs Plan (HOP) 1997

Hoeksche Waard Environs Plan (HOP), Zuid-Holland Province, Zuid-Holland South, joint municipalities of Hoeksche Waard, 1997

As a link between Randstad Holland and West Brabant/Antwerp, Hoeksche Waard clearly occupies a position of its own. In the HOP this fact has caused Hoeksche Waard of the future to be seen as a single, indivisible unit. The key task is to combine its strategic situation as regards major economic and cultural centres with the relatively unspoilt state of the region. The inhabitants profit from both aspects: they live in small, quiet communities surrounded by green areas, and a large part of the working population works in the nearby cities.

The special position of Hoeksche Waard is expressed in a number of specific regional characteristics, such as the settlement pattern, the diking structure, the more or less natural creeks and the monumentally planted farmyards and river banks. Characteristics that bring out the island quality.

It is important that the landscape should be experienced. For this purpose panoramic lines will have to be kept open, points presenting a prospect and/or experience will need creating, and cycling and walking routes laid out. According to the HOP nature can be protected best by zoning. Besides, it proposes the development of visitors' centres, a recreational network of elements having a public function in the nature reserves, and zoning within the nature reserves for the sake of quiet secluded areas.

The water management of Hoeksche Waard is under threat of silting up. If the lock sluices of Haringvliet are to be opened permanently, except during storm floods, Haringvliet will once again be subject to the tides, and salt and brackish water will flow further inland. In order to reduce these effects, more fresh water will have to be supplied from elsewhere. It will then be necessary to construct a freshwater channel between the waters of Binnenbedijkte Maas and Bernisse. The HOP combines the ensuing expansion of the surface water with recreational and natural functions, such as restoring the old course of creeks.

The shores and banks, from which Hoeksche Waard derives its identity as an island, are somewhat fragmented as a result of their several functions of nature, recreation, harbour and dwelling. They are to be made more accessible and better utilized for a wide variety of use types. The pattern of independent cores, each with its own identity, is absolutely fundamental to the spatial design of Hoeksche Waard. The HOP strives for a greater complementarity between the cores in terms of function, facilities and image (so-called 'core specialization').

Development Plan Hoeksche Waard Region 2010-2030
Province of Zuid-Holland, 1998

This long-term study – a consequence of the government's Randstad Report in preparation for the Fifth Report on Spatial Planning – explores the future of Hoeksche Waard in four spatial models.

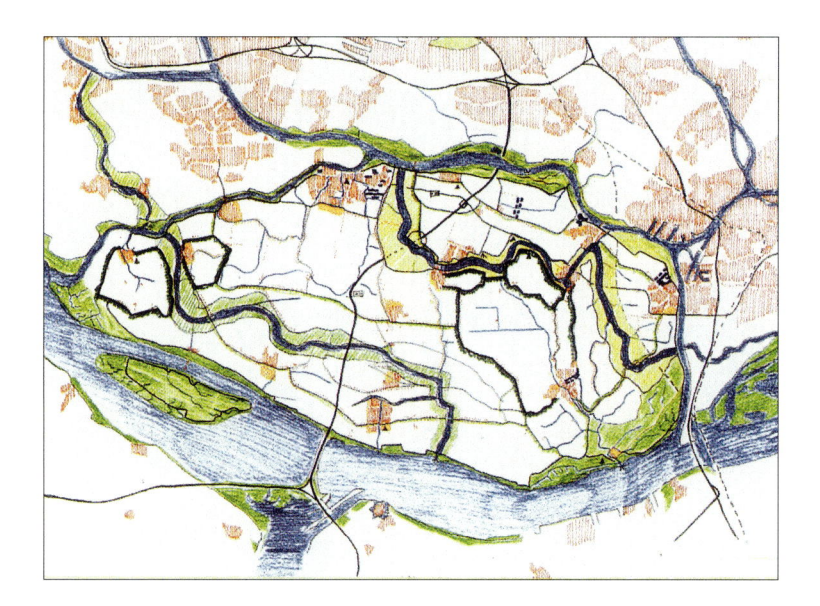

Open Waard
Hoeksche Waard is recreated as a green oasis for the south wing, where agriculture, nature, leisure and cultural history are uppermost. The rural character is reinforced by preserving the open quality of the polders and by highlighting the dikes, creeks and river banks in the region. Residential development adheres to the pattern of villages.

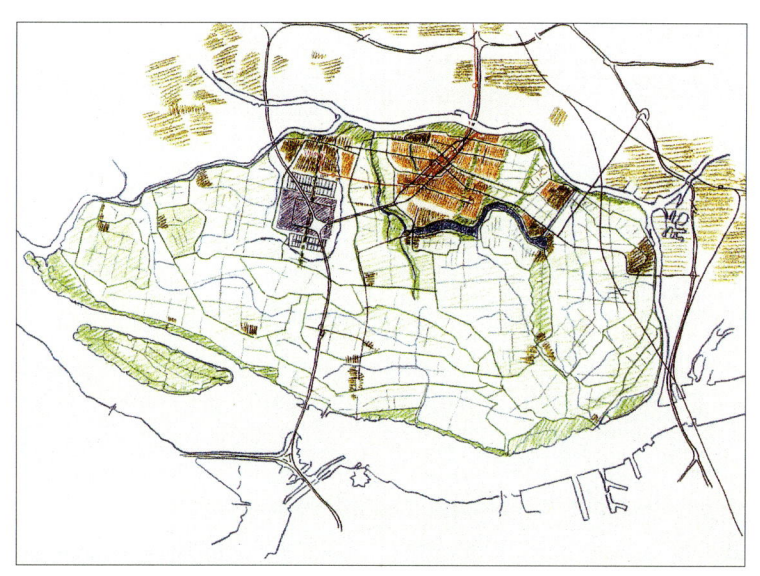

Hoeksche Town
A new town of approximately 30.000 dwellings is to be developed in the north of Hoeksche Waard. The southern part is to remain completely open. Furthermore, there is room for a large harbour-related business park and a concentration of glasshouses. Construction of the A4 and a regional rail link with Rotterdam are incorporated in this model.

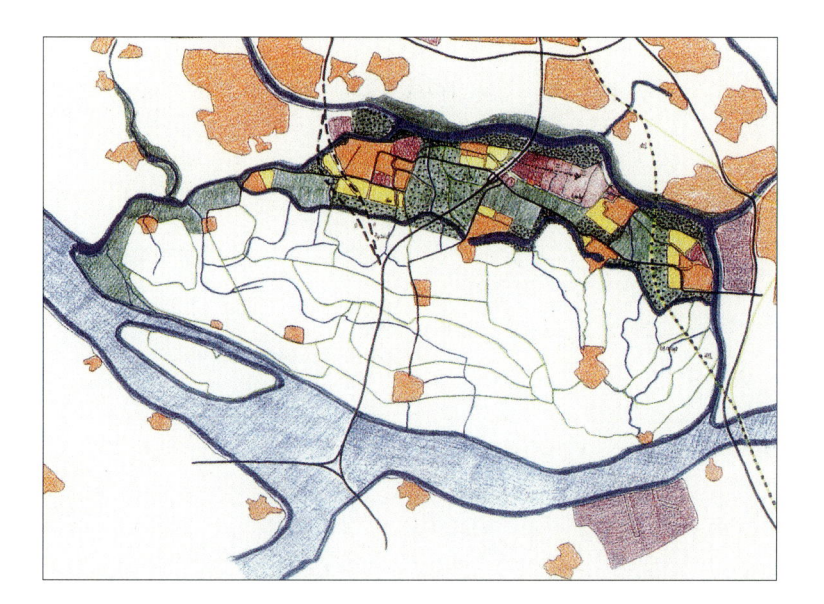

North Park
In the northern part, urbanization can take place within a robust green structure. In the southern part, landscape and agricultural use remain uppermost. The form urbanization in the north is to take depends on the market demand. There is space for a maximum of 20,000 dwellings and approximately 400 hectares of business land.

Work Park
Hoeksche Waard is chiefly developed as a link in the North-South corridor. There is space for businesses (up to 700 hectares) and glasshouses in connection with the economic transportation axis between the ports of Rotterdam and Antwerp. Beyond this, the green and open character of the landscape is to be retained.

AIR-ZUIDWAARTS / SOUTHBOUND

AIR-Zuidwaarts/Southbound focused on the area between Rotterdam and Antwerp, the Rhine-Scheldt delta and Hoeksche Waard. The central question was how to give shape to the relation between the urbanized region of Rotterdam and the landscape of the Zeeland delta in the long term. This question was posed in the light of transformation processes in the region due to increasing urbanization (living, working, leisure time and recreation), increasing mobility, changing agricultural use and greater attention for nature and environment. The design commission comprised the development of new concepts and strategies for the region selected focusing on a synthesis of new urban functions and the cultural-historical and scenic values of the rural region.

DESIGN TASK

SJOERD CUSVELLER/
ANNE-MIE DEVOLDER

The design task

In spite of its situation directly south of the south wing of the Randstad as a densely populated urban area and the proximity of the port of Rotterdam as a significant economic centre, Hoeksche Waard so far has been safeguarded against intensive urban development. This does not imply that plans to that effect have never been made.

Attempts in the past at utilizing the potential space of Hoeksche Waard were either superseded by social developments, such as the ambitious plan Rotterdam 2000+, or never attained their expected breadth, as was the case in the construction of the Kil Tunnel. Only in the northern part of Hoeksche Waard did an overspill of marginal functions from the Rotterdam agglomeration take place, such as the recreational second-home development around the Binnenmaas. The suburban expansions notably near Nieuw-Beijerland are also relatively modest in comparison to Spijkenisse on the opposite bank of the Spui. Lying in the lee of the dynamics of the Rotterdam agglomeration Hoeksche Waard has developed at its own pace as an area where agriculture is still a dominant factor. However, its position on the leeside of that agglomeration only partly defines the meaning of Hoeksche Waard. Regarded from a different perspective Hoeksche Waard is a component of the vast Rhine-Scheldt delta. As a part of the delta, Hoeksche Waard occupies a sheltered position. Recreational and tourist development of the delta is notably taking place along the coast of the Zuid-Holland and Zeeland islands and the waters between the islands. Hoeksche Waard is chiefly a transit area on the route to the islands, with just a few water sports facilities to be found along Haringvliet. The main significance of the delta, however, is its great natural and ecological value. The closing off of Haringvliet within the framework of the Delta Act signified the end of the Rhine as a tidal river. The intended (partial) reopening of Haringvliet to the impact of the sea and the transformation of the island of Tiengemeten into a nature reserve illustrate the recent vision of Hoeksche Waard as part of the ecosystem of the Rhine-Scheldt delta.

Finally, the meaning of Hoeksche Waard is defined by its situation between the port complexes of Rotterdam and Antwerp. It is particularly the eastward connections that have always been important to the ports. The great importance of connections with the hinterland is illustrated by the construction of the Betuwe rail-freight link and the plan to reopen the so-called 'Iron Rhine', the old rail link between Flanders and Nordrhein-Westfalen in Germany. The interrelationship and cooperation between the ports require an ever more intensive infrastructure in a north-south direction. In this light the construction of the HSL (High Speed Line) through the eastern part of Hoeksche Waard is significant. Hoeksche Waard lies exactly in the crook of the north-south and east-west aligned infrastructure and is therefore eminently accessible.

In the opinion of many planning organizations the relatively large quantity of rural space in Hoeksche Waard renders the area highly suitable for spatial-planning developments that can no longer be realized in the south wing of the Randstad, notably the establishment of glasshouses as an overspill area for the Westland horticultural industries and the setting up of logistic and distribution facilities for the port of Rotterdam. The latter issue is even intensified by the increasing importance of the north-south corridor. Notably the port of Rotterdam insists on extending the A4 and establishing a large distribution centre for road transport.

In other words, the pressure put on Hoeksche Waard is rapidly in-

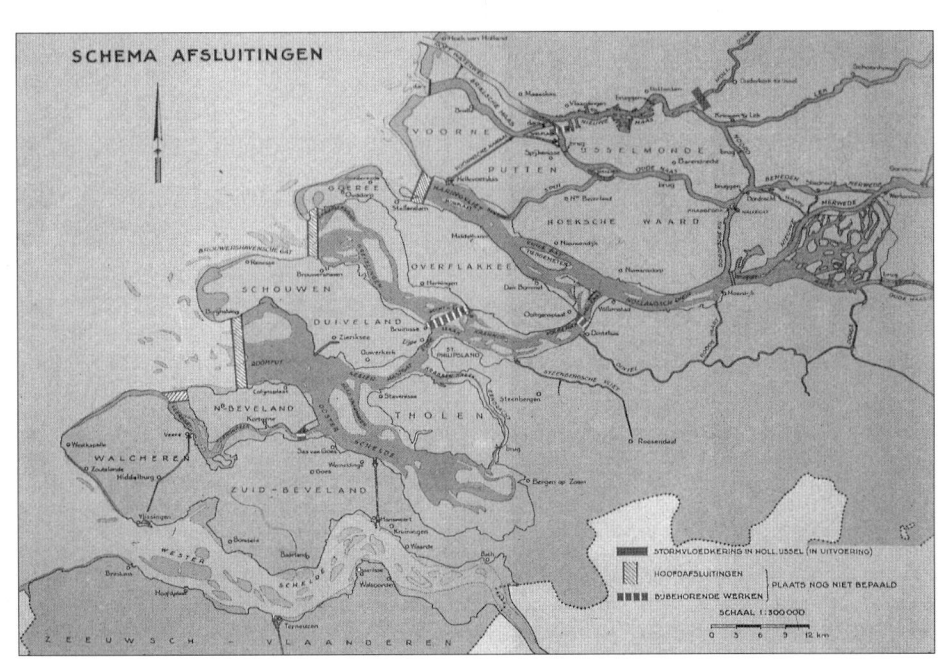

Delta Plan 1956

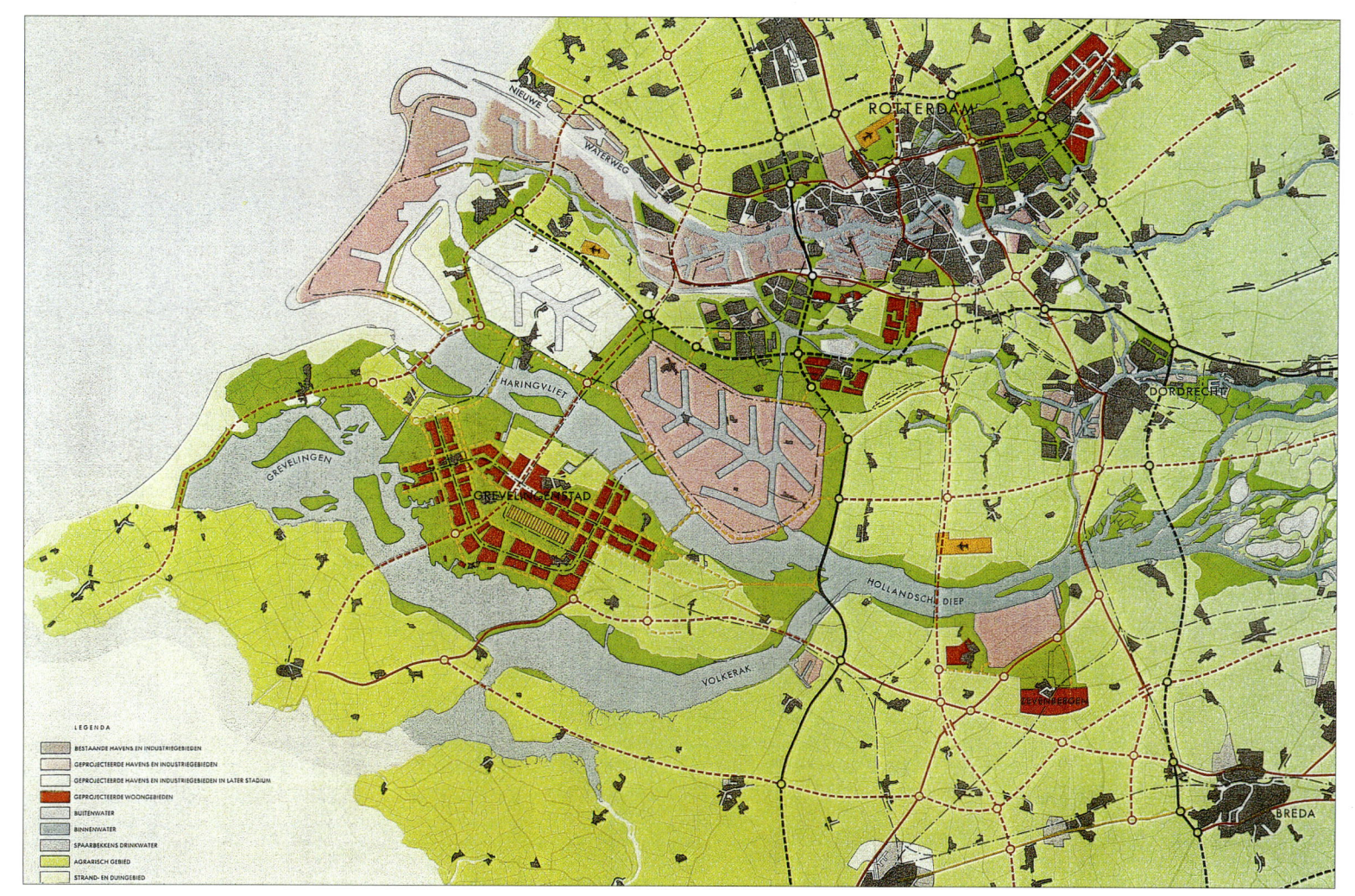

Rotterdam 2000+ 1969

creasing. Hoeksche Waard itself responds to this pressure from outside by stressing its own characteristics and qualities and laying them down and preserving them in the form of a plan.

Scales

The three views – Hoeksche Waard as overspill area for the south wing of the Randstad, Hoeksche Waard as part of the ecosystem of the Rhine-Scheldt delta, and Hoeksche Waard as a rural area to be protected – are based on a conception of the rural area-urban area relationship as one between mutually exclusive antitheses. The principal objective of AIR-Zuidwaarts/Southbound is to reformulate that relationship and explore the specific meaning of Hoeksche Waard as an intriguing meeting-point of conservation, urban development, economic development and nature development.

This is possible by approaching Hoeksche Waard not just from the perspective of the Rotterdam Agglomeration, or just from the perspective of Hoeksche Waard itself, but also from that of the Rhine-Scheldt delta: Hoeksche Waard between Rotterdam and the Zeeland islands on the one hand, and Hoeksche Waard between the urban networks of Rotterdam and Antwerp on the other. Apart from approaching the issues concerning Hoeksche Waard from the three related scales referred to, it is important to approach from three programmatic layers too. The first layer is the long-term changes in the subsoil, the altering relationship between land and water and the balance between fresh and salt water in the delta. The development of infrastructural networks and the nodes in these networks form the second layer. Finally, the relatively rapid shifts in the use of the ground plane constitute the third layer. In each programmatic layer transformation processes are taking place, processes that do much to explain the current pressure on Hoeksche Waard.

Transformation processes

The farthest-reaching transformation process is the expected climatic change in the coming decades. The rise in sea level is one of the consequences. However, this rise is not so considerable that the main dikes of the Netherlands will all at once need heightening. The main consequence is that the rivers in the delta can drain off their waters less quickly, whereas the quantity of water the rivers have to drain off is increasing. (Temporary) storage of river water in order to accommodate the peaks will be one of the major themes for the Netherlands these coming years. This storage will have to be realized chiefly in the upper reaches of the rivers; the possibilities of doing so in the Rhine-Scheldt delta appear to be minimal. However, something that does have a great impact in the delta is the relationship between fresh water and salt water. If policy remains unchanged, the boundary between fresh and salt water is going to be much more inland than it is now. This will have major consequences for the intake of fresh water for agricultural purposes and for the quality of the seepage water. In order to keep the water quality up to standard for the agriculture in Hoeksche Waard, a large freshwater intake is required to counterbalance the expected salt seepage.

A second far-reaching transformation process in the subsoil of the delta is nature development. These past years have seen a process get under way in which the Rhine-Scheldt delta is being developed as a more or less natural delta area again, where the tidal effect and the fluctuating ratio of fresh to salt water are the major ecological factors. The rigorous closing off of Haringvliet as a result of the Delta Plan is to be replaced by partial opening. The degree of opening is still under discussion, but the intention to transform Haringvliet into a tidal river again is there. This implies that the dike as a clearly defined boundary will have to give way to a much more differentiated transition between water and land. The question is how Hoeksche Waard can profit from this transformation.

On the infrastructure front, the most manifest transformation is intensification of the north-south corridor, the bundle of infrastructure between Rotterdam and Antwerp. From the point of view of efficient operation the ports of Rotterdam and Antwerp consider a rapid centre-to-centre connection indispensable. This does not automatically imply that extension of the A4 is inevitable. The centre-to-centre connection ought to be regarded as a multimodal logistic network. The question as to whether the A4 is to be extended or not evolves from a clear vision of this network of existing and possibly new infrastructure and transportation management, that treats transportation by underground, mainline rail and water and the approach to the target groups of road traffic as key elements. The position of Hoeksche Waard with respect to the north-south corridor and the possibilities of development entailed by this, depends on the future design of this logistic network. The network also determines the location, character and planning of the transportation and distribution facilities required for the Rotterdam port.

The transformation process related to the ground level concerns in particular the transformation of agriculture. Agriculture in Hoeksche Waard is not competitive enough on a European scale, and so different production forms are sought for it. The key words here are specialization and intensification; specialization in the form of cultivation under contract of specific products for the food industry or for so-called biological agriculture. Cultivation under contract will also lead to a much more intensive use of farmland on an almost industrial basis. This also obtains for the shift to glasshouse cultivation, as overspill area for the Westland horticultural industries. This cultivation under glass has turned its gaze on the use of residual heat from the industrial site of Moerdijk. The question is whether Hoeksche Waard will be the designated location or whether the western part of North Brabant may be more suitable. The switch in agriculture will have great consequences for the spatial planning of Hoeksche Waard.

Other developments that may have consequences for occupying Hoeksche Waard have not really been expressed yet. However, it goes without saying that in the near or foreseeable future Hoeksche Waard will also be considered for accommodating the expansion needs of the south wing of Randstad, if only because the land is relatively cheap. The port of Rotterdam has already articulated the necessity of an industrial site for transportation and distribution facilities in Hoeksche Waard. However, as mentioned before, its location depends on the design of the infrastructural network between Antwerp and Rotterdam. Another question is whether, and if so how, Hoeksche Waard can integrate a (future) need for housing locations. And how housing for the benefit of the population of Hoeksche Waard itself is to take shape.

Planning processes

The aforesaid transformation processes and the pressure for urbanization on Hoeksche Waard require a clear vision on the meaning of Hoeksche Waard with which to give direction and form to the planning processes. At the level of the Rhine-Scheldt delta, Hoeksche Waard has the position of a link between the south wing of Randstad and the Zeeland islands. The RSD constitutes a complex combination of cultural history (towns), nature and ecological values, coast/dunes and water recreation. Water is an important linking factor in this. The task is to seek out a form of reinforcement for the present structure and the contribution Hoeksche Waard might make to this. Possibilities are particularly to be found in extensive recreation in combination with landscape and nature development. The said effects of climatic change encourage further development of the RSD as a nature reserve and increasing its ecological value. In line with this is the conversion of Haringvliet into a tidal river. This requires a large freshwater buffer in order to prevent salt seepage and a different use for the river banks in connection with nature development within Hoeksche Waard itself.

Hoeksche Waard is situated in the north-south corridor between the urban networks of Antwerp and Rotterdam. Designing the future development of this network and formulating the position of Hoeksche Waard there, is another significant task. Its position with respect to the network does much to define the possibilities of developing Hoeksche Waard and the extent to which Hoeksche Waard is the designated location for accommodating urban expansion needs (housing sites, business sites, glasshouse cultivation, recreational and open-space planning). The north-south corridor will at any rate have to accommodate a business site of approximately 300 hectares for transportation and distribution facilities.

However, the major assignment is probably to establish the significance of Hoeksche Waard. Does Hoeksche Waard possess an identity of its own, what does it consist of, what are the bearers of its identity and how could these develop further?

The draft design brief

The pressure on Hoeksche Waard is considerable. In Hoeksche Waard Environs Plan (HOP), the threats issuing from the urban region have been translated into opportunities for the area itself. The HOP is the basis for revising the regional plan for Zuid-Holland South. The dynamic of the revised regional plan is, for Hoeksche Waard, mostly determined by the Randstad's need for space, in particular for port-related activity for the Rotterdam economic region and for cultivation under glass, as a result of the restructuring of the Zuid-Holland glasshouse industry. The A4 motorway south between Hoogvliet and Klaaswaal, the high-speed rail, a complex for storing polluted sludge in Hollandsche Diep and the landscape quality of Hoeksche Waard are also key factors in this revision.

The southern wing of the Randstad is one of the urban areas to test the current compact urban policy. If urbanization were to extend into Hoeksche Waard, the area would lose its potential, which the Randstad's southern wing will need in the future to improve the quality of life, especially on the recreational front. This is one of the reasons why AIR questions the Dutch compact urbanization model. As a result of the 'VINEX' operation this model is generally diagnosed as a matrix for sectoral planning resulting in the same residential environments everywhere. Which is why the design brief has been defined in terms of the capacities and qualities of Hoeksche Waard, and not as a potential for expansion or a settlement strategy regarded from the perspective of port, industry, distribution or the city. The departure-point here is that the area's intrinsic value does not, a priori, make for good short-term growth planning. As the focus is on redefining Rotterdam Mainport's position in the outer ring of the Randstad, the definition of the design brief will not only concentrate on the various aspects, layers, scales, places, identity or character at Hoeksche Waard scale, but also at the scales of the Randstad as an urban system, Antwerp-the Rhine-Scheldt delta-Rotterdam and the extensive landscapes of southern Zuid-Holland and Zeeland as a assemblage of places and atmospheres. All this should be balanced against:

1. The amount of 'fullness' that may be built in Hoeksche Waard in order to preserve its 'emptiness'.
2. European pressure on restructuring the agriculture in Hoeksche Waard, enabling the development of a new cultural landscape where food production, leisure and ecological recycling could present a new equilibrium.
3. The many barriers around Rotterdam (road, water and rail) that separate the city from its surrounding landscape.
4. The scale on which the region's spatial identity becomes manifest;
5. Traffic planning as a spatial design (A4 corridor, HSL, port rail).
6. Rotterdam Mainport's spatial impact (expansion of Maasvlakte) on development in Hoeksche Waard.

After the conference

In the draft design brief as it was defined in the reader of the international conference of October 1998 transformation processes of agriculture, nature and water, urbanization and infrastructure were placed within a larger context. At the conference a fourth layer was added to the existing three (subsoil, infrastructure, occupation), this being a cultural, non-spatial 'cognitive' layer comprising the research material of the artists and scientists.

A significant recommendation was that the programme of the design brief should not be determined by programmes issuing from current plans (cf. pages 54-65), but by three all-inclusive issues that require space in the long run:

1. The shortage of water basins and the rising sea-level, the demand for new water and nature management.
2. The issue of whether the future of a coherent landscape will be dependent on the fortunes of agriculture. This sector has to contend with dwindling subsidies, competition from Eastern Europe and increasing environmental regulations.
3. The quality of the southern wing as an urban/agricultural area: extreme compaction of the existing urban area versus the quality of life in general. This leads to demands for agricultural strategies premised upon long-term processes relating to nature and agriculture.

Compared with other areas in the Netherlands the southern wing is lagging behind in natural development. The low-lying delta has traditionally been undervalued for recreational purposes compared with the forests in other parts of the Netherlands. Besides, there was until then little concern for in-depth green investments. Thus the region missed out on a number of economic investments, so that the southern wing as a region for economic and residential settlement is lagging behind other comparable regions elsewhere in our country. Attractive areas for such settlement are now being developed in Utrecht, Brabant and the Betuwe region.

As to recreation and leisure in natural areas, short holidays spent not far from home in the Veluwe, on the Wadden Isles or in the Belgian Ardennes are much in demand. The Rhine-Scheldt delta project group wants to develop recreation, tourism and culture on the delta scale. Though on the scale of the Rotterdam region, the 'Regional Green Structure Plan' (1977) was a first step in that direction. Half of the green wedges proposed in this plan reaching from the city into the country are in place and have since been caught up by urbanization.

The design brief

Food for thought: the urban development of the Isle of IJsselmonde. A rural area in 1900, it is now an urbanized territory comprising a conglomerate of residual areas of which the administrative borders no longer coincide with the spatial units.

Define the position of Hoeksche Waard, given the pressure of urbanization in the southern wing of the Randstad and the landscape value of the delta between Rotterdam and Antwerp. What developments are possible in view of this position? Other than in current practice and the discussion on benefit and necessity, AIR poses the question of the form spatial development can take, from the vantage point of the region's qualities.

Develop concepts and strategies that take into account the possible weakening of landscape-related use forms. Develop concepts and strategies for long-term reinforcement of the large-scale landscape with few hard-and-fast programme details, where large residential districts are far from being an obvious solution.

AIR-ZUIDWAARTS / SOUTHBOUND

The presentations of the research by artists and scientists at the international conference and in the reader, maps and documentation, the historical physical-planning research, the design commission, the many excursions and the discussions with experts were the major parts of an elaborate briefing of the four national and four foreign design teams. The outcome is eight different approaches to the design commission.

DESIGN RESEARCH

FRITS PALMBOOM/JAAP VAN DEN BOUT
PETER CALTHORPE/MATTHEW TAECKER
STEFANO BOERI
FRANÇOIS ROCHE
DETTMAR/BEUTER/FRITZ/HASTENPFLUG
BINDELS/GIETEMA/HARTZEMA/KLOK
MARIEKE TIMMERMANS
DIRK SIJMONS/YTTJE FEDDES

The Time Machine

In Dutch urban development it is either-or, according to urban planners Frits Palmboom and Jaap van den Bout and their team. One area is designated to urbanize, in the other the emptiness must be protected to the extreme. For Hoeksche Waard the choice shouldn't be either-or, but and-and. Both accelerating and slowing down, both increase and decrease in scale. The island will be divided in layers. The northern side can accelerate. A renewed N217 which is extended to Spijkenisse will become the new southern border of the Rotterdam conglomerate which accommodates all sorts of activity. In the middle of the island large polders, which are systematically parcelled out, provide space for hi-tech agriculture geared to the world market. The south side of Hoeksche Waard will slow down. It will be detached from the regional and international infrastructure. In the landscape with ash dikes on the line Strijen – Zuid-Beijerland is space for small-scale agriculture and dwelling. The polders – situated at a lower level – along the Haringvliet and the Hollandsch Diep will become overspill areas which will occasionally be completely flooded.

Hoeksche Waard
Elementary landscape

The landscape in Hoeksche Waard is elementary: vast and bare at the same time. Its overwhelming flatness accentuates the play of the elements: light, air, wind and silence. The cultivation of the land has drawn sharp lines on it: the ridges of dikes, the grooves of ditches and creeks, furrows in the fields. Sometimes buildings and vegetation are dwarfed by these surroundings, sometimes they elevate the landscape into impressive architecture, or stand inalienably and lonely as independent entities.

Space and land

The sensory perception of the landscape as emptiness coincides with the recognition of the landscape as economic good. The surface area of Hoeksche Waard has been entirely parcelled out as an agro-industrial estate. In this respect, one could rather speak of fullness, the land being used to the full. The enjoyment of the space and the cultivation of the land belong together but, being inseparable, are also vulnerable. Transformations beyond the range of this perfect functionality infringe on its beauty. It is where the fields of sprouts have been transformed into fields of houses that purity becomes bareness. The existing landscape of Hoeksche Waard is a prisoner of its perfect functionality.

Time at a standstill

It seems as if time has been brought to a stop in Hoeksche Waard. Traces of the age-long process of colonization – the gradual draining and rational parcellation – have been almost literally imprinted in the landscape. This standstill, however, is only superficial. Underneath, there is friction and dispersion. Things are often no longer what they seem to be; caravans stand in glasshouses, a small dike house becomes a country seat.

Dispersion

It is difficult to point out the reasons for dispersion. The infrastructure of new bridges, tunnels and roads has ended the island's physical isolation. Together with the globalization of information and the omnipresent availability of facilities, it has led to insidious changes in the ways of life and work of residents and users. Changes that are not tied to a particular area and occur elsewhere too.
These changes scarcely have the form of a planning project. They sometimes take place slowly, sometimes by fits and starts, simultaneously in countless places, or consecutively. Some are triggered by the physical presence of a town or motorway, whereas others may occur mainly due to the relative isolation.

Elementary landscape

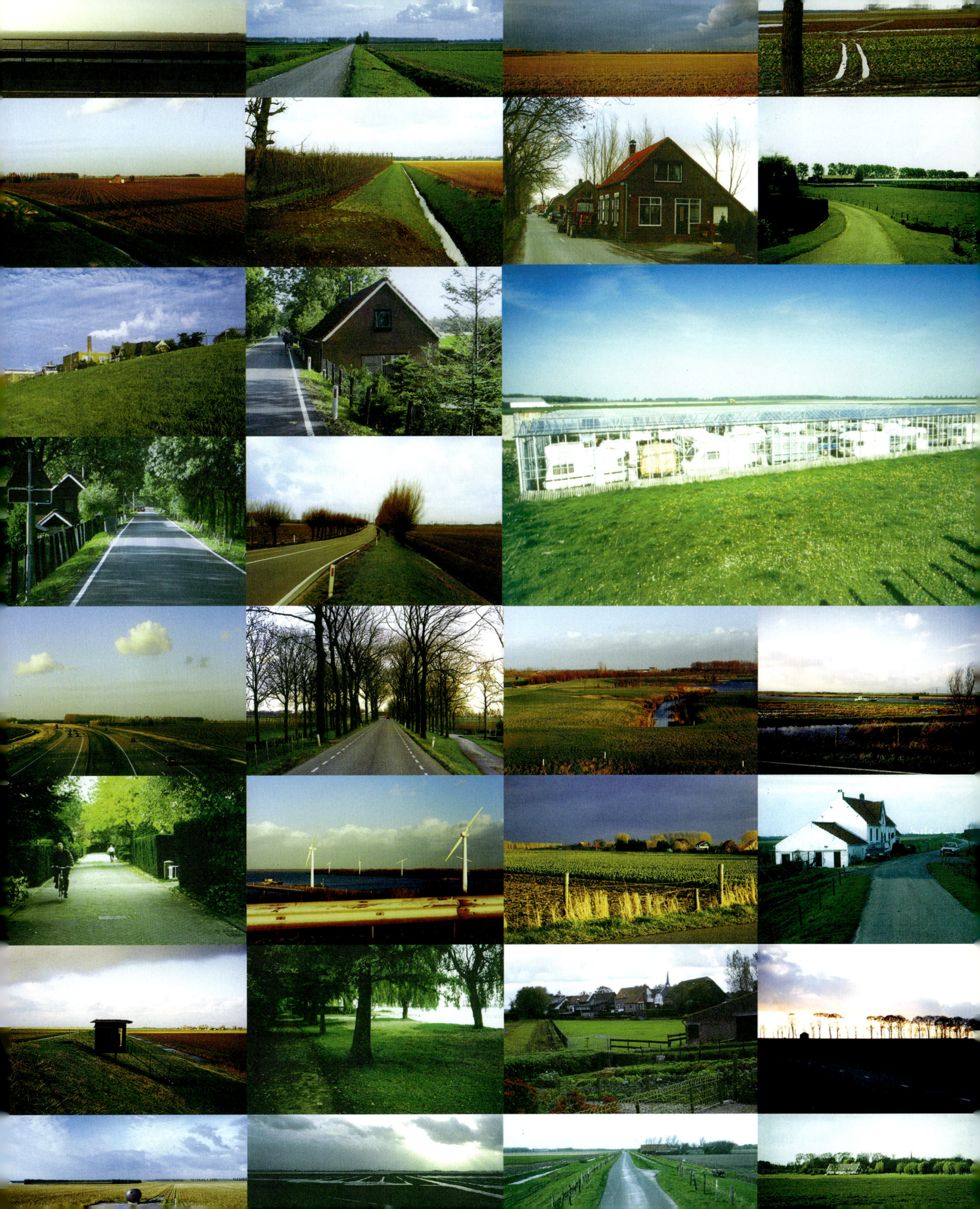

AIR-ZUIDWAARTS / SOUTHBOUND

DESIGN RESEARCH

FRITS PALMBOOM/JAAP VAN DEN BOUT
PETER CALTHORPE/MATTHEW TAECKER
STEFANO BOERI
FRANÇOIS ROCHE
DETTMAR/BEUTER/FRITZ/HASTENPFLUG
BINDELS/GIETEMA/HARTZEMA/KLOK
MARIEKE TIMMERMANS
DIRK SIJMONS/YTTJE FEDDES

The urge for planning
Nevertheless, maps with drawings of a new future for Hoeksche Waard circulate in many institutions. The motives for these planning options lie largely beyond the transformations in Hoeksche Waard itself. They concern the new infrastructure for the Rhine-Scheldt delta, the demand for space from the surroundings (companies, glasshouses), and invisible processes such as land subsidence and climatic change, which influence the water management in the delta. These planning notions have not yet taken shape in a concrete scheme or programme: there are no swarms of house hunters, no VINEX, and the A4 has a long way to go. So far, the urge for planning has scarcely got a grip on Hoeksche Waard.

Assignment: vagueness
Is it possible to make a plan for Hoeksche Waard in this vague situation? We think that this requires a different kind of urban planning. An urban planning that neither justifies its drive to want to fill everything in with renewal projects and alterations, nor wants to limit or camouflage change with restrictive regulations. An almost programmeless urban planning that does not fix the end result but considers the facilitation of time, money and decision-making to be the main issues. An urban planning that appeals to the basic skills of land surveying, the organization of access and land, the bringing about of changes in daily life in the easiest possible way.

Short circuits
A plan for Hoeksche Waard cannot be a blueprint; it can merely serve as a hypothesis for a methodology. In our plan we are seeking short circuits between the planning notions at the scale of the entire Rhine-Scheldt delta and the insidious changes in Hoeksche Waard.
We make no new proposals for the Rhine-Scheldt delta; we juggle with ideas that already circulate. For Hoeksche Waard itself we have developed a time machine that modulates changes in the area in time and space. Our aim is to make this area suitable for a wider range of ways of life and work.

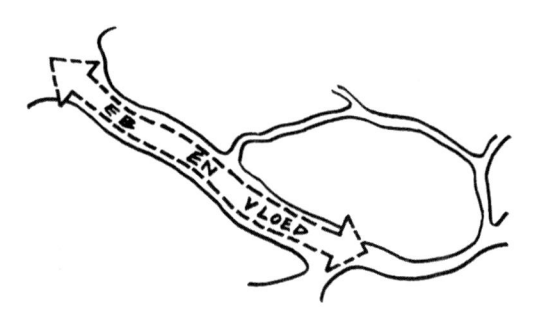

Tidal movements

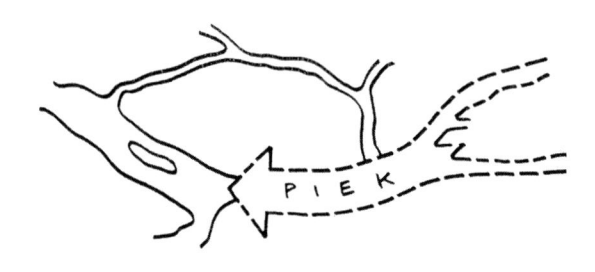

Peak supply on the rivers

Fresh-water buffer

The Rhine-Scheldt delta
Land and Water

The aim of the Delta Works and the dike heightening after 1953 was to draw a sharp and compact border between land and water. In recent years a more dynamic land-water relationship has been sought at various levels. Three options are topical in this respect:

1. The reintroduction of the tidal movement in Haringvliet has been proposed as a means to increase the ecological value of the delta.
2. The rising sea level and the growing peak supply of river water require a different water management approach; instead of the constant heightening of dikes, it is more effective to allow excess water to flow incidentally into previously designated polders.
3. The shift from fresh to brackish water in parts of the delta necessitates the polders to manage their own stock of fresh water in a better way.

These three processes converge in Hoeksche Waard. We assume that this will have the following effects on the island:

1. The shores of Hoeksche Waard island and the whole Tiengemeten island will eventually become a tidal area.
2. Several southern polders will be made suitable to serve as overfalls in periods of excessive supply of river water.
3. Oudeland van Strijen will be designated as a reservoir of good quality fresh water.

As a result of these measures new forms of land use will appear, especially along the south edge. Complemented by the other banks of Haringvliet and Hollandsch Diep, this will be the most valuable asset to Hoeksche Waard for the development of nature and recreation; an asset which is important for the entire Randstad.

Link new developments up with extension secondary network of regional infrastructure

Infrastructure

The infrastructure that was built after the war in the western part of the Netherlands connected town centres. In the King Atlas (a very basic atlas, published in the 1960s to advertise a brand of mints) the motorways and railway lines leaped side by side from town to town. The nature of the contemporary motorways is more diverse. On the one hand, they form a network through urban regions, programmes in the form of high-profile locations that feed on it. Motorways with lots of junctions, like the A16, belong to this network. On the other hand, they operate as connections between distant economic hubs, like the (air)ports of Amsterdam, Rotterdam and Antwerp. Motorways like the A29 and the future A4 are looking for the shortest route between these cities, passing over rather than opening up adjacent areas, Hoeksche Waard being one of them.

We argue for a further differentiation of the infrastructure by designating roads that provide access and roads that pass over. Our plan contains the following starting points:

1. We assume that intensive urbanization will continue in the Dordrecht-Breda-Roosendaal zone. This zone is not only easily accessible by the A16 and A17 motorways, but also by a network of railway lines. There are urban cores in the area; the transition to the sandy ground of Brabant offers favourable conditions for business development. The lack of a good railway connection in Hoeksche Waard makes it less suitable for intensive urbanization.

2. We expect that the A4 will be realized one day, although we consider the exact moment extremely uncertain. The most important underlying motive for the A4 is the fact that the ports – Rotterdam, Maasvlakte, Moerdijk, Sloe area, Terneuzen, and Antwerp – are operating increasingly as a network and should be interconnected. As a motorway that passes over, the A4 is of marginal importance for Hoeksche Waard.

3. We propose combining new developments primarily with the extension of the secondary network of regional roads. Within the limits of Hoeksche Waard, we propose extending the N217, linking Dordrecht with Oud-Beijerland, to Spijkenisse. This infrastructure should be made suitable to accommodate local and regional programmes.

Investing in the secondary network kills two birds with one stone. Firstly, it offers space for programmes which focus on the international scale of the network of motorways and simultaneously operate at the level of a regional or local labour market. Secondly, it offers opportunities for incorporating residential cores, which are now linked to the central city (Rotterdam) only by a single route, into a regional network. The suburbs of Spijkenisse and Oud-Beijerland will escape their destiny as residential enclaves and will become part of the contemporary city. The new regional road acts as a catalyst, stimulating the dynamics at the interface between place of residence, region and network of motorways.

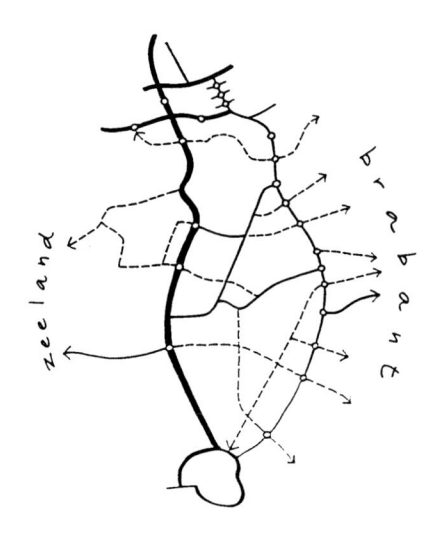

Regional network

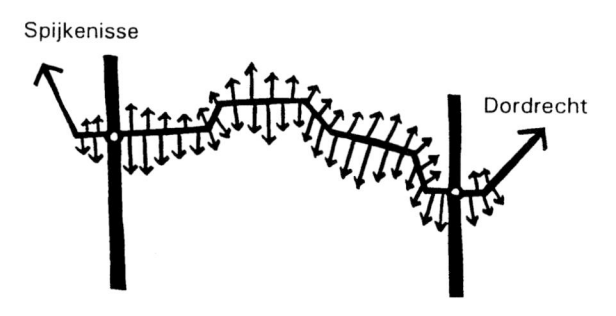

Regional road

The Time Machine

Our plan for Hoeksche Waard consists of a territorial division (zoning) and an accompanying set of rules (strategy). The plan operates like a time machine that modulates potential changes in Hoeksche Waard in time (pace) and space (scale).

It will be possible to decide by area whether to speed up or slow down the pace and whether to differentiate or integrate the scale.

Speeding up will be achieved by looking for a connection with the infrastructural network at the regional and international scales. The modernized and extended N217 will be the spine of this development. Slowing down will be achieved by looking for a connection with the slow cycles of the delta, and/or by disconnecting areas from the regional and international infrastructure. Several fragments of the landscape will neither speed up nor slow down; they will be brought to a standstill as cultural-historical monuments.

The differentiation of the scale means that the landscape will develop towards a more varied combination of different elements.

Integration, on the other hand, means that different parts of the current landscape will be put together and will blend into a greater whole. Instead of becoming more varied, the landscape will become even more homogeneous.

The set of rules entails disassembling and redefining Hoeksche Waard. With the assistance of the time machine the parties operating in Hoeksche Waard will be able to decide who should cooperate with whom, when local authorities or other parties can operate independently, and when coalitions will have to be formed with areas or organizations outside Hoeksche Waard. As a result, the time machine entails both an agreement about decision-making and claims to potential flows of funds.

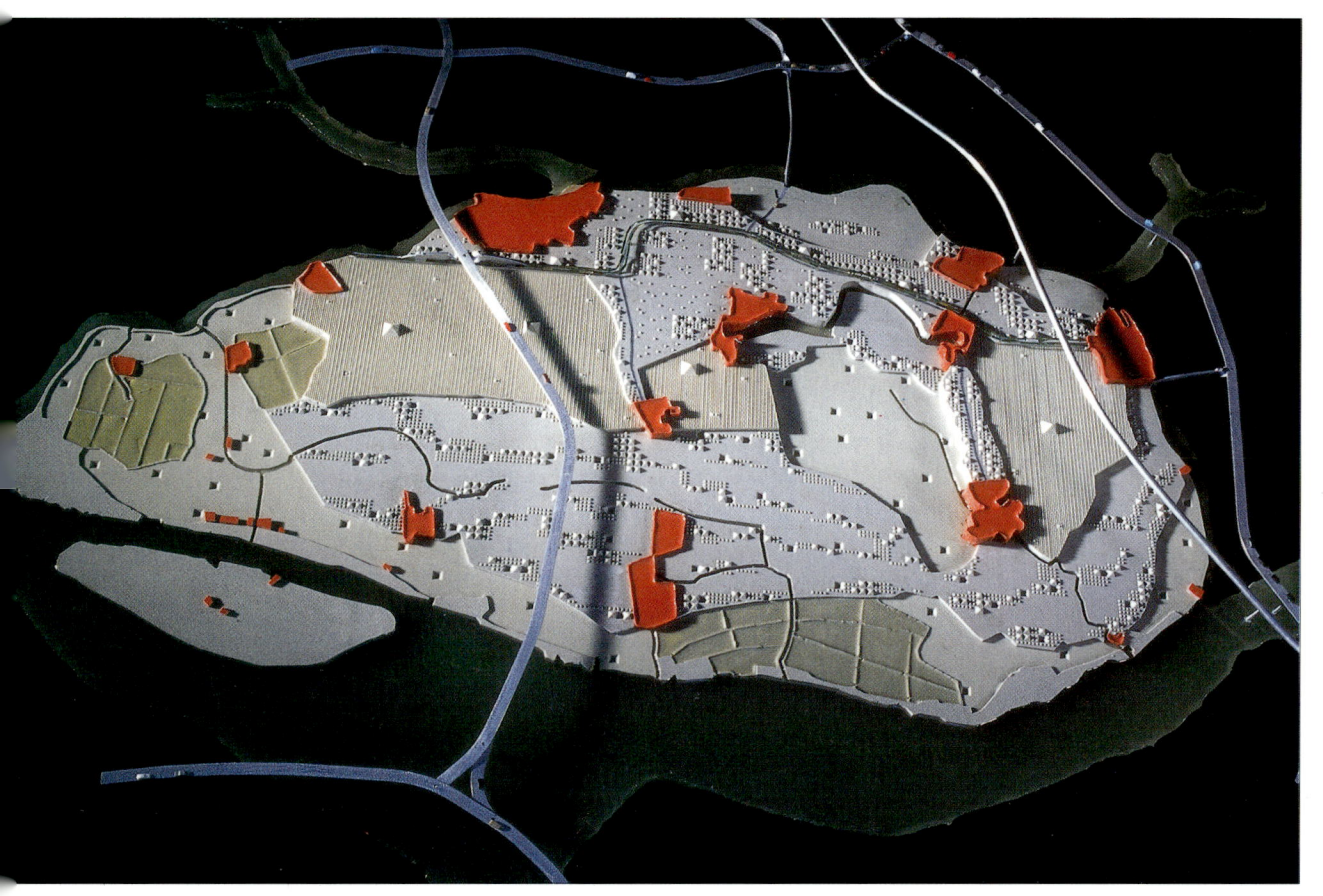

Acceleration-differentiation

Acceleration-integration

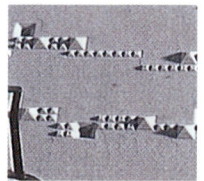

Deceleration-differentiation

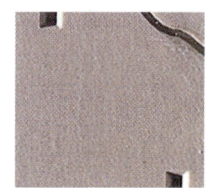

Deceleration-integration

The Time Machine

AIR-ZUIDWAARTS / SOUTHBOUND

DESIGN RESEARCH
FRITS PALMBOOM/JAAP VAN DEN BOUT
PETER CALTHORPE/MATTHEW TAECKER
STEFANO BOERI
FRANÇOIS ROCHE
DETTMAR/BEUTER/FRITZ/HASTENPFLUG
BINDELS/GIETEMA/HARTZEMA/KLOK
MARIEKE TIMMERMANS
DIRK SIJMONS/YTTJE FEDDES

Acceleration and differentiation north of N217

Speeding up and differentiating
In the north, Hoeksche Waard seeks contact with the fast pace by transforming the N217 into a regional road which is linked to the A16 and the future A4. Thanks to a clever access system, rows of plots can be located along this road. The northern part of the road can develop into a strip with a great variety of urban and rural functions. The southern part can accommodate plots and enclaves geared to recreational and residential programmes. The inhabitants of the region will meet one another in a computer megastore, a beer garden, a mosque, and on a golf course. Life will be dominated by the everyday bustle.

Speeding up and integrating
Being easily accessible, the large polders south of the N217 are suitable for specialized agriculture geared to the world market. By removing or privatizing country roads, the scope of operational management can grow without restrictions. This is where tractors leave their mark in the fields.

Acceleration and integration south of N217

Deceleration and differentiation in southern Hoeksche Waard

Slowing down and differentiating
The landscape with ash-lined dikes in the south of Hoeksche Waard is the most suitable for small-scale diversification of farming on the one hand and unorthodox housing on the other. This mix of farming and housing will result in a rural residential landscape. A certain degree of peace and slowing down will be guaranteed by removing the connection with the A4 near Numansdorp. This is where peripheral city-dwellers, second house owners, managers of storage places for caravans, agri-tourists, cheese makers, and biodynamic farmers will meet. Life will be determined by the rhythm of the seasons.

Slowing down and integrating
The southernmost polders along Haringvliet and Hollands Diep as well as Oudeland van Strijen will be given a function in the large-scale water management and conservation of nature in the river delta. Parts of these polders can periodically flood; other parts will become completely or partly inaccessible to motorized residents, visitors or passers-by. Silence, wind, water, reeds, birds and recreational vagrants will dominate this area. The heartbeat of the delta will measure time.

Deceleration and integration in the southernmost polders along Haringvliet, Hollandsch Diep and 'Oudeland van Strijen'

AIR-ZUIDWAARTS / SOUTHBOUND

DESIGN RESEARCH

FRITS PALMBOOM/JAAP VAN DEN BOUT
PETER CALTHORPE/MATTHEW TAECKER
STEFANO BOERI
FRANÇOIS ROCHE
DETTMAR/BEUTER/FRITZ/HASTENPFLUG
BINDELS/GIETEMA/HARTZEMA/KLOK
MARIEKE TIMMERMANS
DIRK SIJMONS/YTTJE FEDDES

Interventions

The regional road

The regional road spans the local and regional road networks between the A16 and the future A4. Once the A4 has been completed the south part of the A29 will be removed. The road through the Heinenoord Tunnel will become a city road, extending as far as Zuidplein and the Erasmus Bridge in Rotterdam. A sophisticated system of sliproads and service roads along the regional road will offer an opportunity for locating series of plots and enclaves here.

To introduce rhythm into this zone, lanes of trees and windbreaks will be planted in a pattern. A roof of ashes will cover the length of the road. The road will run through Hoeksche Waard like a tunnel forest from east to west; a large-scale architecture of vegetation.

This zone is an alternative to the common high-profile sites and industrial estates that are frequently linked to motorways. Thanks to its location between two motorways, the zone will serve both the local and/or regional and the international scales. A public transport route will offer the inhabitants of, for example, Spijkenisse, Rotterdam and Dordrecht easy access to the zone. These conditions can initiate a bustling mix of as yet unpredictable functions.

Large-scale agriculture

The large polders bordering on the modernized regional road offer optimum conditions for large-scale agriculture. The dikes around the polders are built up and will be left as they are. There are hardly any buildings along the small country roads. If necessary, they can be removed from the public road network. The farms operate on the world market. They transcend the scale of a family business. The ties between house and work weaken.

Rural residential landscape

The landscape of ash-lined dikes in the south is the most beautiful part of Hoeksche Waard. The large empty expanses of fields – monochrome, neatly organized, furrowed, inaccessible – contrast sharply with the voluptuous lines of the dikes – colourful, anarchistic and individualistic. Here the cult of one's own estate reigns supreme. The individual domain stands in direct relation to the largest conceivable scale: a simultaneous experience of intimacy and panorama. The extremely elongated polders form a recurrent spatial pattern. Roofs and edges of trees lend this landscape overwhelming and monumental architectural features.

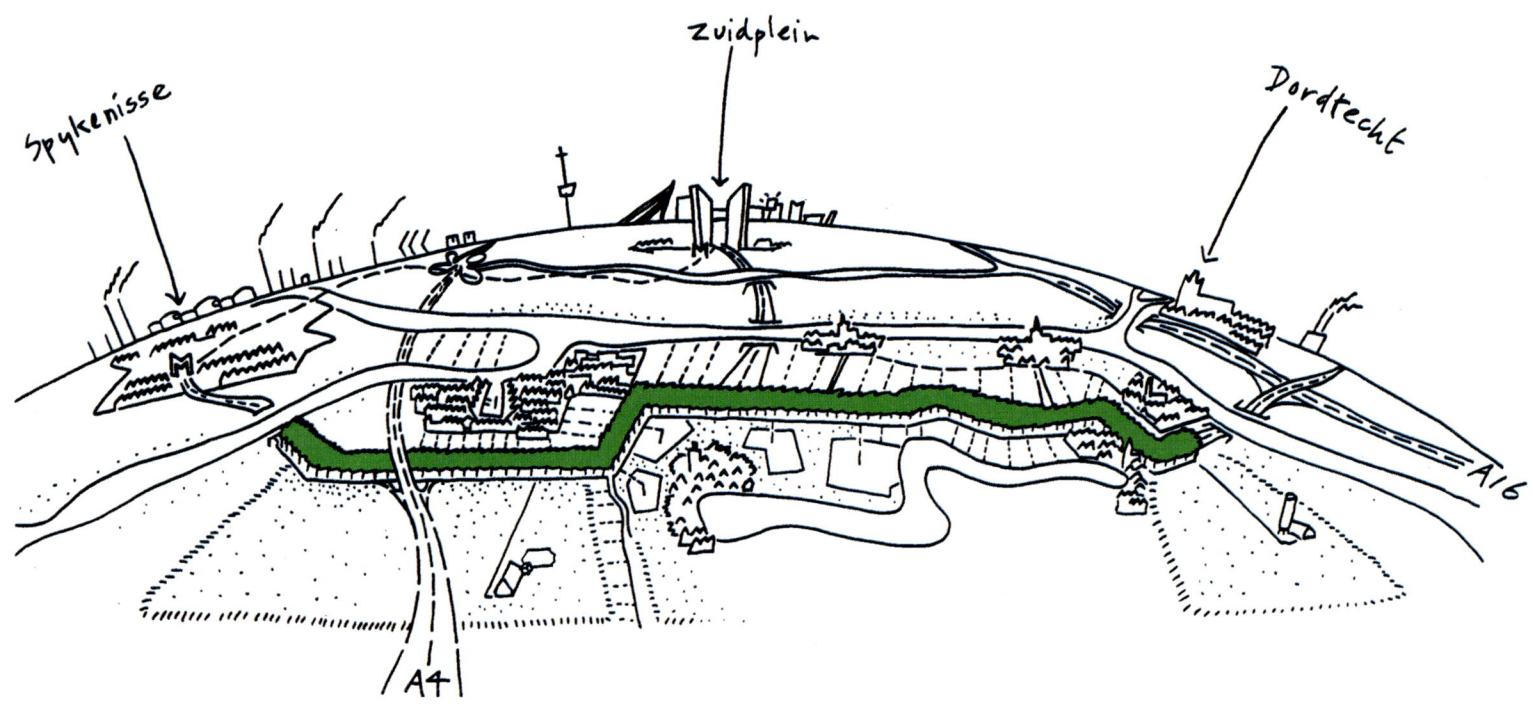

Regional road between Spijkenisse and Dordrecht

Rural residential landscape

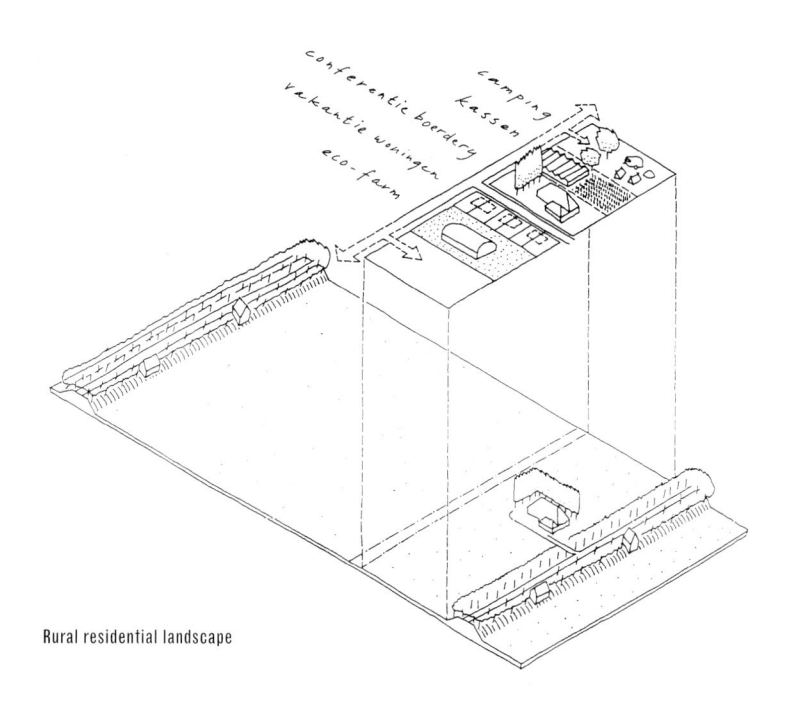

Our plan combines the desire for a more relaxed residential culture with opportunities for a diversification of farming. Instead of drawing up a clear-cut plan, we postulate a set of rules and agreements.
Since time immemorial, labourers' cottages have stood on the south flank of the dikes. New houses may be built here, on condition that enough ashes are preserved. Each house will have a splendid view of the open country. The north side of the dikes has always accommodated large estates. This is where considerable densification and diversification will be made possible within a given zone. A strip of land reserved for a road will limit this zone. The property-owner can build a road to provide access to a camping site, a caravan storage site, a workshop, a group of (second) homes, a party barn, or a biodynamic discount store. The authorities can decide to link these access roads if the traffic load on the narrow dikes becomes too heavy, thus effectuating a parallel road. Those who pre-invest will be reimbursed, while those who profit afterwards will have to pay.
Such a system allows the agricultural monoculture to evolve into a rural residential and work landscape. It offers new opportunities for a relation between home and work, for the farmer who operates in many market segments, for new deals between city and countryside, between consumers and producers.

Large-scale nature
The southern edge of Hoeksche Waard and Oudeland van Strijen will become the domain of a large-scale policy of conservation. Not so much the colonization of land, but the control of water is the driving force behind a slow transformation of the landscape.
The outermost rim of polders, mostly located beyond the main dike, will be integrated into the tidal landscape of Haringvliet. This is where the natural course of alluvion and erosion will determine the contours of the coastline. A strip of thinly populated polders behind the main dike will be adapted to function as an overfall during extreme peaks in the process of discharging river water. Several small sluices in the river dike will serve as controlled water inlets. Wide quays will protect existing villages and farms when the polder is incidentally inundated. New facilities that focus on recreation and conservation in the area will be located on mounds. At odd periods of inundation, the polders of Oude Korendijk and Ambachtsheerlijkheid van Cromstrijen will lie like serene monuments of the area's cultural history, enclosed by a vast water landscape.
The whole southern edge of Hoeksche Waard will be incorporated into the slow rhythm of the delta. This relative isolation will put up a natural barrier against further densification. Due to its low position in the patchwork of clay polders, the peat polder of Oudeland van Strijen is suitable as a reservoir for rainwater. During rainy periods water will be stored in the polder for the irrigation of Hoeksche Waard during dry spells. Thoroughfares will be removed. The bare grassland of Oudeland van Strijen will evolve into a waterlogged peat bog where a few eccentrics will live in seclusion.

Epilogue
This urban development plan creates conditions for changes in land use. Such a commonsensical land surveying approach is not imageless but has its own architectural dimension. This dimension has been made explicit in the impact the regional road will have on Hoeksche Waard. More implicit is the architectural quality hidden in the way spatial contrasts are revealed and variation is added. They form a composition that accentuates the characteristic motives in Hoeksche Waard: the parallel and elongated patterns in the organization of space and its use. In this way, a grand context is created for taking advantage of changes that are scarcely tied to a particular area.

Urban Revitalization, Rural Diversification and Environmental Rehabilitation

Architect Peter Calthorpe is one of the leading lights of the American New Urbanism movement which tries to make suburbs 'healthy' again. According to him, Matthew Taecker and their team cities should become more urban and the countryside more rural. Rotterdam and the Drecht towns should exploit their territories much more intensively. In this way the countryside remains protected from undesired urbanization. Rotterdam should get a more clearly defined boundary: the Oude Maas. According to Calthorpe the future of Hoeksche Waard is primarily to be found in new perspectives for agriculture, fishery and recreation. He proposes to partly open the Haringvliet sluices. The delta then becomes a more natural tidal area again with an extensive system of 'wetlands'. Thus he solves many problems at a time. With regard to nature wetlands are one of the richest landscape types. At the same time the area serves as a reservoir that can receive threatening sea water as well as excess river water and a 'living-machine', purifying waste water biologically. In the wetlands people can live, cultivate and recreate in a pleasant way. All the villages and towns will be by the water and get an attractive waterfront. Their waste matter will be processed locally in biological systems. Fish and oyster farms provide new economic perspectives. If in addition the farmers switch over to ecological cultivation and supply the local and regional market with high-quality products, Hoeksche Waard will become much more diverse and less dependent on the world market.

Regional plan

Hoeksche Waard represents an unparalleled opportunity to define sustainable urban and rural development patterns and practices. This island sits at the nexus of competing systems. To the north lies the port city of Rotterdam, where the expanding industrial might of the Rhineland meets the sea. To the south lies the Rhine-Scheldt delta, and within it vast ecosystems which have gradually declined through human activity.

We support the five primary goals expressed in the Province of Zuid-Holland Discussion Report advanced in 1994: restructure the city to maintain its built quality, improve residential opportunities, stimulate the urban economy, safeguard rural areas for their environmental and aesthetic values, and reinforce transit, especially on a regional scale. However, we disagree with the assertion that Rotterdam must move beyond its compact fabric to achieve these goals. Pressures to urbanize the delta region are expected to mount and are threatening to merge Amsterdam, The Hague, Rotterdam, Antwerp and Brussels into an unbroken megalopolis. And our technical and economic capacity for settlement will only improve, fuelled by our increased mobility and a desire to 'spread out'. But doing so threatens to deplete resources at an ever-increasing rate and will undermine our ability to offer 'the good life' to future generations.

Urban limits and opportunities for growth

Containing growth and reinforcing existing urban neighbourhoods are essential to counteract the decline of the cities and avoid dependence on highways and cars. Highway dependent systems of urban expansion are resource intensive and lead to gridlock and the permanent loss of open space. They also decant economic activity to the edge of regions and reduce our ability to maintain compact neighbourhoods that support walking and transit for many trips.

Growth should be harnessed to revitalize existing neighbourhoods and remake underutilized lands. Aging industrial blight should be transformed into active mixed-use districts. Dysfunctional building stock should be replaced and the 'leftover' spaces of the modern city put to use. Parking lots and excessive building setbacks should be redeveloped to support pedestrian connections and urban vitality.

At the urban edge, new growth should be used to consolidate cities, using natural constraints as permanent boundaries. In Rotterdam, open areas are available north of the Oude Maas River. Developing these sites will avoid the need for expensive river crossings and highway extensions.

New industrial growth should be directed into the A-15 corridor where rail, highway and transit are in place. Industrial growth south of the Oude Maas will only set in motion a demand for nearby

Regional vision: water determines the islands' new nature and economy

Growth develops in the existing town

INFILL

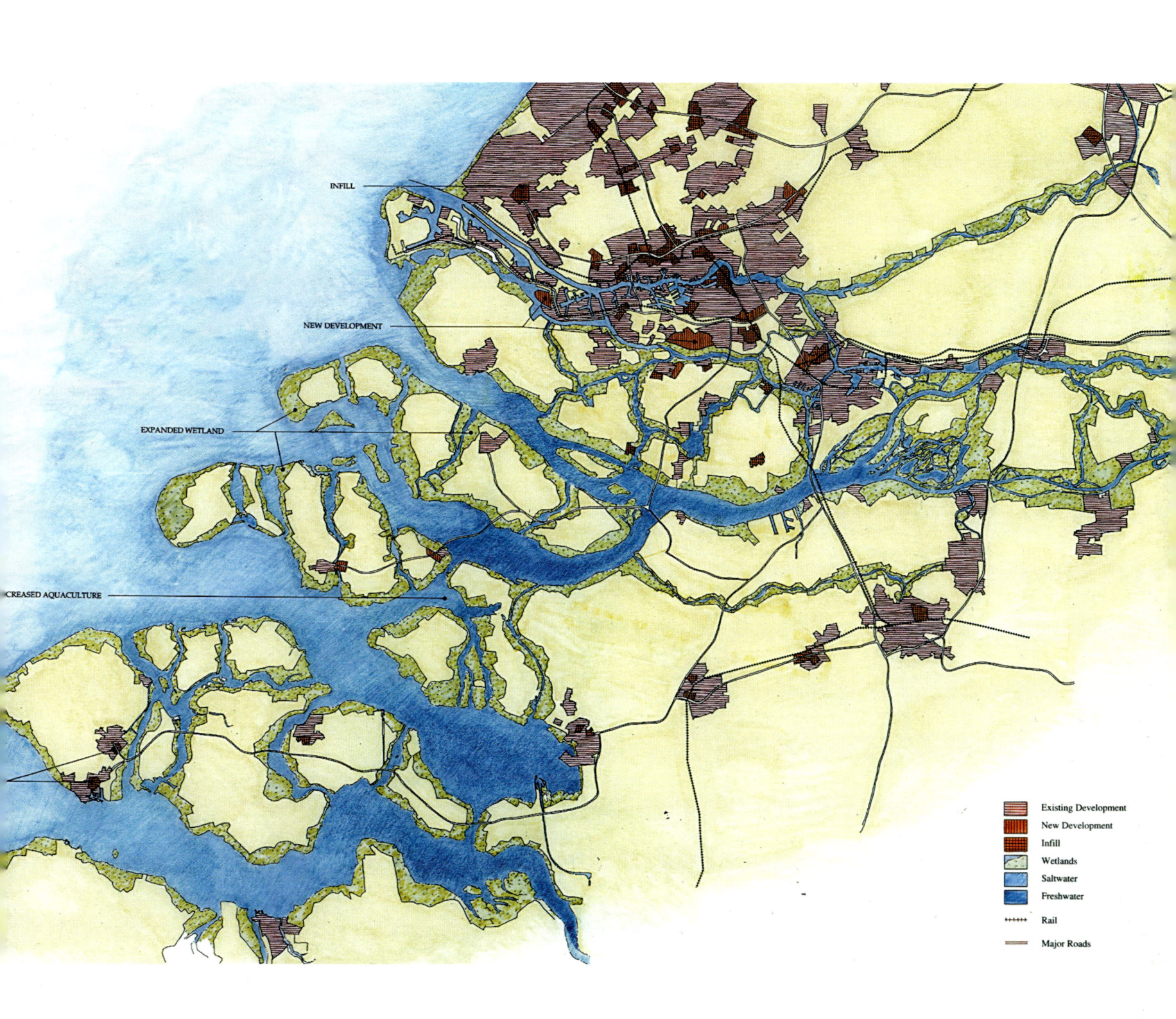

NEW DEVELOPMENT

EXPANDED WETLAND

CREASED AQUACULTURE

- Existing Development
- New Development
- Infill
- Wetlands
- Saltwater
- Freshwater
- Rail
- Major Roads

housing and shopping centres, which will erode the economic vitality of the city and consume valuable agricultural and environmental resources.

Hoeksche Waard and Rhine-Scheldt delta

Containing urban growth is best for the city and permits the continued use and enjoyment of nearby open space. But the future of agriculture in Hoeksche Waard and the Rhine-Scheldt delta is far from certain. The farm economy of the delta is in decline. Agri-businesses are supplanting the family farm, and the prices of goods from Poland and other developing markets threaten to undermine cost-competitiveness of local goods.

To survive, agriculture must focus on high-value niche markets such as organic produce and dairy. Organic methods are cost-effective, improve water quality, and support a larger workforce – halting the outward migration and economic decline of many rural towns.

Large portions of the delta's islands should also revert to freshwater lakes and natural wetlands. The environmental degradation of the delta estuaries has been long documented. Dams have eliminated tidal forces and led to the continued erosion of riverbanks. Fish stocks have declined as natural habitat has been consumed by dikes and polders. Global warming may raise sea levels, increase flood surges from upland areas, and necessitate large water storage areas. Land is also expected to subside, as peat layers oxidize due to diminishing water tables.

Extensive lakes and wetlands offer major environmental and economic benefits. Paired with the Haringvliet lock sluices, they provide important flood and storm damage protection by avoiding bank erosion and by providing areas that can accommodate high flows during surges or heavy rains. Wetlands filter out pollutants that degrade water quality and remediate decades of pollution. Increased hydrostatic pressure from lakes and wetlands also recharges local aquifers, offsets saltwater intrusion, and halts the oxidation and subsidence of peat soils.

Wetlands can also play a central role in the region's economy by supporting intensive aquaculture. Fish farms and fish ranches will be increasingly profitable with the global decline of fish harvests. Fish farms would occur in contained ponds, and a range of aquaculture activities would be supported by wetlands. Wetlands are the foundation of the food chain and provide vital 'nursery' areas for organisms and young fish. Wetlands can foster abundant harvests of fish, shrimp, molluscs and crabs. The wetlands also provide important nesting and mating areas for a wide variety of resident and migratory birds, and would greatly enhance tourism in the region. Towns and villages will also benefit from the new lakes and wetlands. Waterfront development, nature trails and labour-intensive farming will boost local economies. New pressures for growth should be harnessed to revitalize existing neighbourhoods and town centres and support a rich mix of uses and activities.

The south wing of Rotterdam
Urban limits

Rotterdam's southern edge should advance only up to the Oude Maas River. Redevelopment of underutilized areas is already under way and should be further encouraged. New neighbourhoods are also possible and can absorb sizable development. Growth should be concentrated where there is already existing infrastructure. An intensive system of industries, roads, rails and transit now extends from the western harbours toward inland destinations along the Rhine. Development should take advantage of this existing infrastructure and avoid expensive new river crossings. New industries should be organized about the east-west spine of infrastructure and port-related activities that already exists. By doing so, the region can avoid the cost and destructive effects of extending the A29 through Hoeksche Waard by way of an expensive river crossing. Concentrating businesses within the east-west corridor will also make the new jobs accessible to employees via transit. Rotterdam must fight the temptation to build a large industrial park in the large open areas of Hoeksche Waard. 'Leapfrogging' into this undeveloped area will force an absolute reliance on cars and trucks that will exacerbate traffic congestion, necessitate growth-inducing construction of highways and infrastructure, and lose for ever the island's scenic character. The ongoing monetary and cultural costs of an island industrial park dwarfs the modest initial savings from cheaper land.

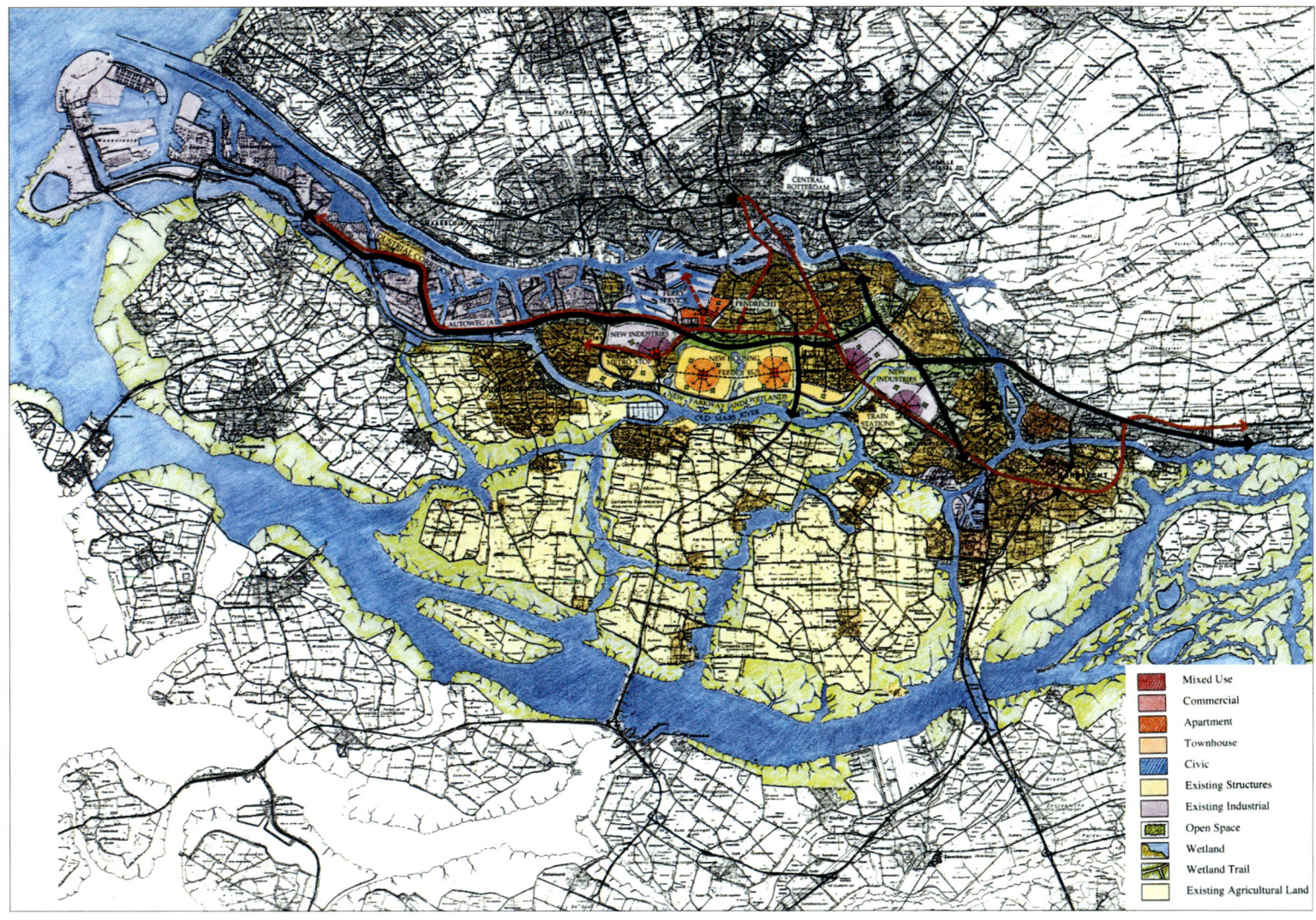

Rotterdam's expansion is halted by River Oude Maas, new industrial and residential zoning along the existing east-west infrastructure. The port is modernized by redevelopment of the old port

Increase connectivity and pedestrian-supportive environments

Without the construction of a large industrial park on Hoeksche Waard, the capacity of existing highways is expected to be adequate for the next twenty years, negating the need for the A-4. In the meantime, efforts should be made to enhance the existing network of urban roads. Where possible, additional connections should be made to distribute traffic among multiple routes. Enhanced road connections will improve the capacity of the transportation system and reduce traffic volumes to levels that can encourage pedestrian and neighbourhood activities. With lower traffic volumes, roads will be transformed from hostile urban highways at the edge of neighbourhoods to urbane boulevards at their centre. Large undeveloped setbacks from the highway turn into development opportunities within the city. One important new connection includes a new 'parkway' along the southern edge of IJsselmonde. The parkway should be designed to permit easy pedestrian movement from the new neighbourhoods to the open spaces that are proposed along the river.

Development opportunities north of the Oude Maas

With the modernization of the Port further west, exciting possibilities exist for the redevelopment of harbour-front land into mixed-use districts. Substantial residential and employment growth should occur in these and other underutilized areas throughout Rotterdam.
Rotterdam's edge follows natural boundaries and existing infrastructure. North of the Oude Maas, new neighbourhoods should be built in ways that maintain connections to open space. Recreation and naturalized detention areas should extend along the river and define the edges of neighbourhoods.

AIR-ZUIDWAARTS / SOUTHBOUND

DESIGN RESEARCH
FRITS PALMBOOM/JAAP VAN DEN BOUT
PETER CALTHORPE/MATTHEW TAECKER
STEFANO BOERI
FRANÇOIS ROCHE
DETTMAR/BEUTER/FRITZ/HASTENPFLUG
BINDELS/GIETEMA/HARTZEMA/KLOK
MARIEKE TIMMERMANS
DIRK SIJMONS/YTTJE FEDDES

Urban growth through redevelopment
Remaking underutilized land

Underutilized areas exist throughout Rotterdam. One redevelopment opportunity exists on the harbour, west of Pendrecht. This area is characterized by aging wharves and single-storey structures, and by fast-moving roads edged by barren parkways. It is difficult to get to, except by car or truck, and the area is void of the most basic conveniences. In our proposal the heart of the district is an intimate boulevard, connecting Pendrecht to the east with the harbour to the west. Mixed-use buildings with ground-floor retail and housing or offices above would frame this shopping street. Where the two boulevards join, an existing lake – a neglected asset within the community – can be combined with a park and community centre to create a civic focal point. Transit service intersects the east-west boulevard where it meets the harbour. Multi-modal connections to ferry services are possible – quickly transporting residents, workers and visitors to and from the city's major destinations. Associated with the transit station, an oval park forms a symbolic and functional heart of the mixed-use district. Mid-rise apartment buildings, office buildings and major hotels face the oval park, the waterfront and the east-west boulevard. The ground floors of these buildings would contain street-facing shops, restaurants and cafes. A broad range of housing opportunities should be contained within every neighbourhood. In this plan, mid-rise towers face the boulevards, new townhouses frame streets and open spaces, and detached single-family homes utilize neglected areas at the neighbourhood's edge.

Waalhaven reorganization

Existing situation

A new boulevard with mixed destination

Hoeksche Waard islands; villages and towns will be on the water, new rural economic, natural and environmental developments go hand in hand

Hoeksche Waard
A new rurality

The future character of Hoeksche Waard becomes, therefore, a question of the future of agriculture and the small towns within the Rhine delta. In the 21st Century, agriculture and the rural landscape will reflect a shift toward sustainable practices that use resources efficiently and ecologically. The new landscape will stress the interconnectedness of urban, agricultural and natural systems and the benefits each system offers the other. Our proposal for Hoeksche Waard emphasizes: the creation of lakes and wetlands (to increase biological and economic diversity); a growing global demand for aquaculture (fish farming and fish ranching); niche agricultural markets (organic farming and glasshouses); and connections between urban and rural systems (biological wastewater treatment).

The creation of lakes, wetlands and aquaculture

The creation of lakes and wetlands within and around Hoeksche Waard offers major environmental and economic benefits, and is a central element in our proposal. Extensive wetlands provide important flood and storm damage protection by avoiding bank erosion and by providing areas that can accommodate high flows during surges or heavy rains. Wetlands also filter out pollutants that degrade water quality, and could remediate decades of pollution if constructed throughout the delta region. By increasing the hydrostatic pressure of freshwater impoundments, wetlands and ponds also help recharge the local aquifer, offset saltwater intrusion and halt the oxidation and subsidence of peat soils. Wetlands can also play a central role in the island's economy by supporting fish farms and fish ranches. Wetlands nourish fish and other aquatic organisms by serving as a nursery area for larval and juvenile fish as well as a key source of nutrients that support the food chain. The production of phytoplankton, zooplankton, shrimp, molluscs, barnacles, crabs, snails and many other creatures thrives in healthy wetlands. Plankton are consumed, in turn, by benthic (bottom dwelling) organisms such as clams, crustaceans and a variety of worms, cover many surfaces and are embedded in the mud. These filter-feeders help maintain water quality and feed a wide range of fish and birds. Tidal and seasonal wetlands also provide important nesting and mating areas for a wide variety of resident and migratory birds. Sustainable commercial fisheries nurtured by healthy wetlands are likely to be increasingly profitable. World fish stocks continue to decline and current conditions indicate substantial price increases for all forms of fish in the future.

Niche markets: organic farming & glasshouses

For Hoeksche Waard, the competitive advantage of other agricultural areas in Europe requires an emphasis on the production of high-value crops for niche markets. Niche crops for the island include fresh market vegetables, fresh culinary herbs, cut flowers and other ornamentals, speciality dairy products, and fresh fish and shellfish from aquaculture. A high potential also exists for emerging niche markets for agricultural products not consumed directly by humans, such as fingerlings and seed stock for aquaculture or ecosystem restoration, production of plants for ecological restoration projects, and value-added products processed locally.

Organic farming systems send no pollutants into surrounding ecosystems or into the crops themselves. Organic farming enriches the soil using natural processes and materials, encouraging healthy plants that resist attack by pests. Additionally the agro-system maintains a wide range of plants, habitats and organisms in an interrelated web of life. Ecological stability is thus achieved, resulting in fewer interventions by the farmer, reducing the need for pesticides and reducing the level of nutrients and other soluble chemicals that escape to water bodies, groundwater and the air.

A modest increase in glasshouses can boost year-round production and employment and increase incomes of farm operators. Organic production techniques can be effective and are adaptable to glasshouse use. Rather than interrupting the scenic vistas of the island, glasshouses should be located proximate to the urban silhouette of villages and towns.

Village growth
Revitalization and redevelopment

The transformation of the landscape from conventional farms into ecologically diverse systems presents profound opportunities for the typical community. Currently surrounded by a uniform landscape of conventional farms, towns can remake themselves into 'seaside villages' by relating directly to the scenic wetlands and lakes that will be created. With plentiful wildlife, fresh seafood, scenic trails and water recreation, the villages will be enormously attractive.

Redevelopment is especially important for the revitalization and expansion of each village's centre, where a rich mix of uses should be encouraged. In the village centre, future streets should be framed by ground-floor shopping with new apartments and businesses on the floors above. Civic buildings, like new libraries or day care centres, should be incorporated within the village centre and be accompanied by small parks for rest, recreation and special events. Farmers' markets should showcase local organic produce and aquaculture.

A hotel, auditorium or other civic and commercial uses should take advantage of places where the village centre meets the new lakes.

A broad range of housing opportunities should be generated. To succeed economically, affordable housing must be included to accommodate the larger workforce necessitated by organic farming and aquaculture – workers who will help support the economic resurgence of each town. Higher income households should also be encouraged and can be attracted by the unique lifestyle the new towns will afford.

The system of lakes and wetlands offer new possibilities for housing. In Holland, townhouses and shops have long faced directly onto waterways for commercial trade. Future housing will take advantage of views and recreation. Townhouses can be built on 'piers' extending into the water. Houseboats can further broaden housing opportunities and remind us of Holland's strong connection to water and the sea.

Under this proposal, each village would have its own waste recycling facility in proximity to it. The liquid-borne waste stream would then go into a biological filtering type treatment with aquatic and biological digesters in the form of linked, attractive ponds or glasshouses. Water plants are a by-product and can be used for feed or compost. Flower, shrub and tree seedling production can be incorporated into the treatment process. Bio-gas is also generated and can help heat and light the glasshouses.

Agro-tourism and eco-tourism

Agro-tourism and eco-tourism opportunities can be created at the village's edge, where visitors can enjoy open spaces and can walk to the village centre to shop, dine or enjoy a show. Where farm meets town, tourists can engage in the life of a farmer and can also learn organic farming processes. Where lake meets town, tourists can enjoy waterfront promenades and a range of water sports. Where marsh meets town, tourists can enjoy nature and learn ecological processes along an extensive network of trails.

The presence of the strong local economies creates opportunities for farmers to gain increased income directly from tourist services as well as from increased direct sale of farm products to visitors. Such sales are usually made at current retail prices, which allows the farmer to increase the economic returns by avoiding the costs of packaging, storage and shipping.

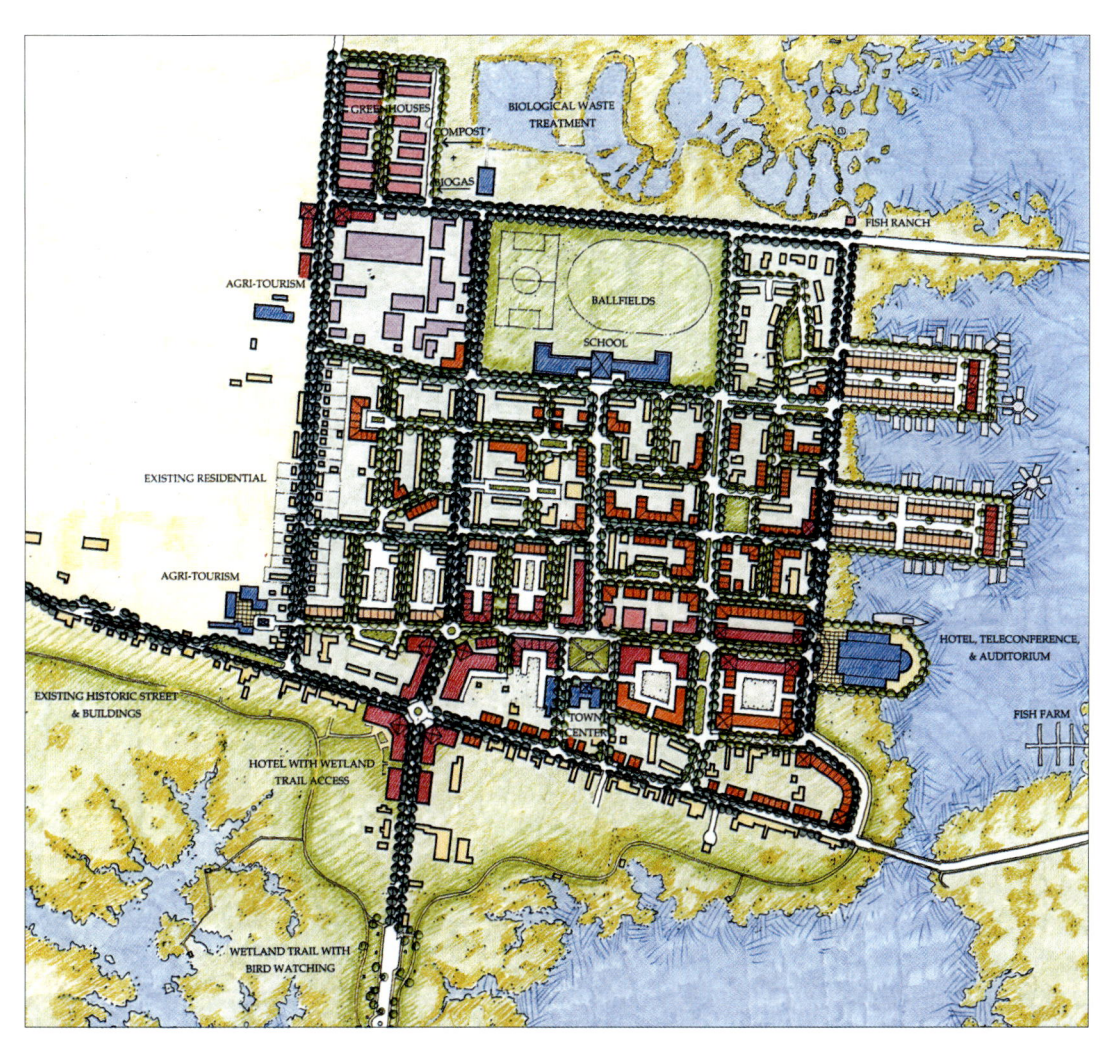

Revitalized village, new waterfront activities, agro-tourism and eco-tourism

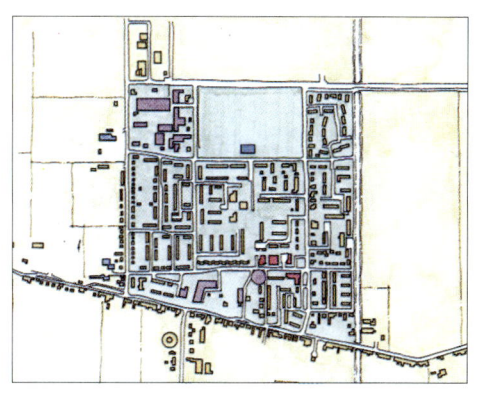

Existing situation

Historical relation between living and water

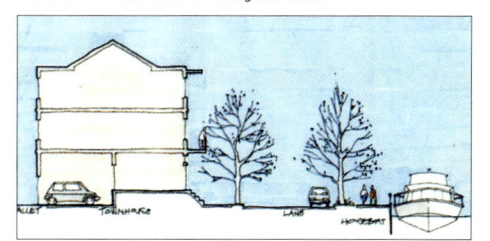

Construction of new houses on a pier

Filament City

Hoeksche Waard, according to the Italian architect Stefano Boeri, is a fascinating laboratory for new dwelling forms. Like many other parts of Europe lying in the shadow of a major city, the island has the benefit of urban facilities and an extensive network of roads, though itself remaining pleasantly rural. The proposal of Boeri and his team proceeds from a special type of dike development. The 'Filament City' consists of eleven sections of dike each several kilometres in length, along which various combinations of houses and other functions can evolve. Each 'filament' gets its own function. On one dike (Numansdijk) the emphasis is on dwellings and glasshouses, on the other (Westdijk), houses in combination with facilities for walking and birdwatching. This will steadily give rise to a varied landscape that is at the same time a genuine city, in that each function is to have its own location. As the development is concentrated along dikes, the landscape is kept open and the views across it are maintained. A far cry from the uniform sea of single-family houses in the Dutch VINEX developments.

Differences and variations in the contemporary city

Hoeksche Waard project is an attempt to deal with the radically altered relationship between the principles of difference and variation in the contemporary city.

Today the principle of difference no longer acts between big and homogeneous parts – the 19th-century city and the Renaissance city, the public spaces of the periphery and the great industrial zones – but between the individual molecules of an urban organism that has expanded enormously: between the suburban house and the adjoining shopping centre, between the terrain vague and the adjoining block of apartments, between the car wash and the industrial shed with attached residence, between the bypass and the area of farmland.

In the same way, the principle of variation no longer operates within broad territorial sections (as a declining of the individual components of the city block, or of the linear fabric), but through surprising jumps and extemporary solutions among the few categories of 'urban features' that make up the emerging city: the variation is reduced to innumerable adaptations that can be assumed in different territories by the single-family house or block of apartments or container for a leisure facility/commercial undertaking. An excess of versions, then, that does not produce typological inventions and that appears to reflect the need for over-representation of the individual in a society made up of a plethora of minorities, loath to accept unitary and aggregated designs. Hoeksche Waard project is an endeavour to accept the new principle of difference and orient it into specific evolutionary rules. The idea of a 'Filament City' is an attempt to use the claim to an individualistic lifestyle and transform it into a syntax of physical variations in the new Hoeksche Waard urban settlement.

MID-lands

Like some other spaces along the major infrastructural corridor that spans Europe from North to South, Hoeksche Waard is the potential space of a new form of urban habitat: close to the big European metropolitan areas, yet immersed in the countryside and nature; grounded on single-family housing and tangential to the big networks of continental mobility.

Hoeksche Waard, like other intermediate territories of high environmental value, could become the laboratory of a new urban lifestyle far away from city centres and next to networks, where the domestic realm attains intimacy with natural and agrarian landscapes, as well as with the territory of fluxes.

On the scale of the Netherlands, Hoeksche Waard is itself in an intermediate condition, where no single system (agricultural, metropolitan, infrastructural, local) prevails. This is emphatically not the result of a lack of control, rather the unintended consequence of the process of construction of the contemporary territory in the Netherlands. More intensively than elsewhere, this springs from the interaction of multiple sectorial rationalities and expertises, each one exerting its power over a well-delimited portion of space. This leads to an overall condition of instability and uncertainty, no one of the extended resources being able to emerge over the others. Indeed, the regional space of economical, social, historical and urban relations seems not to be the adequate scale on which to orient the future in Hoeksche Waard.

The island should recognize its references at two utterly different scales: access to the emergent network of new urban/landscape habitats in Europe and local establishment of a new model of non-deterministic urban growth.

Authentic landscapes along the Blue Banana

The Trossachs

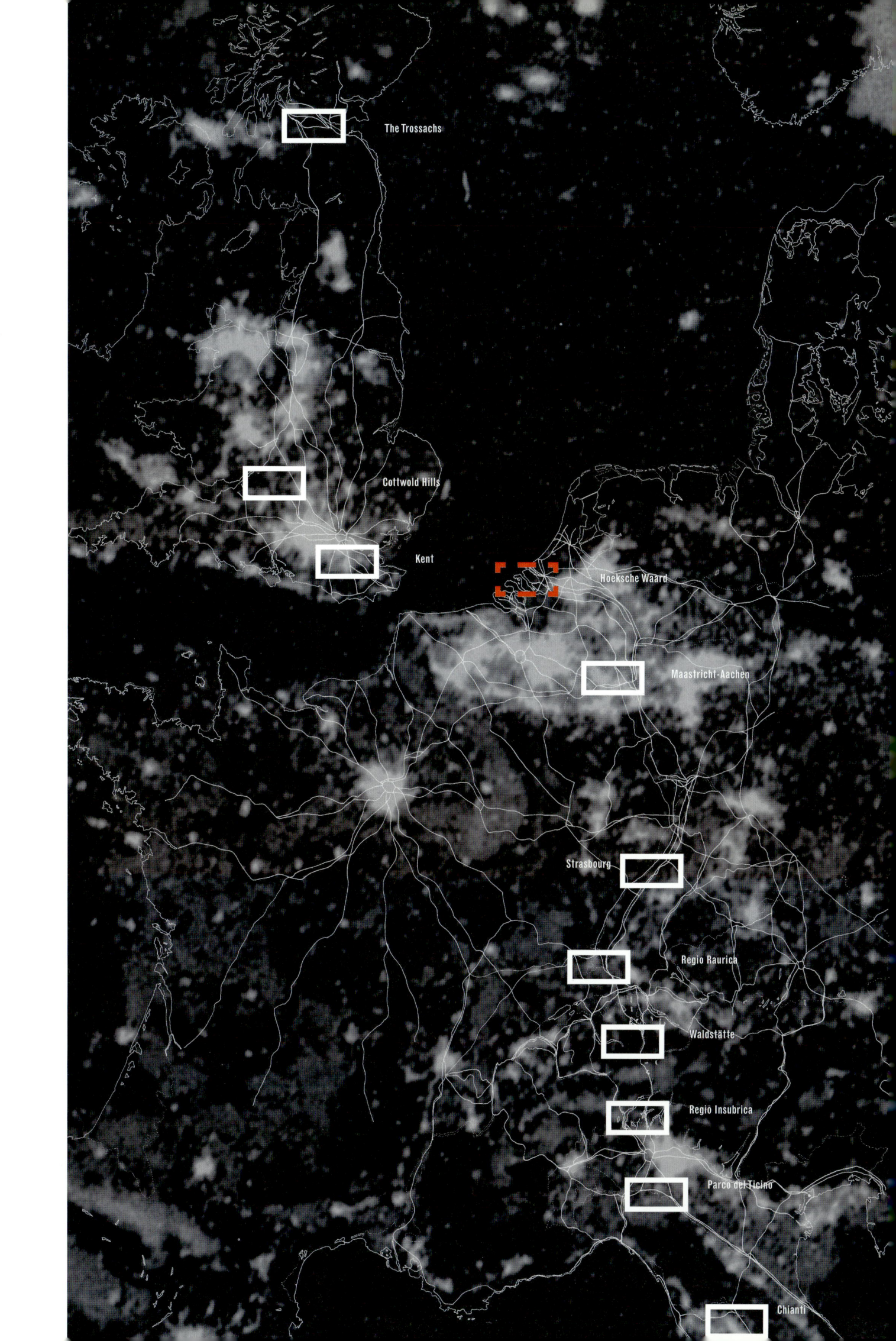

Cottwold Hills

Kent

Hoeksche Waard

Maastricht-Aachen

Strasbourg

Regio Raurica

Waldstätte

Regio Insubrica

Parco del Ticino

Chianti

DESIGN RESEARCH

FRITS PALMBOOM/JAAP VAN DEN BOUT
PETER CALTHORPE/MATTHEW TAECKER
STEFANO BOERI
FRANÇOIS ROCHE
DETTMAR/BEUTER/FRITZ/HASTENPFLUG
BINDELS/GIETEMA/HARTZEMA/KLOK
MARIEKE TIMMERMANS
DIRK SIJMONS/YTTJE FEDDES

Living and filament city

In opposition to the VINEX model, which proposes mono-functional and peri-urban residential settlements, the new Hoeksche Waard habitat unwinds through the countryside in bands of differentiated population density.

In each of the eleven filaments that compose the new city of Hoeksche Waard, single-family housing hybridizes with a particular activity: small industry, retail services, spare-time facilities, offices, sports, experimental agriculture, etc. The specific predominant activity which characterizes each one of the eleven filaments is a guarantee that we are not building eleven villages but one whole city.

The entire Hoeksche Waard can become a single big city divided into eleven specialized districts; some of them will run between two polders, others will encircle wide natural areas, others still will be scattered along a linear infrastructure. Here will be districts variously populated but all hosting sufficiently intense interactions to inform you that you are in one and the same city. In particular, the specific activity characterizing each filament ensures that the intense relationships between the different filaments converge to form a single, very active urban habitat.

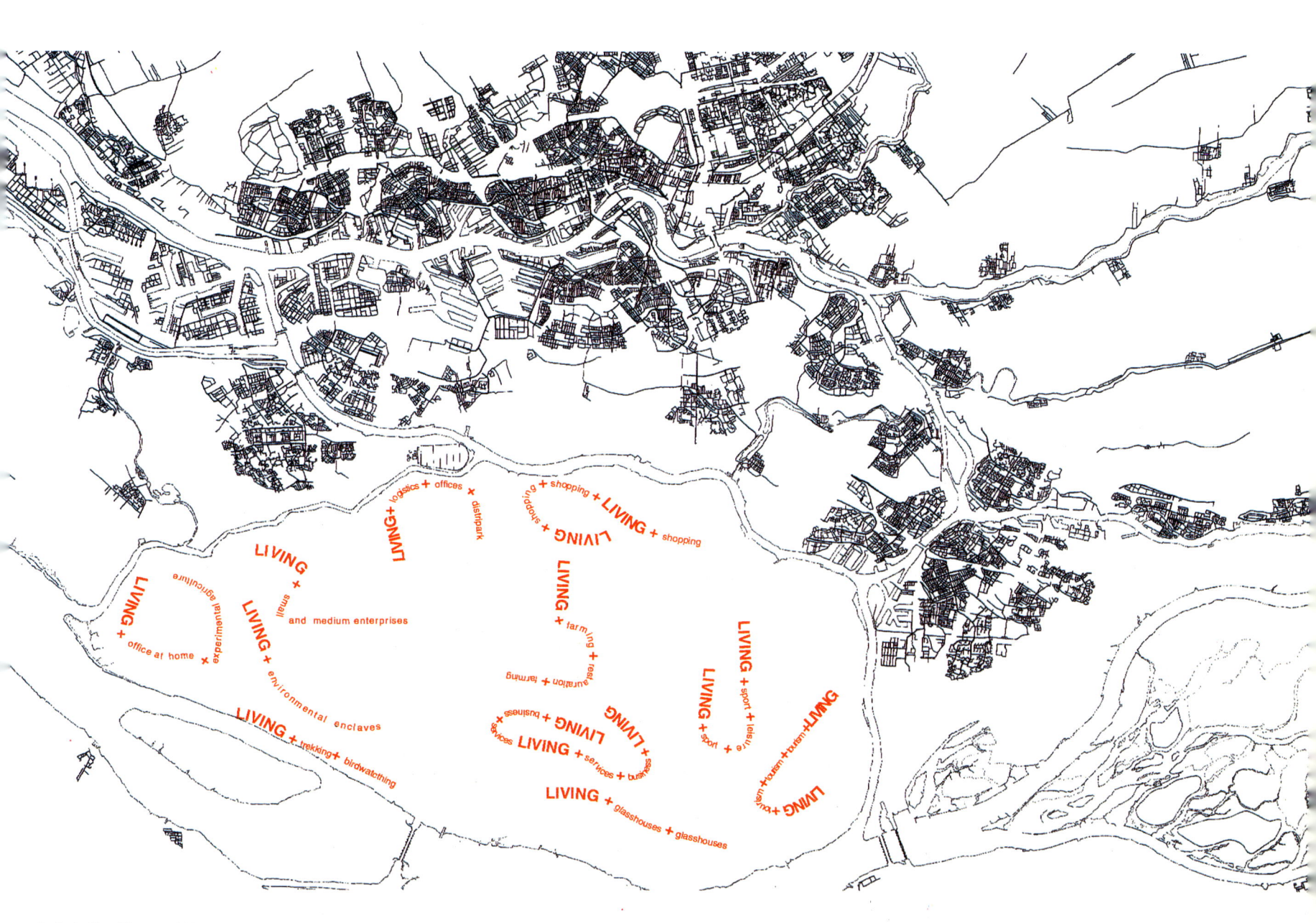

Hoeksche Waard line-town: Living +

Bands of differentiated density

The construction of this new city will not follow a linear path, where every step is clearly set in advance and the overall asset is in a condition of equilibrium. The new structures will interact with the existing processes of construction of the landscape, generating local intensifications of the urban flow and reacting back on the new structures themselves, accelerating the process at times, inhibiting and slowing it down at others. The gradual evolution of the filaments uses and intercepts pre-existing conditions and the constraints of the territory: the dike pattern, the villages, waterlines, infrastructures, natural reserves, as well as institutional conditionings. The territorial constraints guide the unstable and unforeseeable evolution of the eleven filaments amidst a wealth of possibilities.

Each filament runs along and progressively covers the profile of the dikes according to general rules of extension and population density. Yet, as with the genetic code of living forms, it is not possible to completely predict their evolution. A hindrance, a veto, an obstacle, can make the filament change its direction, which can indeed generate multiple figures in the territory. There is no unilinear development track, but different paths can coexist in the same space interacting with one another, to form a stratification of fluxes and environments within a single 'intermediate' urban habitat. Each filament grows according to its own rhythm and the new city in Hoeksche Waard represents in its totality the general dynamic of the interaction of these different ambits, a dynamic that can organize itself in numerous different ways during the various moments in its evolution. Hoeksche Waard becomes the experimental ground of a non-deterministic urbanism, one that accepts and re-elaborates hindrances even when pursuing a stable, optimum configuration.

Ways of changing

Each urban filament follows an unforeseeable evolutionary dynamic. In order to orient this growth, it is only possible to prefigure a limited number of ways of changing, and some general construction diagrams. We may recognize four main ways of changing: first, unitarian interventions (promoted by single large developers and organized as a whole), allotments (the subdivision of land in different similar portions characterized by a spontaneous order), repetition (engaged by a multitude of individual tremors), and intertwining (the addition of new buildings and extensions into the existing urban fabric).

These four ways of changing are composed and recombined in at least eleven diagrams of evolution – Autocatalytic Loops, Hysteris, Extension, Feedback, Inertia, Intensification, Slowing Down, Embedding, Densification – each one dealing differently with the various urban processes.

Territorial intimacy

Against the mono-functional and peri-urban model of row-housing pursued by the VINEX Programme, the evolution of Hoeksche Waard generates a stratification in the landscape of complex built filaments, differentiated by a functional propensity and characterized by an elevated typological variety.

Running through different environmental conditions, and accumulating the entire complexity of a multi-functional urban fabric within the corridor along the dikes, each linear settlement acquires emergent environmental qualities from the various combinations of activities and their multiple relations with the wide open spaces that separate the filaments. For the inhabitants of a space that alternates contemplation of the landscape with automobile movements, day-to-day life is organized by differentiated physical and perceptive bands. Starting from a domestic intimacy with open landscape, each movement through and within the new urban habitat of Hoeksche Waard produces a particular sequence of filaments, a particular succession of resources and urban facilities, a particular sequence of perceptions.

Filaments of various densities

Oude Korendijk	Total length: 11,000 mtrs	Population: 826
	Density: 75 inh./km	Amenities: 22,400 m²

Numansdijk	Total length: 14,000 mtrs	Population: 4,660
	Density: 332 inh./km	Glasshouses and trade: 390,000 m²

Zuidzijdse dijk	Total length: 9,100 mtrs	Population: 3,180
	Density: 349 inh./km	Small and medium-sized businesses: 87,000 m²

Westdijk	Total length: 7,000 mtrs	Bird-watch towers: 6
	Picnic areas: 450,000 m²	Natural restoration: 600,000 m²

AIR-ZUIDWAARTS / SOUTHBOUND

98

DESIGN RESEARCH

FRITS PALMBOOM/JAAP VAN DEN BOUT
PETER CALTHORPE/MATTHEW TAECKER
STEFANO BOERI
FRANÇOIS ROCHE
DETTMAR/BEUTER/FRITZ/HASTENPFLUG
BINDELS/GIETEMA/HARTZEMA/KLOK
MARIEKE TIMMERMANS
DIRK SIJMONS/YTTJE FEDDES

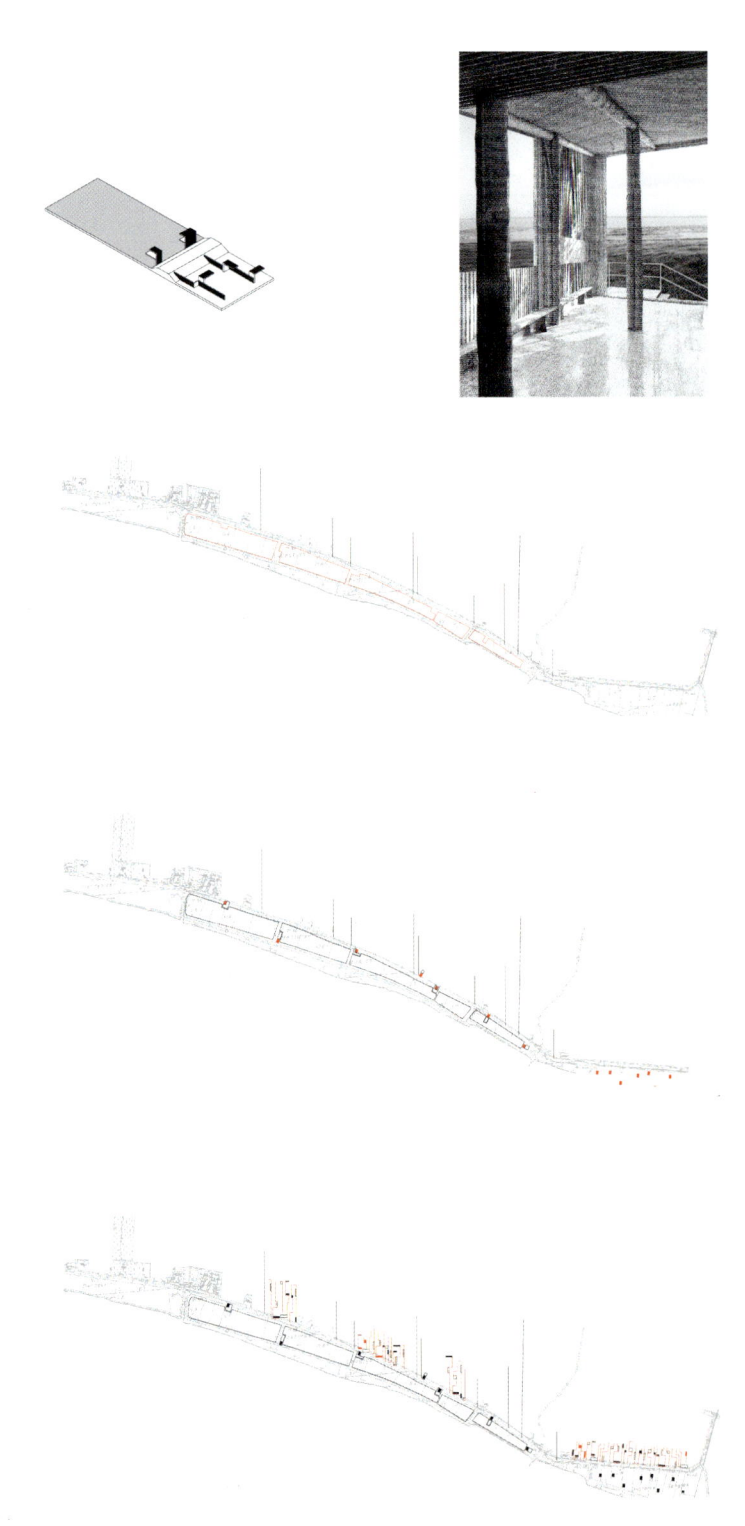

The town as an individual construction

Living and glasshouses: phase 1, 2 and 3

Living, camping and bird watching: phase 1, 2 and 3

99

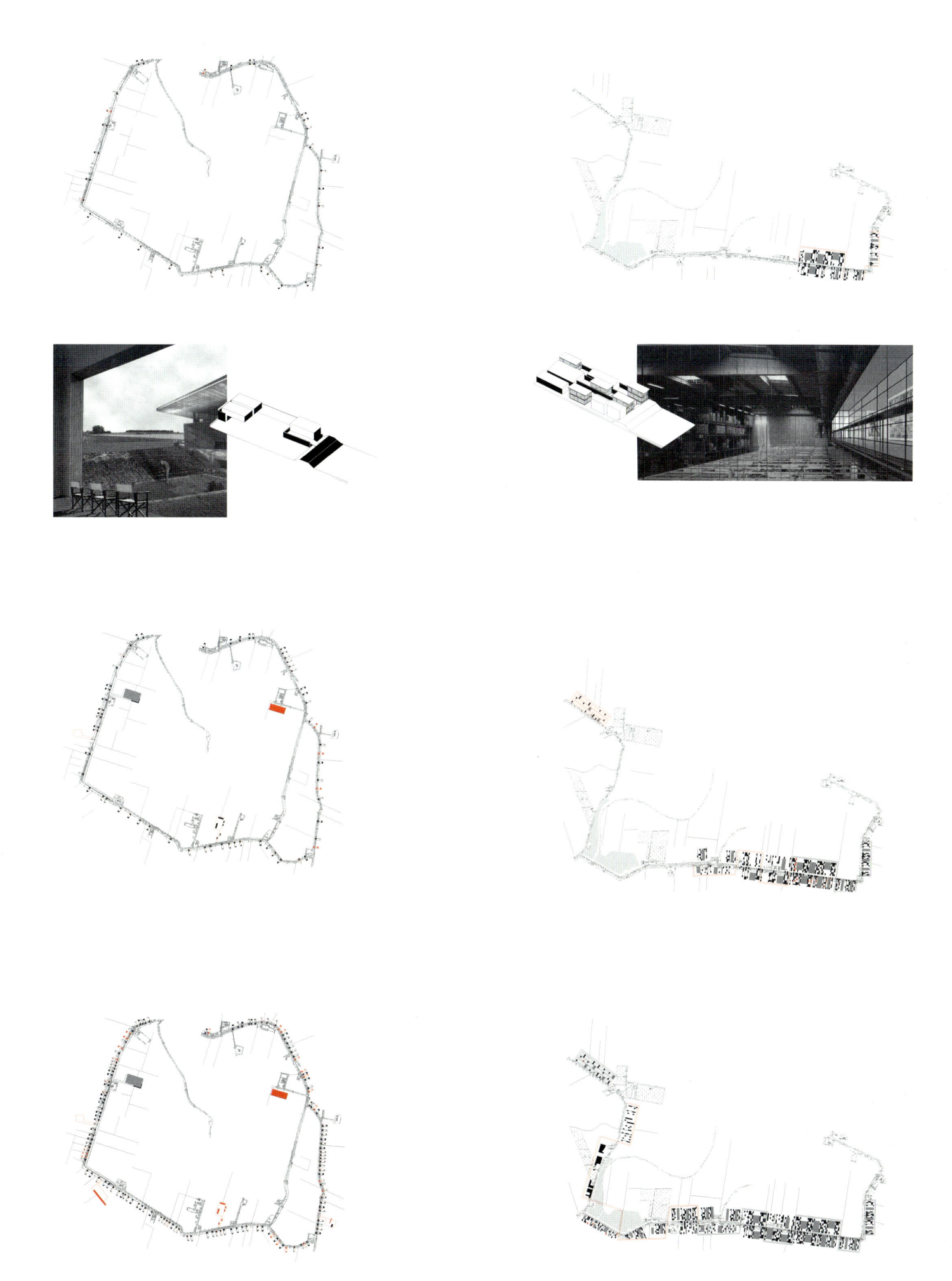

Rooms with a view

Living, office at home and experimental agriculture: phase 1, 2 and 3

Living, small and medium-sized businesses: phase 1, 2 and 3

Unfolded landscape

According to the French architect Francois Roche urban development still hasn't done with the medieval notion that city and countryside are eachother's opposites: the city is packed and lively and the country is empty and isolated. While, thanks to the Internet, villages and secluded farms are now as accessible as offices in a metropolis. Roche and his team call this dissolution of city and country 'fractalization'. Spreading building more across the land is an attractive alternative for the process in which the city expands by way of VINEX-lumps and eats up pieces of the landscape. For Hoeksche Waard they will to entirely dissolve the boundary between building and open land. With the current construction equipment this is quite possible according to him. The interpretation of the ground as an elastic plane which can be lifted, cut open and folded, enables the earth to encompass buildings. Roche comfortably shoves three-storied buildings and 80 m^2 in such a fold. A unit of 500 houses has a front of one and a half kilometres with sunlight and a view. The dark parts in the back provide room for storage, technical installations and a small cinema. In this way urban development and agriculture literally coincide and the building density on the island can be increased considerably without affecting the landscape or extending existing villages.

Situation

In the first phase of a commission of this kind one is faced with the choice between two different models of territorial intervention. The first model consists of the input of Euclidean forms, reasoned and permitted, a model directly arising from geometrical abstraction. These forms are applied to the planning area as a conceptual raster. The second model is of a totally different character and will enforce an answer that is in line with the complexity of the planning area as such. The one model dominates the area so as to prove man's superiority over the situation; the other is introverted, like a sunken relief, so that it can be assimilated within the previously existing balance.

The first model is a pure projection of the mind, within reach for the consumption of concepts and images, like decorative wallpaper, and in line with modern ideals. The second model is a mutant, withdrawn from the existing but more complicated to effect. However, it invites us to think that 'if we have no ideas, we should observe'. The project proposed here was developed from the point of view of this second hypothesis.

Previous history

The concept of the 'city' arose at a time when its contours coincided with its apparatus of military protection. This resulted in merely dividing between full and empty, inside and outside. As far as the evolution of the city is concerned, the Netherlands differs from the rest of Europe in the sense that the protective dikes (regions reclaimed from the North Sea) formed the national borders. Moreover, the dismantling of these dikes was often used as a means of protection (remember the Napoleonic armies with their feet in the water). The political identity of the nation coincides with and follows the lines of this region, having a territorial identity and being a geographical entity without a hierarchy of oppositions between rural and urban, but one that connects and disperses. The road network in the Netherlands is proof of this.

Concepts

Our proposal consists of reinforcing these specific characteristics by 'fractalizing' the expansion of Rotterdam in and along the built-up regions. The entropic movement ensuing from the growth of a city must be uniform and unequivocal, comparable to a shock wave. In this case the point is to look in another manner: as an interweaving flow, between full and empty, between what constitutes urban density and its contrast, rural emptiness.

The hypothesis of a transformation of splitting up through hybridization offers the opportunity to have these two identities, these a priori separated bodies – urban planning and agriculture – exist side by side. Moreover, 'fractalizing' the 'overspill' makes us inclined to maintain the existing road network on the dikes: an extremely dense but limited network that would not allow any change in extent (destruction of the scale-economy). The region folds and unfolds itself so as to be able to itself define the dimensions of the structures. Seen from an aeroplane nothing changes; only the shadows of the elevations betray the mutations, the carvings. And emptiness remains empty.

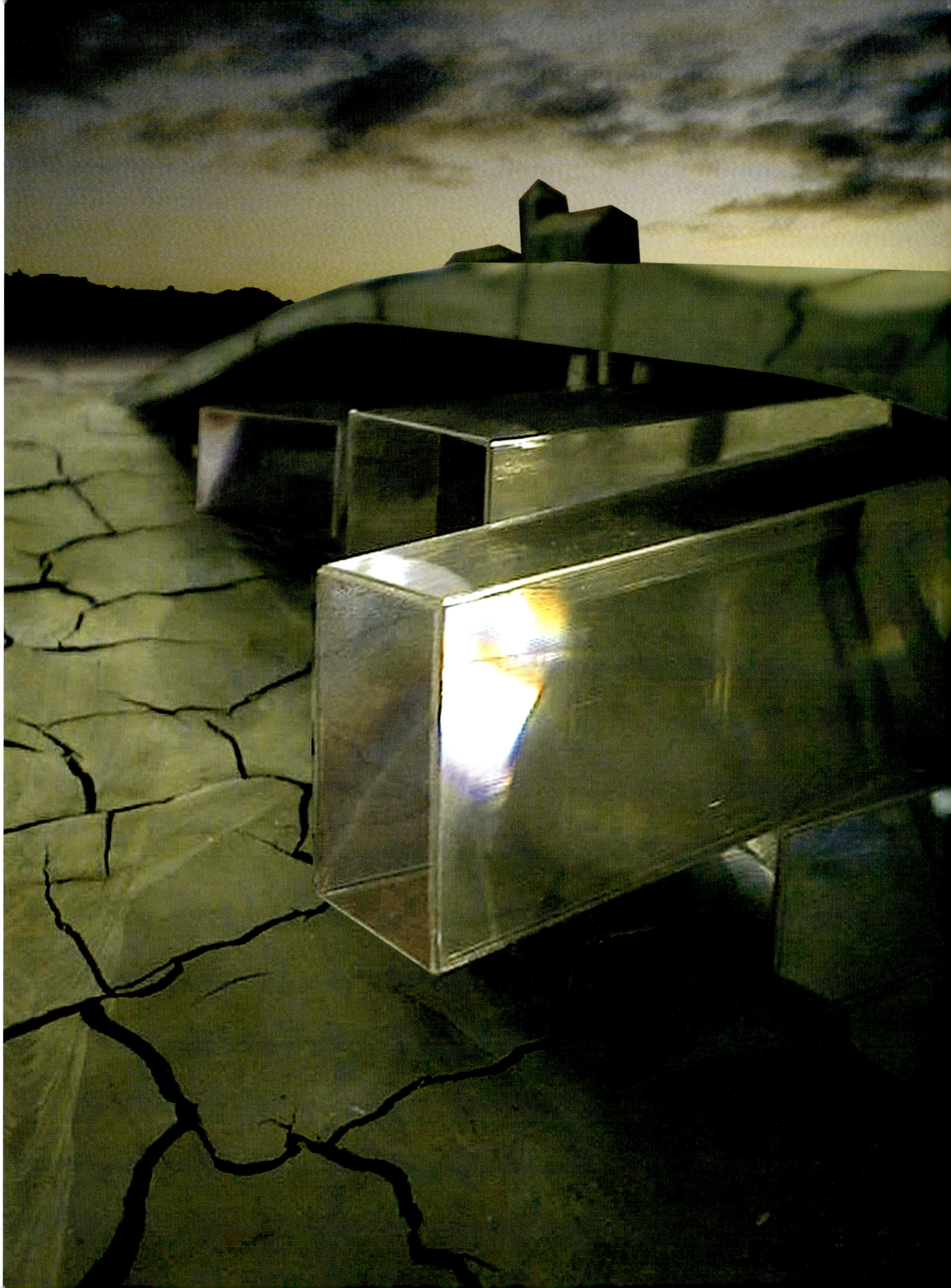

DESIGN RESEARCH

FRITS PALMBOOM/JAAP VAN DEN BOUT
PETER CALTHORPE/MATTHEW TAECKER
STEFANO BOERI
FRANÇOIS ROCHE
DETTMAR/BEUTER/FRITZ/HASTENPFLUG
BINDELS/GIETEMA/HARTZEMA/KLOK
MARIEKE TIMMERMANS
DIRK SIJMONS/YTTJE FEDDES

Ambivalence

These elevations of earth and architecture are indecipherable anyhow. Does it concern an intensification of the local identity here, a genetic disease of the earth's crust, a spontaneously growing dike, a way of making the territory habitable, a hypodermic piercing?

Critical density

Pre-modern thought (Fourier, Owen, Considerant) shook off the hypothesis of critical volume. Naturally, modernity did not take this into account, in view of the fact that it only took over the models, without imposing the related obligations on itself. In the first place we want to work out the various density scenarios in a region like Hoeksche Waard without overburdening the existing villages and with maximum respect for the existing regional structures.

The proposal consists of taking advantage of the rural regions and peripheries by dividing the required densification of the polder into the demarcated urban structures (2000 to 3000 persons) and by intertwining urban and rural economies. The form of the existing villages and dike villages will be retained and any changes to them brought to a halt. The volume per entity amounts to 2.5 km^2, with a maximum occupation surface of a fourth part for construction and a three-fourth part for agriculture. The urban entities of 2000 persons cover about 5.5 km of the main light-receiving frontage (500 families consisting of 4 persons per 80 m^2 dwelling). Or: for a height of R+2 (three levels), 1.5 km of urban facades with natural light incidence. Where the earth has been raised, the functions for storage, technical buildings or even buildings with a cultural destination are integrated in the depth thus acquired.

Scenario

1. Defining the existing villages and demarcating their geographical expansion in the rural regions.
2. Defining the interstitial development areas (fractal) between the areas of spatial density.
3. Working out a critical volume of planting and development.
4. Defining the rural division into parts.
5. Numerical raising (soil displacement) of the parcels.
6. Working out a programme for the surface created below the fields.

Models: construction in and out of sight

Territorial infrastructural network

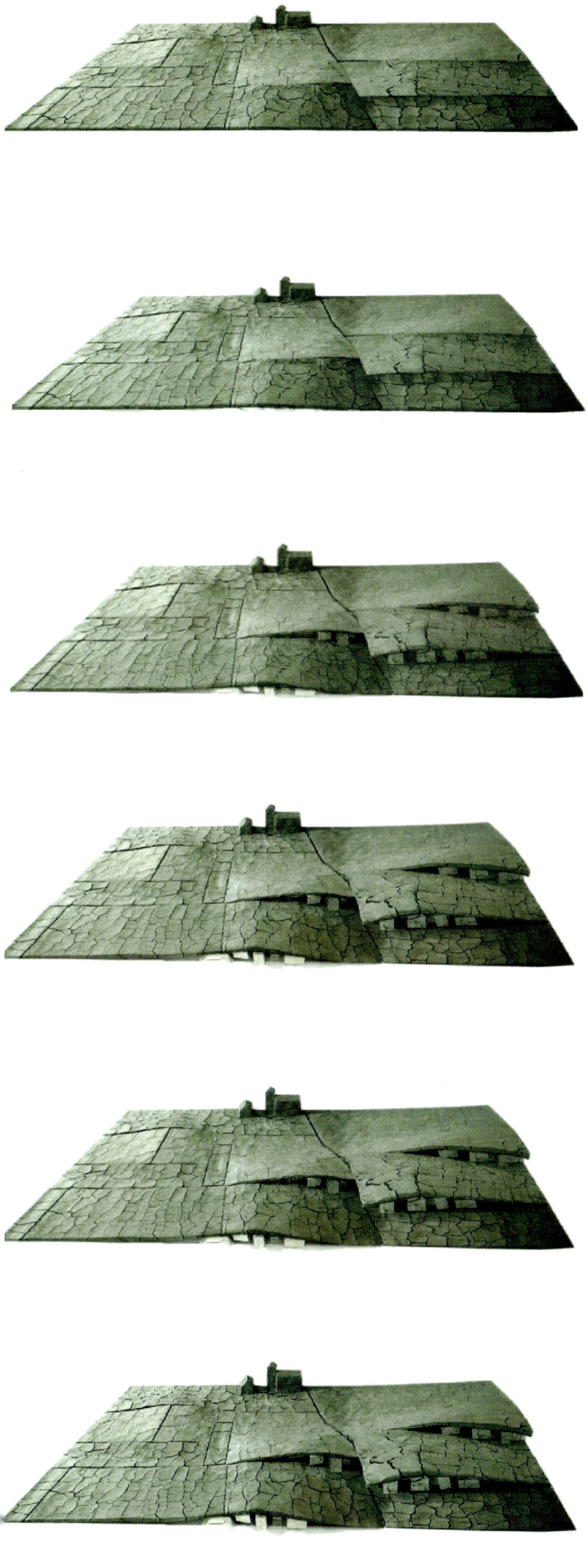

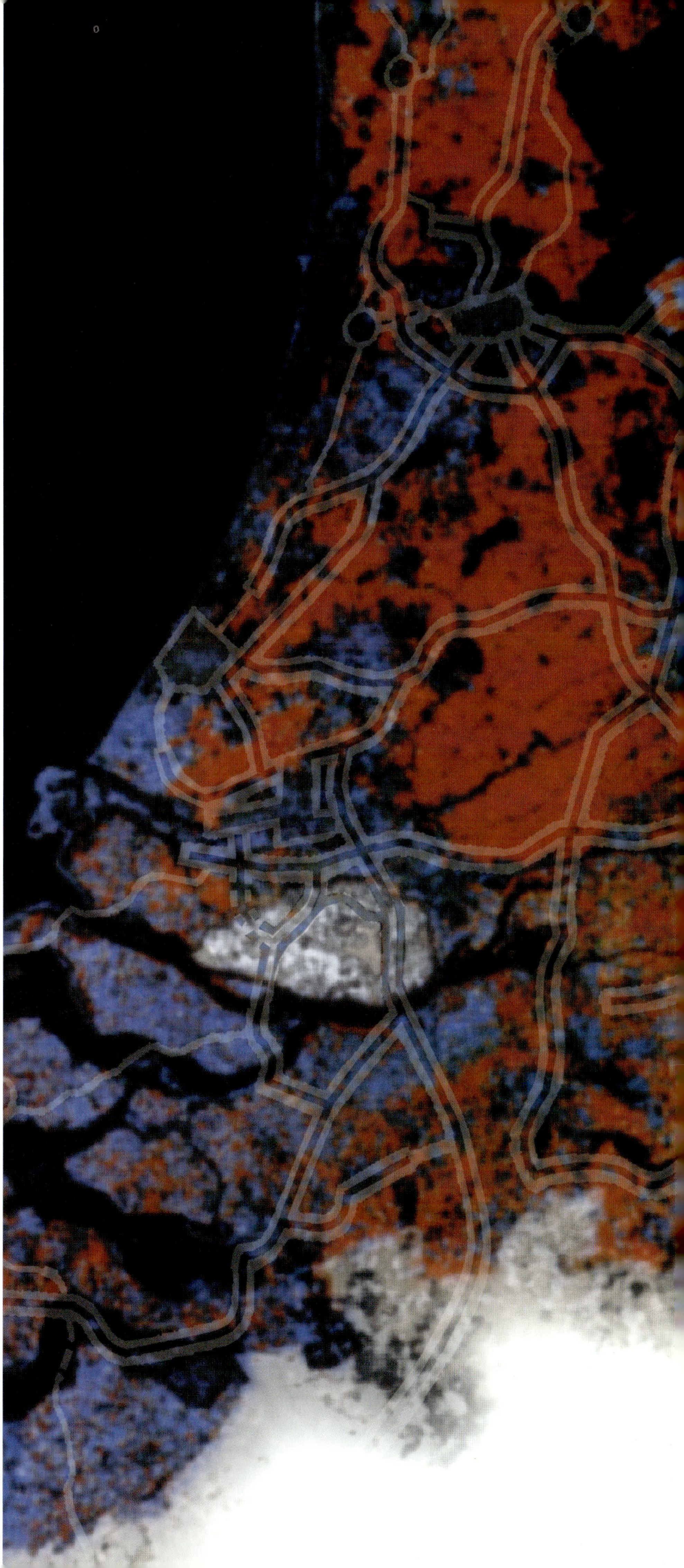

AIR-ZUIDWAARTS / SOUTHBOUND

DESIGN RESEARCH

FRITS PALMBOOM/JAAP VAN DEN BOUT
PETER CALTHORPE/MATTHEW TAECKER
STEFANO BOERI
FRANÇOIS ROCHE
DETTMAR/BEUTER/FRITZ/HASTENPFLUG
BINDELS/GIETEMA/HARTZEMA/KLOK
MARIEKE TIMMERMANS
DIRK SIJMONS/YTTJE FEDDES

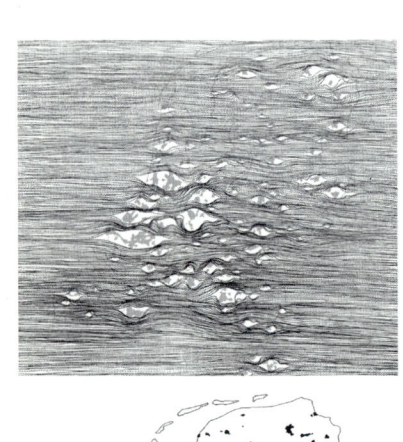

Critical size town

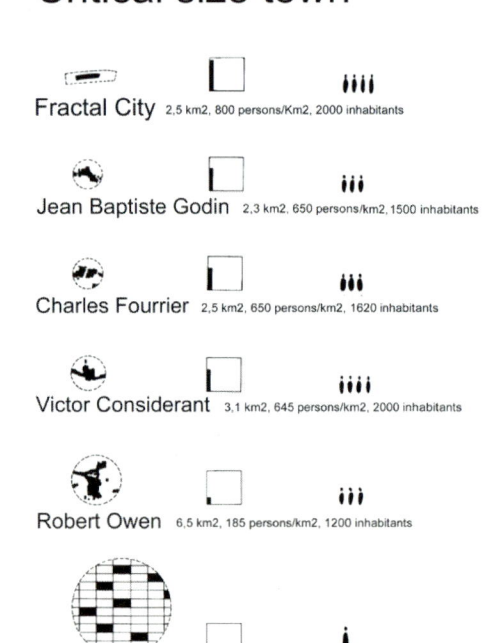

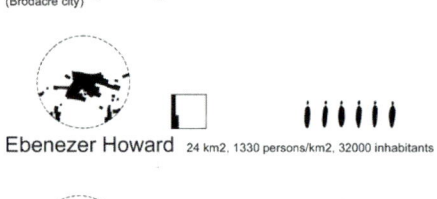

Fractal City 2,5 km2, 800 persons/Km2, 2000 inhabitants

Jean Baptiste Godin 2,3 km2, 650 persons/km2, 1500 inhabitants

Charles Fourrier 2,5 km2, 650 persons/km2, 1620 inhabitants

Victor Considerant 3,1 km2, 645 persons/km2, 2000 inhabitants

Robert Owen 6,5 km2, 185 persons/km2, 1200 inhabitants

Frank Lloyd Wright (Broadacre city) 26 km2, 190 persons/km2, 5000 inhabitants

Ebenezer Howard 24 km2, 1330 persons/km2, 32000 inhabitants

Benjamin Ward Ridchardson 20,8 km2, 4810 persons/km2, 100 000 inhabitants

Unlimited size

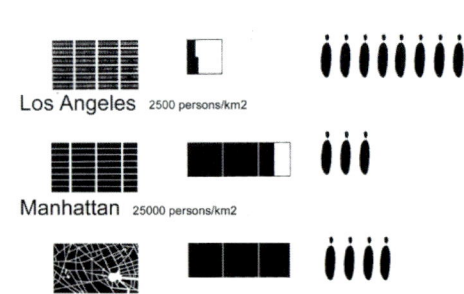

Los Angeles 2500 persons/km2

Manhattan 25000 persons/km2

Paris 30000 persons/km2

The Netherlands: new densities as a result of entropic and fractal processes

Critical densities

From an existing density to more than 800 inh./km^2 (i.e. population increase from 120,000 to 320,000 in Hoeksche Waard)

Computer comparisons between entropic
and fractal processes

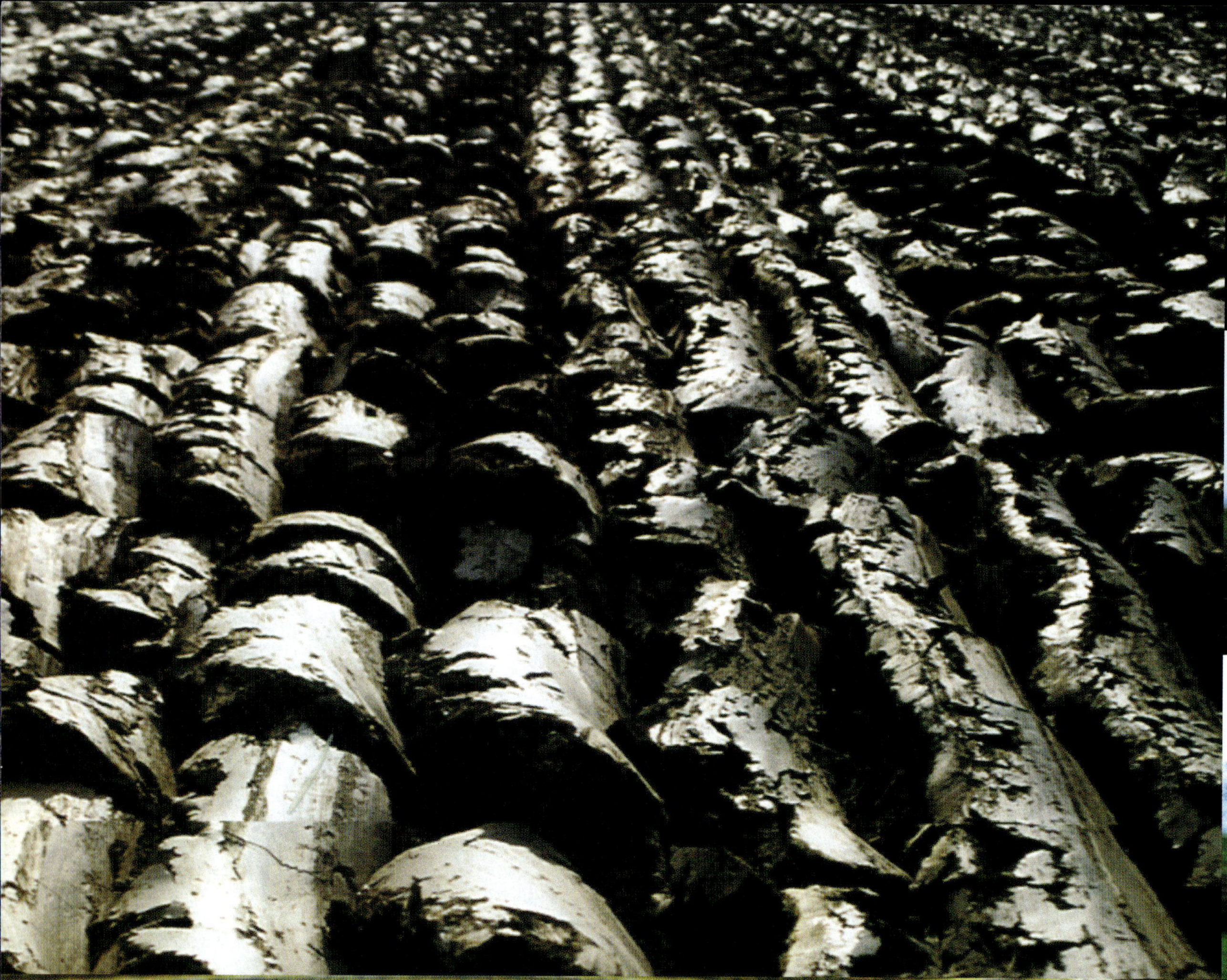

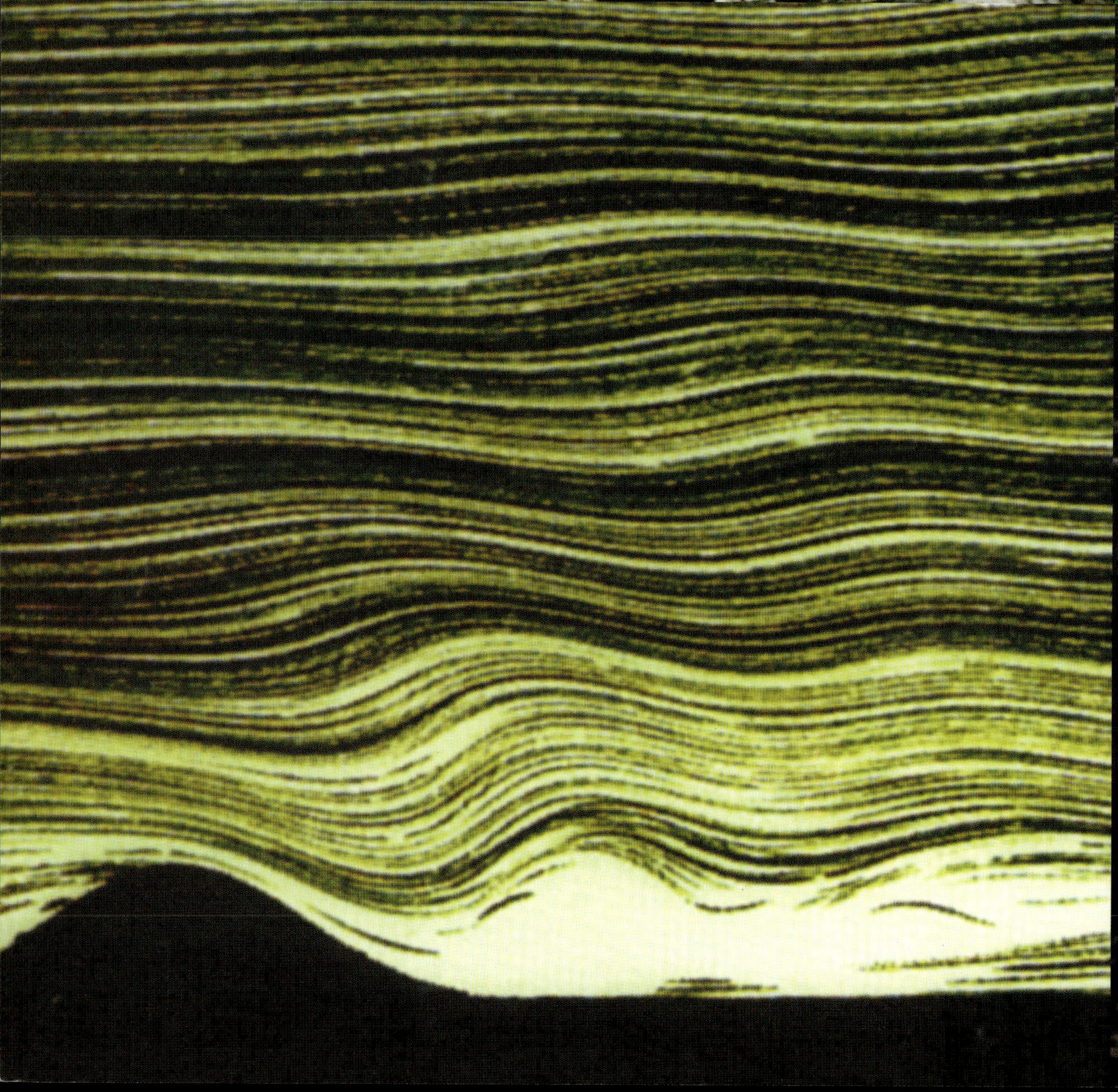

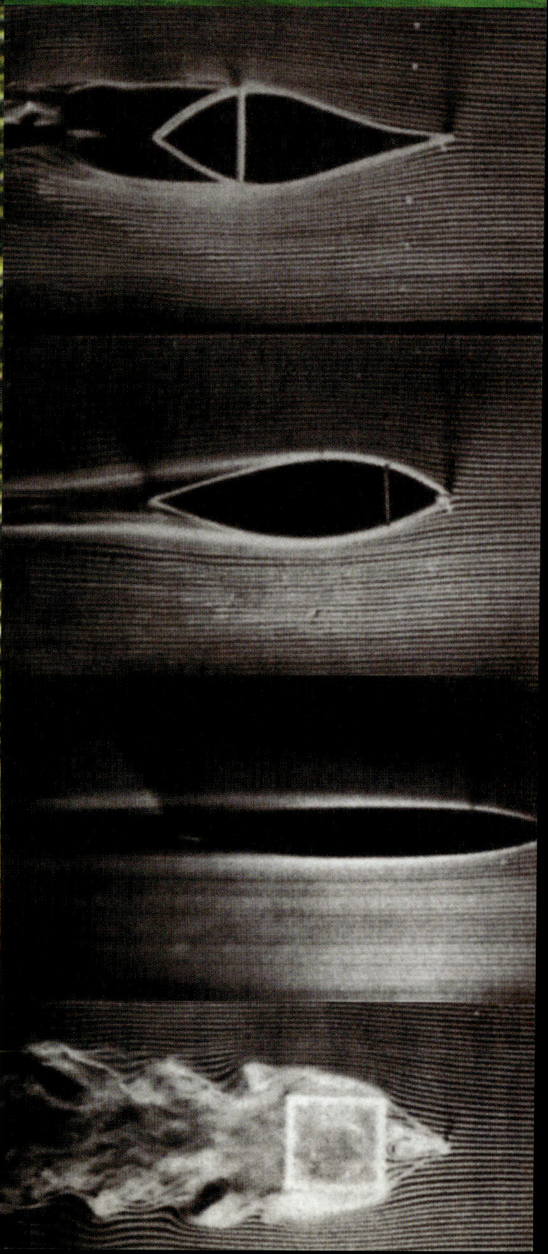

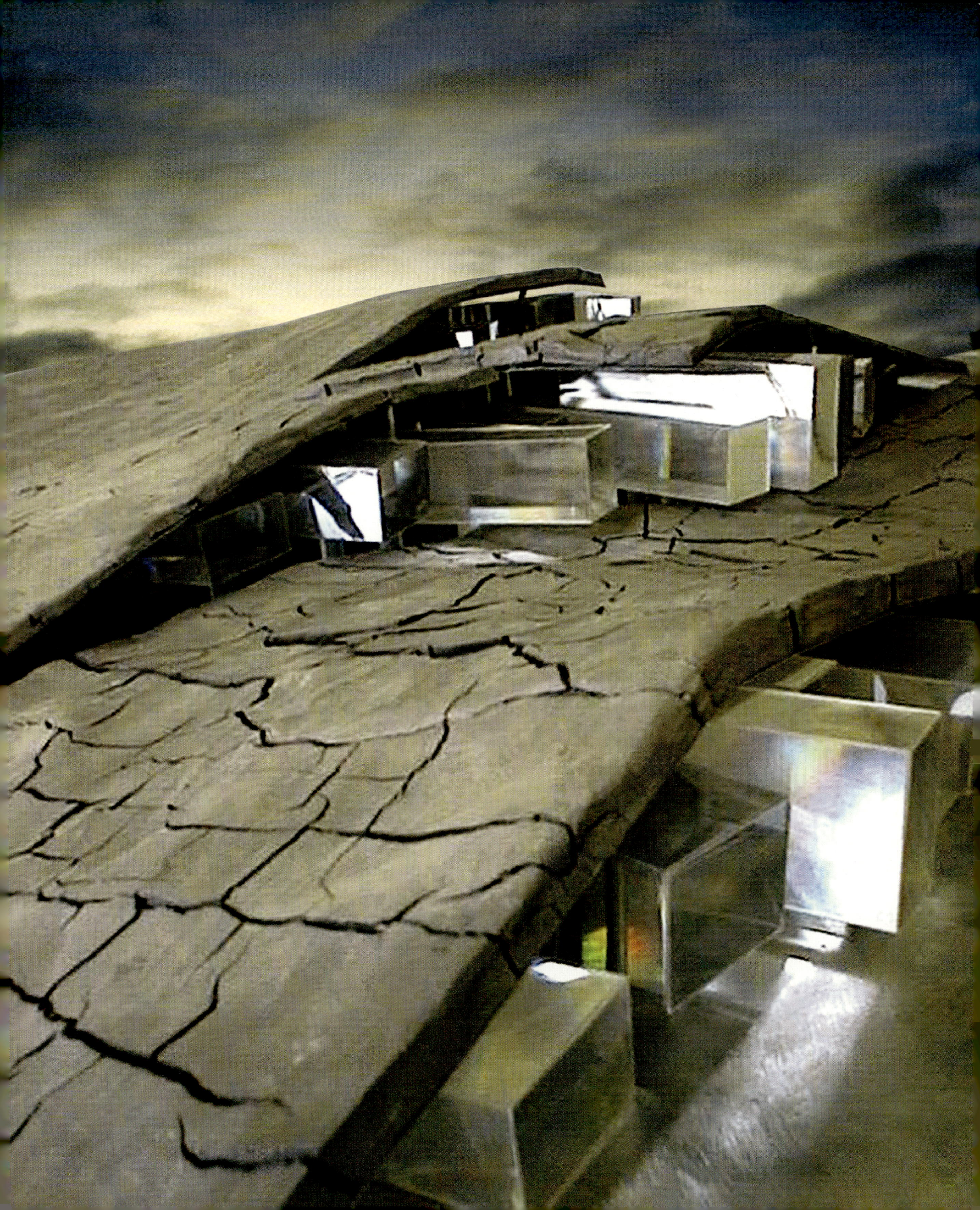

The garden of Rotterdam

The urban planner Jörg Dettmar and the landscape architects Ulrike Beuter, Harald Fritz together with Simone Hastenpflug conceive Hoeksche Waard as 'the garden of Rotterdam', an area providing that city with leisure activities, nature and food. If it is to attain this status, the landscape will need to diversify further. This it can do by switching over to eco-farming and giving nature a fresh opportunity to develop. It is so that river banks and shorelines gradually become overgrown whenever agricultural activity eases up. So in two polders, St. Anthony and Oudeland van Strijen, agriculture needs to literally give ground to nature. To compensate, agricultural activitity can be stepped up elsewhere. Dettmar believes in agro-tourism: sightseeing, shopping and perhaps even giving the farmers and market gardeners a hand. All future built development should follow the typical linear structure of dikes, drainage ditches and avenues of trees, with new linear elements needing to be added to supplement the inadequate existing ones. Sun lounges, solar energy panels and orientation to the south will keep energy consumption down to a minimum.

The reality of the European agglomerations of today

There are only a few agglomerations left in Europe that show an increase in population. The Randstad in the Netherlands is a good example, and Rotterdam in particular. As a consequence one can understand the prognosis of a continuously growing demand for further development areas. It is also a known fact that even if the population stagnates there is still a burgeoning demand for new developments in western agglomerations. Rural areas are becoming more and more urbanized. Endless cities are developing everywhere.

The reasons for this massive consumption of former rural areas are sufficiently known. Changing life styles, more space to live, and a steady increase in commercial areas, even though there are fewer jobs, play a major role. The negative ecological side effects of this land use are obvious. Sociologists too are critical of the social consequences of the endless city. The objective aesthetics of the uncharacteristic and uniform 'in-between cities' in Europe make the more sensitive of us feel depressed. But there seems to be little we can do about it. Neither the idea of compacting the cities nor the urban planner's perpetual desire for new developments of an urban density, let alone nature conservation and landscape planning, have been able to change anything.

There is a contemporary movement in urban planning that views this process pragmatically, simply as unavoidable. It is looking instead for solutions which work for sustainable suburbs (ecosuburbtopia). In fact from our point of view there are many reasonable arguments for giving up the idea of separating urban and rural areas in some European agglomerations. This is especially necessary for the Randstad in the Netherlands. It has to make way for rururban development, which aheres to the principles of sustainable development. Whether this is not a contradiction in terms, and what it will look like in detail, are open questions. Our proposal, however, is an attempt in this direction.

Future demands for a sustainable development of European metropolises – a scenario

There will be higher taxes on fossil energy in Europe within the coming decades. Because of the price increase it will be necessary to lower energy consumption. There will be higher taxes, too on land use, because land is a resource that cannot be increased. The re-use of brownfield sites will continue. The more functions that are combined on one surface, the lower the tax burden will be. Functions in this sense are first of all the production of energy (the use of regenerative energy, the production of biomass), and secondly the organization of closed cycles of water and nutrients including the production of food.

Those cities able to close their ecological cycles will have an environmental advantage. As a consequence they become more independent of the surrounding areas, as far as the import of energy, water and food is concerned. All these factors are getting more and more expensive, just like the export of waste. Thus it is becoming necessary to create room for ecological turnover processes especially within the densely built-up cities. Such turnover processes include the cooling effect of water evaporation, and energy and food production. All these functions require suitable locations. At this point, less densely built-up city structures have significant advantages.

The attractiveness of the cities/metropolises/agglomerations depends particularly on the quality of life for its inhabitants. The quality of life

Future of the delta and the Randstad: sustainable towns and suburban ecotopia

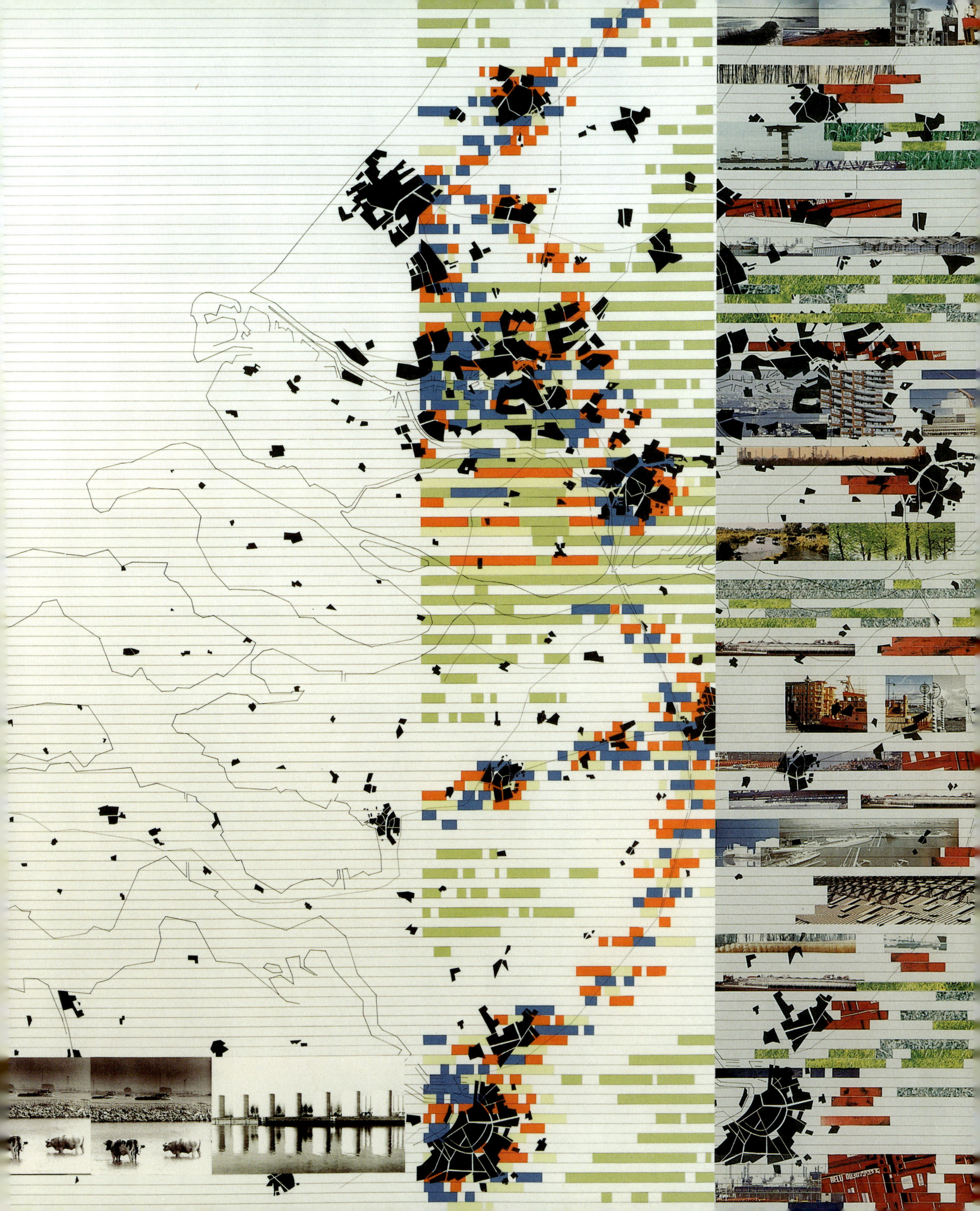

in turn depends on the supply of leisure facilities and employment opportunities, cultural events, the range of goods on sale, the transportation system and the quality of housing. The supply of leisure activities is playing an ever more significant part, bringing with it the need for serviceable open spaces (parks and sport facilities). The so-called 'soft infrastructure factors', such as landscape quality (in this case quality of the urban landscape) are important factors when choosing one's place of residence. Attractiveness is becoming a key competitive factor between cities and agglomerations, with good ecological quality a fundamental precondition.

The urban landscape's appearance must be pleasant and distinguishable, and must create identity. Identity needs history, making it necessary to preserve the old urban and rural landscape structures. Those areas of cultural value in the old rural landscape where further development is prohibited (taboo areas) are also important ecologically.

The future of Delta-Randstad

The Randstad will continue to expand in all directions. It is essential to declare more areas taboo for further development. Major 'taboo areas' are central parts of the Green Heart, and the delta area south of Haringvliet as far as the Biesbos. These are unique areas of landscape with diverse ecological functions, and possible retention areas. They serve several functions simultaneously. One is to give identity, another is historical importance, while psychologically they constitute a key leisure and breathing space for the population. The future urban planning of Rotterdam's periphery needs to focus on preserving connected open spaces more than it had to in the past. It must additionally create connecting corridors from the large taboo areas to the centre of Rotterdam.

As a consequence of the new high speed rail link between Amsterdam and Paris, developing Brabant and especially the area around Breda will become a more attractive proposition. This process will be accelerated by the two ports of Rotterdam and Antwerp which are growing together. New settlements will be established along the A16 motorway, that will lead to a kind of 'Delta Randstad'. Especially here, it is important to fix the taboo areas and the necessary landscape corridors well in advance.

It is more logical to further urbanize the area south of the Oude Maas river, particularly in Hoeksche Waard, rather than the Green Heart or the delta region. If one is to avoid a repetition of developments in IJsselmonde, the approach to Hoeksche Waard should take a strictly sustainable line. This new urban landscape type should also be attractive, to lower the pressure on the defined 'taboo areas'. Attractiveness has a lot to do with preserving and upholding an independent landscape type. We think that the future of Hoeksche Waard lies in the possibility of it becoming the 'garden of Rotterdam'. A garden supplies food, enjoyment of nature and leisure facilities. A garden, however, has to be cultivated carefully, which requires knowledge and love from its user. Should an enduring relationship successfully develop between Rotterdam and Hoeksche Waard, it is possible that this garden can also turn into an urban garden or even a garden city.

Every form of new settlement should have as little effect on the natural balance as possible. At the same time it has to be prepared for future ecological requirements which will be much stricter. This also means that urban development has to be so flexible that it can be adjusted to meet future demands without much effort.

There is no strict separation between settlement, agriculture and areas with more natural dynamics; all of these are elements of the garden. For this a specific settlement structure needs developing, one that meets ecological criteria. However, it should not hinder the necessary flexibility of agriculture. The aim is to develop an attractive landscape structure by combining the more natural dynamics with more urban, leisure-related elements.

Urban meets rural and nature returns

The most valuable parts of the old cultural landscape in the Green Heart and the delta have to be saved from further development. A combination of a more natural dynamic with recreation purposes makes sense here. The way is then open for further sensitive urban development south of Rotterdam as far as Haringvliet. This is relevant for the 'islands' of Voorne, Putter, Hoeksche Waard and the area around Dordrecht. Connecting landscape corridors have to be developed and pre-existing ones kept open. Further urbanization is only acceptable if it succeeds in sustaining settlement structures that show the uniqueness of these islands. The landscape structure and history of these islands differ from one another. Voorne and Putter could become a kind of 'wild garden' and Hoeksche Waard the 'arranged garden' of Rotterdam.

The characteristic landscape structures of Hoeksche Waard are linear because of the dikes, tree lines, ditches, fields and furrows. Agriculture shapes the landscape, which is demarked by dikes. The existing settlement structures are mainly oriented towards the dikes. This suggests a resumption of the old linear principle for future building. Because there is not enough space left along the old dikes for new development, new linear structures need to be established. Ecological viewpoints should play a big role when deciding on areas for new settlements. These will be linked with agriculture, and their boundaries marked by fields. Even the location, size and form of a new commercial area will adjust to this pattern. The plan shows the maximum tolerable settlement on Hoeksche Waard as a kind of final stage of development.

The new settlement accompanies a process of opening up for the sake of a more natural dynamic. Haringvliet is re-opened to the North Sea. The shore in front of the dikes and the island of Tiengemeten are then influenced by the tide. It is possible to open the floodgates gradually to create a situation comparable to former times when there were no such barriers. Of course this cannot be done during storm tides.

More 'nature' is allowed in Hoeksche Waard too. Only heavily cultivated or altogether uncultivated shorelines are being developed along the creeks. They can also gradually be made wider. Intensive cultivation should also cease on the oldest part, the polders of St. Anthony and Oudeland van Strijen. This expansion is combined with the intensified use of groundwater.

There are, besides, fundamental changes in agriculture. Parts of the area, especially in the vicinity of old and new developments, will be converted to sustainable, environmentally compatible cultivation. Health food products can be produced here for the local trade and regional market. Other areas are intensively cultivated according to demand. Larger glasshouses can be built on the Hogezandse Polder, though in combination with new housing developments and leisure facilities. Agricultural areas become more diverse, and intertwined with areas with a natural dynamic. The view of the landscape changes and varies, but does not lose its fundamental character.

It is very important that Rotterdam's inhabitants discover and value Hoeksche Waard as an attractive recreation area at their front door. The improvement of the landscape view along the A29 caused by new

The Hoeksche Garden of Rotterdam

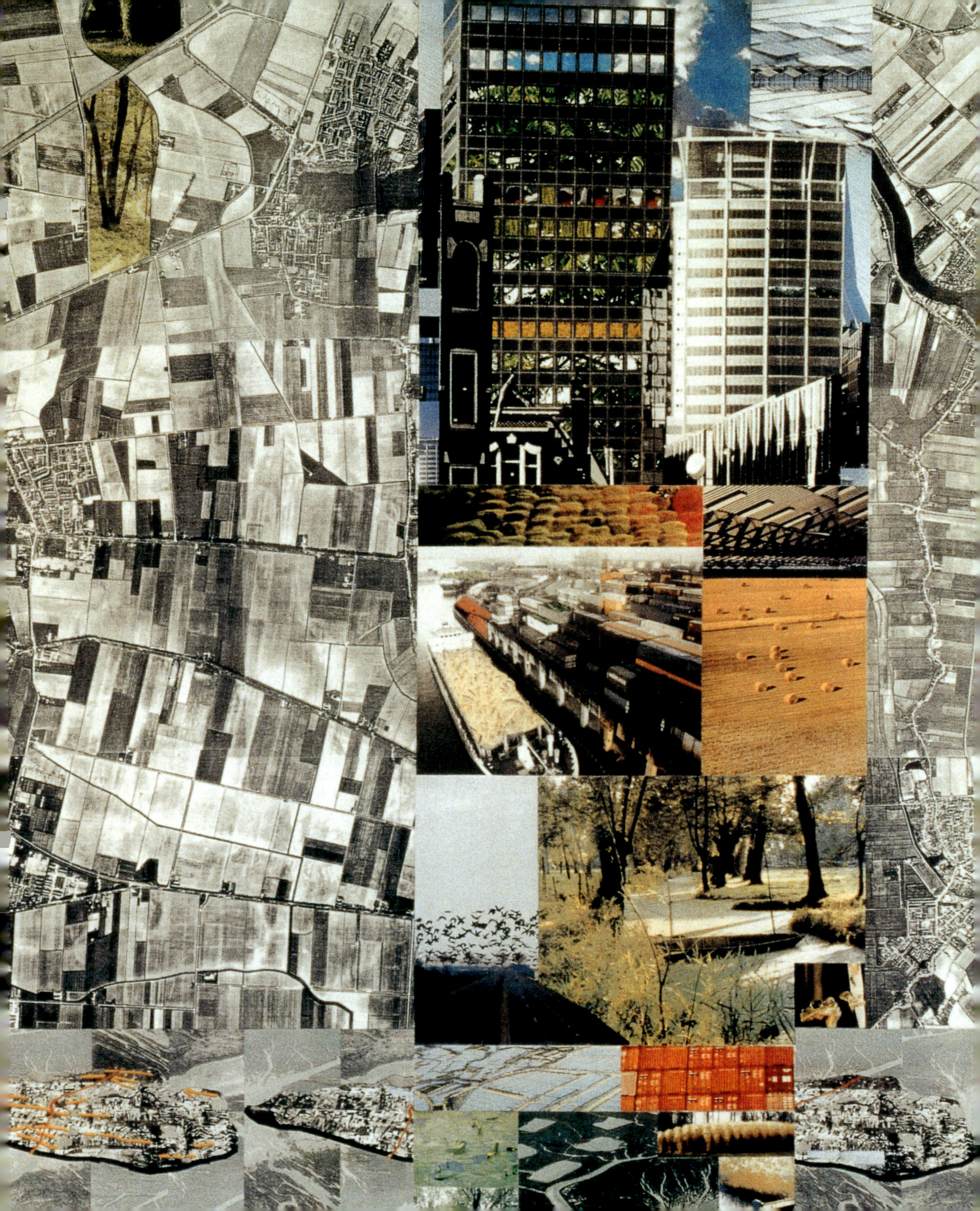

AIR-ZUIDWAARTS / SOUTHBOUND

112

DESIGN RESEARCH

FRITS PALMBOOM/JAAP VAN DEN BOUT
PETER CALTHORPE/MATTHEW TAECKER
STEFANO BOERI
FRANÇOIS ROCHE
DETTMAR/BEUTER/FRITZ/HASTENPFLUG
BINDELS/GIETEMA/HARTZEMA/KLOK
MARIEKE TIMMERMANS
DIRK SIJMONS/YTTJE FEDDES

Town meets country, nature returns

afforestation should be part of this, in that it opens up new and more interesting perspectives. Rotterdam is coming to Hoeksche Waard, but Hoeksche Waard is also coming to Rotterdam.

Rotterdam has to keep changing if it wants to meet the demands of an attractive and sustainable city of the future. If this is taken into consideration, it is not a question of keeping areas dense or open, of planning ideologies. It is the task to establish the right mix of built development and open space. Our goal should be to make the city more and more independent of the surrounding areas in terms of energy, water and waste disposal. Modern architecture, ambitious urban development projects and the restructuring of old port areas alone are not enough. Rotterdam's centre needs a system of qualified green spaces that is able to accept ecological turnover processes. At the same time these spaces should serve as recreational areas and should improve the quality of life for the population.

The Hoeksche Garden of Rotterdam

Hoeksche Waard is to become an eventful landscape and also an attractive place to live. The new linear developments of the first stage enable sophisticated and privileged living. Again, its development is to meet all possible demands made on ecological construction. Only low-energy houses or houses without external energy input are allowed. The lines of the development are strictly oriented towards the south for the use of solar energy. Houses are heated and air-conditioned by winter gardens, and are supplied with photovoltaic cells for energy production. In the beginning only single houses or smaller estates of terraced houses are to be built. The structure, however, has to be so flexible that it can become more dense afterwards when energy and land taxes rise.

In the first stage, open spaces around the houses can serve rainwater management. Washing machines will certainly be able to run on rainwater. Used water is led to small sewage treatment plants located at intersections between the new developments and the old villages. The purified water, which is still nutrient however, is used as a fertilizer in agriculture. The sludge serves as an energy provider, either by burning or by biogas generators. The remaining water is led into the energy system or is directly used in greenhouses. In future, eutrophic water from sewage treatment plants may be used to water sewage filter-beds in greenhouses. And it will be possible to grow vegetables on these filter-beds too.

It is sensible to separate faeces from water by installing compost toilets in the new houses. As a consequence the cleaner water can be led directly into the countryside. The used water will be conducted through ditches with reed vegetation to settling ponds or later maybe directly into the greenhouses. The remaining sludge can be regularly used as a fertilizer on the fields. Despite the increasing density there are still wide enough strips of cultivated land left between the rows of houses for sustainable agriculture. Closed energy and nutrient circles between the built areas and fields are a long-term goal.

The first new housing should be built in the south with a connection to the A29 exit at Numansdorp. Larger glasshouse complexes are already planned east of Numansdorp. This need not be an ecological catastrophe, or an aesthetic one. There is a potential energy link with the industrial area of Moerdijk on the southern part of Hollandsch Diep. In the future, even the glasshouse production will have to follow the principles of sustainability. Useful ecological cycles can be worked into a combination of horticulture, housing and touristic leisure activities. The necessary flexibility of the high-tech production under glass has to be taken into consideration, thus the separation of functions is inevitable. Nevertheless, a new glass village with an 'adventure landscape of horticulture' is a distinct possibility.

In the next stage, further strips for development are established with a new connection to the A29, maybe followed by a new commercial zone. First it needs to be demonstrated that an industrial area like this would not necessarily be more sustainable elsewhere, say in Brabant. So it is unreasonable to assert that the province of Zuid-Holland needs more jobs. The location and design of this commercial area should be orientated to the landscape structure. Inserted into the existing fields, it presupposes standard ecological construction, alternative energy concepts and closed water cycles. Larger glass covers which serve as solar power plants are also likely. Commercial sites can be flexibly designed beneath these glass covers. Even agriculture, housing and leisure activities can be gathered there to encourage interaction.

More and more cultivated areas will be extended or laid out as a consequence of increasing settlement. Biocoenosis is developing in the tidal areas in front of the dikes. The peripheral zones along the watercourses are growing together into an extensively used grassland or wilderness. Diverse structures can develop depending on the efforts of design or maintenance. They are all connected with the polder of Oudeland van Strijen, the 'Green Heart' of Hoeksche Waard. Given the increasing influence of brackish water it is becoming necessary to change the irrigation system in Hoeksche Waard. The new Green Heart plays an important role here.

The stages of development in Hoeksche Waard lead from a garden of Rotterdam to an urban garden, culminating in a garden city of the future. Here, natural dynamics and anthropomorphic use are closely linked in cycles.

The Golden Delta

According to the architects or urban designers, Edzo Bindels, Ruurd Gietema, Henk Hartzema and Arjan Klok, what is most important is that the delta, starting below de Oude Maas, is regarded as an entity. In order to develop it as such, cooperation will be required. The designers propose to establish a development company for the purpose of coordinating sub-projects, if possible combining and gearing them to one another. In order to regulate water management a lot of civil-engineering works will have to be carried out these coming years. Whenever possible, these should be linked with residential and recreational possibilities. To the south of Dordrecht an enlarged Bieschbosch will develop. The Oudeland van Strijen is to become a fresh-water reservoir. From there fresh water will pass straight across the island towards market-gardening in the Westland. Once the foundation is laid, the delta can be further developed into a residential and recreational Walhalla through sub-projects. The designers have all kinds of visions in this respect, varying from floating houses to cube-shaped houses on concrete pillars and vaporettos.

Commission - Scale

So far, Hoeksche Waard has managed to stay clear of from urban expansion, and could indulge exclusively in navel-gazing at the virginity of ploughed fields and dike structures. In the meantime, however, the villages were growing, the roads were being widened, traffic lights were introduced and companies were established on the outskirts of the villages, the greater part of which now consists of residential districts that could be situated anywhere. The never-ending local discussions in this abdomen of Zuid-Holland on the desirability or necessity of industrial sites X at turning Y or a complex of glasshouses at location Z, indicate the utter denial of the situation in which the region has come to find itself. This situation is drowned out by a general sense of doom because the limits to growth are in sight: roads are congesting, open water is getting polluted, the rising sea level demands of the rivers an ever larger drainage capacity, the number of yacht basins and mooring places have reached their maximum, nature is growing scarcer. Proceeding from the serious conviction that spatial planning ought to shift the boundaries for further development of the distinctive landscape of economy, living, recreation and nature, this project establishes the potential of Hoeksche Waard from the perspective of the Rhine-Scheldt delta.

Development Strategy

Without sinking to a call for administrative border adjustments, we offer the conflict-oriented model of a proposed future development company. The aim of the 'Golden Delta Development Company' is to realize projects of a measured scale and with a well-organized time schedule by means of deals between participants with seemingly contradictory interests. Objectives in the fields of environment, public housing, economy and infrastructure are not split up in terms of distinct administrative units and individual commissions, but are investigated for possible alliances, cooperation and combinations: New Deals.

Ambition - Delta 2.0

In the first instance the New Deals are deployed to realize Delta 2.0. This is a package of measures improving the hardware of the river delta on the basis of new insights and peripheral conditions. This update comprises the partial restoration of the tidal system, increased (peak) drainage and storage of riverwater and rainwater and anticipation of the rise in sea level, new saltwater nature, a complementary freshwater supply for the purpose of agriculture and industry, and adapted water works.

Golden Delta

This preliminary investment is the onset of a process which enables cross-overs between a European recreational Walhalla, a nature reserve of unprecedented value, a pragmatic working area and an explicit residential environment for divergent urban demands. These cross-overs irrigate the Rhine-Scheldt delta with a profusion of programmatic uses and at the same time offer the opportunity to widen the palette of urban, city-related and scenic forms of living and working in the Rotterdam-Antwerp region and demonstrate, moreover, that this region has not reached the limits to its growth in any area whatsoever. Agriculture, nature development and housing form the basis for the well-considered construction of a slender vegetal city. For each season this city has wildly fluctuating numbers of users and a hinterland extending as far as Paris and Frankfurt. It offers the perfect basis for a residential, working and recreational area manifesting itself as a 'state' in Europe.

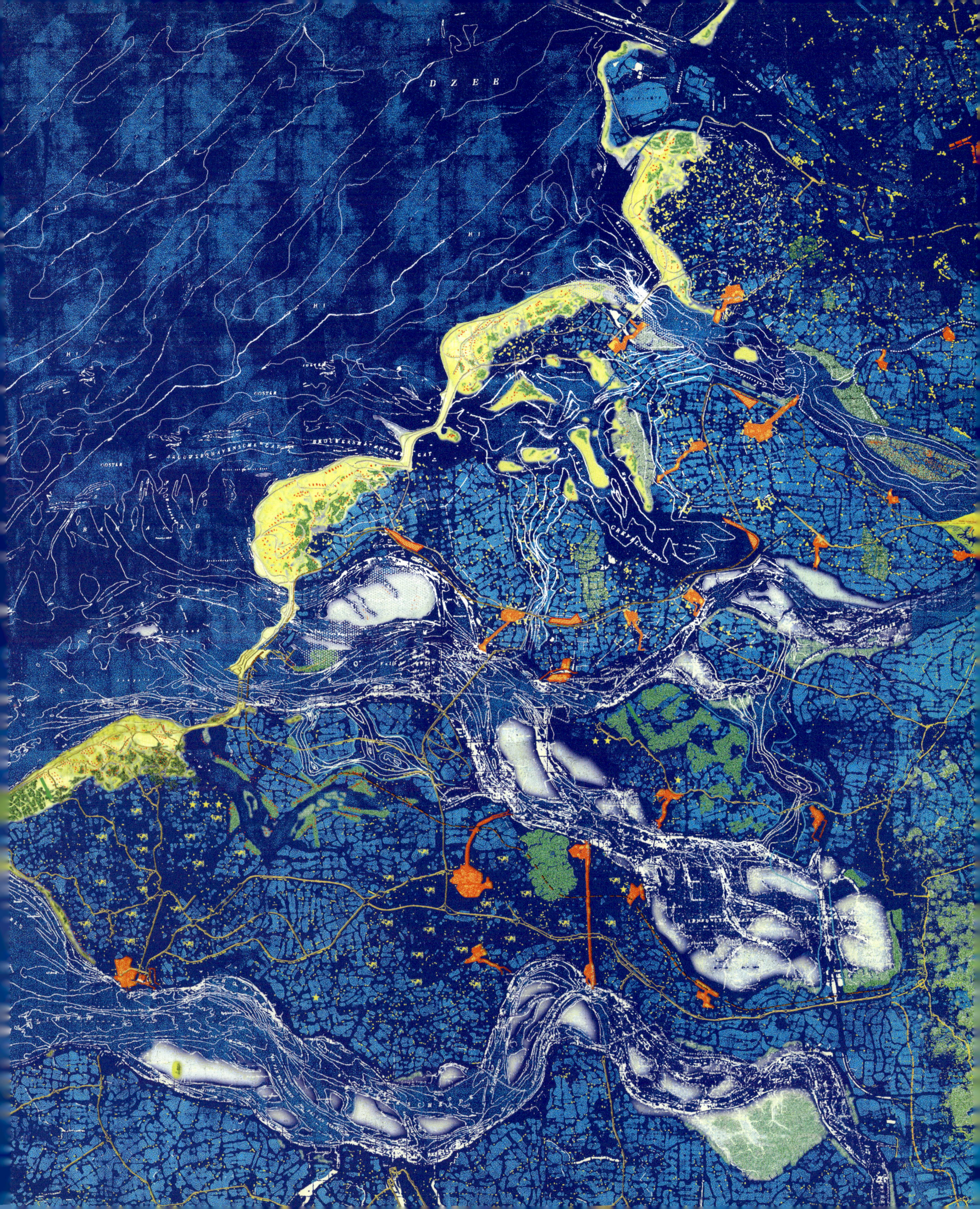
DZEE

AIR-ZUIDWAARTS / SOUTHBOUND

DESIGN RESEARCH

FRITS PALMBOOM/JAAP VAN DEN BOUT
PETER CALTHORPE/MATTHEW TAECKER
STEFANO BOERI
FRANÇOIS ROCHE
DETTMAR/BEUTER/FRITZ/HASTENPFLUG
BINDELS/GIETEMA/HARTZEMA/KLOK
MARIEKE TIMMERMANS
DIRK SIJMONS/YTTJE FEDDES

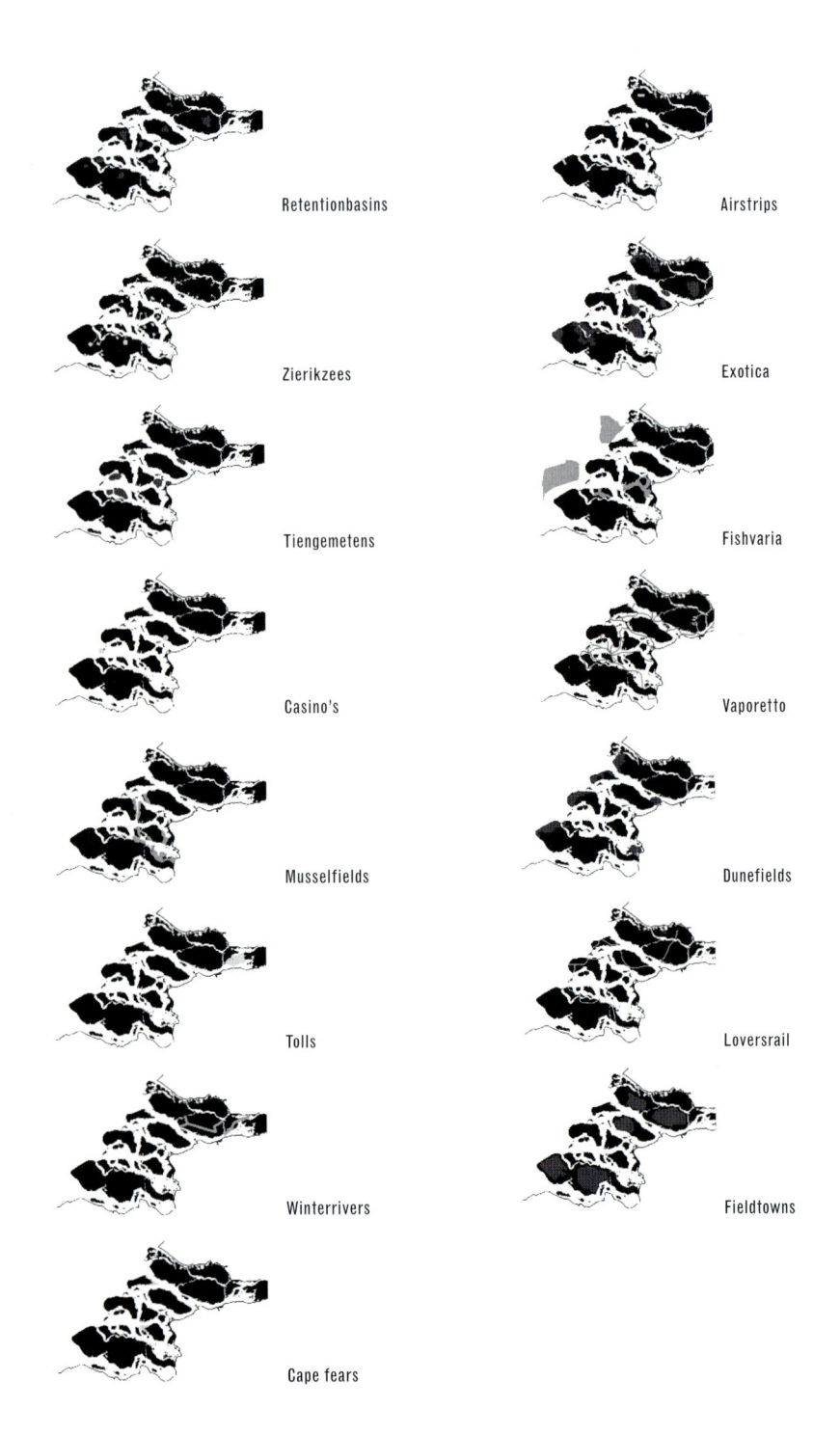

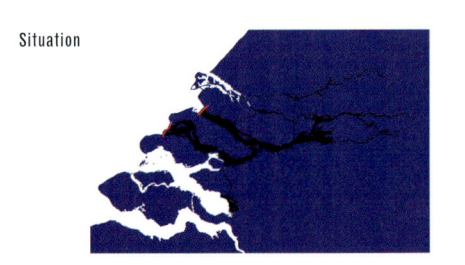

Retentionbasins

Zierikzees

Tiengemetens

Casino's

Musselfields

Tolls

Winterrivers

Cape fears

Airstrips

Exotica

Fishvaria

Vaporetto

Dunefields

Loversrail

Fieldtowns

Golden Delta programme

Situation

Delta operations 2.0

Increased tidal area

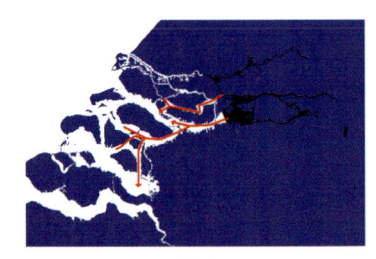

Increased riverwater discharge

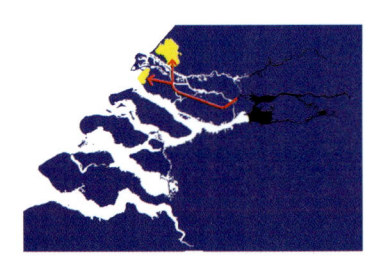

Freshwater supply ports and Westland

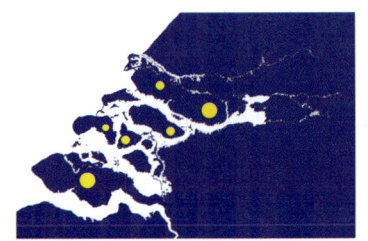

Rainwater retention basins

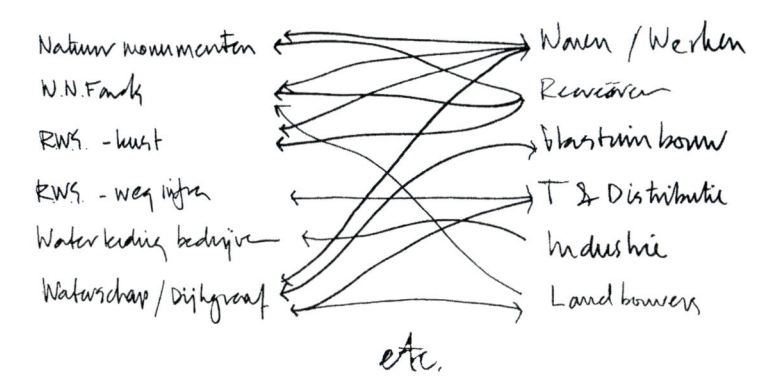

Diamond City

A compact city is in the making, one complementary to the development of the delta. The zone along the Rotterdam infrastructural 'diamond' and parts of the infrastructure between Antwerp and Rotterdam are brought in so that the industrial sites projected in the grasslands and the empty zones around the large-scale infrastructure benefit from one another, with masses of leeway and laissez-faire.

In Rotterdam this implies that services and distribution centres related to the extensive harbour districts are deliberately inserted in the zones along the highway diamond. Development of the residential, working and recreational programme is taken up in its totality. The completion of a ring road – for the greater part already existing – parallel to the diamond sees to it that high-grade addresses for an economic programme will emerge. In cooperation with parties operating in the urban renewal of adjacent districts, the space within the territory of the city is effectively used to give shape to an enduring city life.

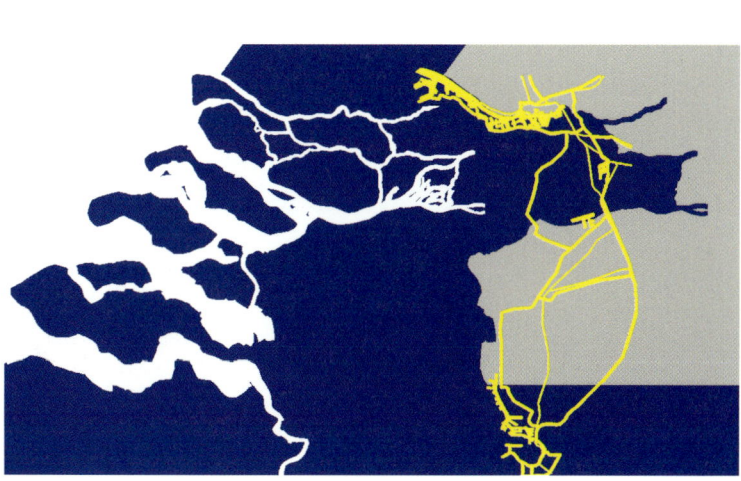

Gap between delta and hinterland

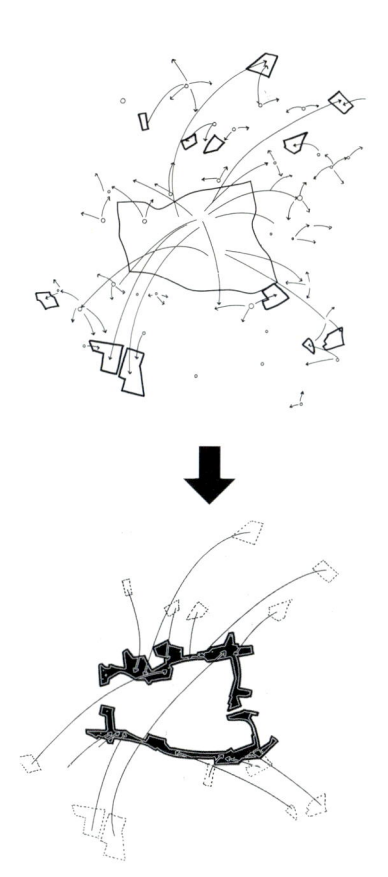

Diamond City development

Attempts to shape the Golden Delta with custom-made projects in a number of places in and around Hoeksche Waard

Winter River

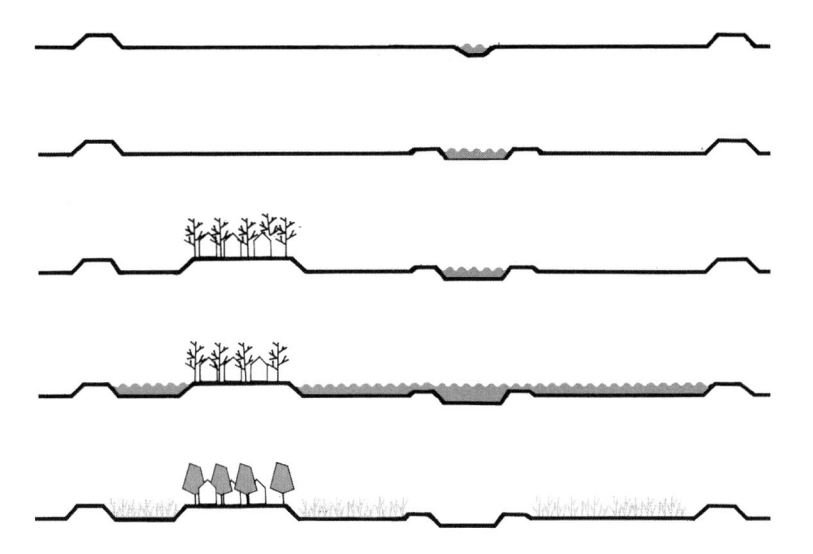

Winter River

2010, the struggle against the flooding of cities along the rivers can no longer be solved by raising the dike another metre. The canalization of the Rhine and Maas is doomed to fail. Instead, the Department of Public Works has opted for a strategy in which the river can expand during peak periods into dozens of rivulets capable of buffering the water and draining it off into the North Sea by way of Haringvliet. All kinds of short cuts for water in search of the sea will unexpectedly arise. One of these flood areas runs diagonally across Hoeksche Waard. Polders designated for the purpose fill up once a year and drain off the water towards the sea. In these regions the fate of flooding presents specific conditions for building (or not building).

In the grassy sheep meadows 'terps' (ancient mounds) and remnants of old dikes stand out against the Dutch sky. Extended driveways leading from the winter dikes open up the dwellings.

On the inside of the summer dikes runs a river providing the Westland and the harbours with fresh water. The industry of Europoort and the glasshouses in the Westland draw fresh water from the Bernisse on a large scale. When the Haringvliet dam is opened, the Bernisse is in danger of becoming a brackish-water river. By restoring the Piershils Gat, Groote Gat, Kleine Gat, Borrekeen and Oude Diep as creeks and connecting them with the channel of Ondergelopen (= flooded) Land van Strijen, a freshwater supply to the Spui can be achieved. The economic central points will continue to be supplied with fresh water through a syphon connection with the Bernisse. Locks in the Bernisse and the Kreek will enable boats to penetrate far into the polders of Voorne-Putten and Hoeksche Waard. A new address in the delta will be the result.

Ondergelopen Land van Strijen

Large retention areas for fresh water will need designating as compensation for the silting-up caused by operation Delta 2.0. In times of drought, farmers will be able to use this water to irrigate their land and to lower the salt level. As the lowest-lying region in Hoeksche Waard, Oudeland van Strijen is the best place to store surface water. Here water retention, housing and nature development are combined. The region is parcelled in lots; a channel connected with the Binnenbedijkte Maas is dug at the centre of the region. The land dug out will be used to reinforce the dikes of the polder. Development proceeds from this channel. The lots can be partly built over with houses, if 60 per cent of the land is levelled. The remaining 40 per cent can be planted with marsh cypresses. Thus a 2000-hectare exotic water forest will rise from the clay polder.

Houses will sail in from the shipyards of Zwijndrecht through the bay waterway and the channel. The floating homes will be moored along the wooded lots. These floating structures allow for fluctuations in the water level from 0 to 1.5 Amsterdam Ordnance Datum.

AIR-ZUIDWAARTS / SOUTHBOUND

DESIGN RESEARCH
FRITS PALMBOOM/JAAP VAN DEN BOUT
PETER CALTHORPE/MATTHEW TAECKER
STEFANO BOERI
FRANÇOIS ROCHE
DETTMAR/BEUTER/FRITZ/HASTENPFLUG
BINDELS/GIETEMA/HARTZEMA/KLOK
MARIEKE TIMMERMANS
DIRK SIJMONS/YTTJE FEDDES

One to Ten

Expansion of the Nieuwe Merwede will relieve the critical path for the peak drainage of river water of the Beneden Merwede/Oude Maas at Dordrecht. The polders to the south of Dordrecht may flood, causing the river forests of the enlarged Biesbos to encroach upon the city. By opening the Haringvliet dam, tidal and river water will wash out the sludge in the Biesbos. Concealed in this water landscape lie sandbanks one to ten, interconnected by bridges and waterways. A tabula rasa for the development and expansion of Dordrecht.

Tiengemeten

After having been worn away by river and tides for ten years, nature on the island of Tiengemeten proves unable to manage without man. The dismantling of the old dikes has given rise to a landscape of channels and creeks. The new pioneers build their pile dwellings in the reeds along the more accessible channels, with the North Sea close at hand at high tide for their yachts. Clustered around the old ferry house is a collection of dwellings, a village on piles. The vaporetto passes Tiengemeten by way of the Grote Geul.

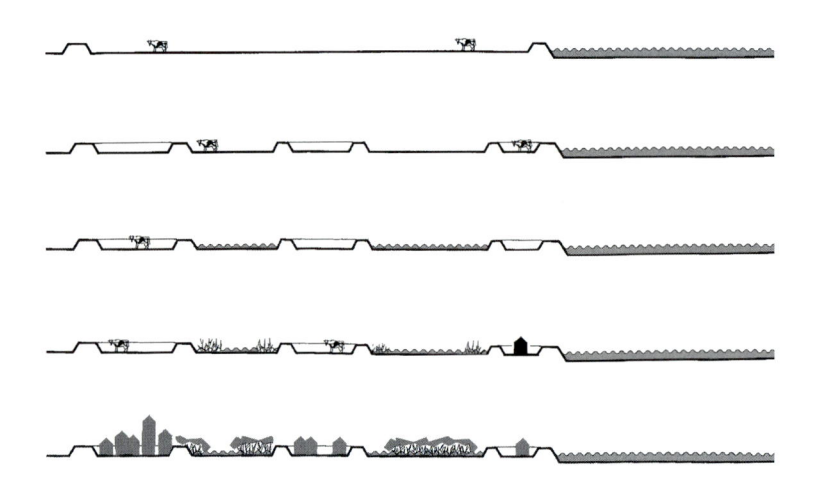

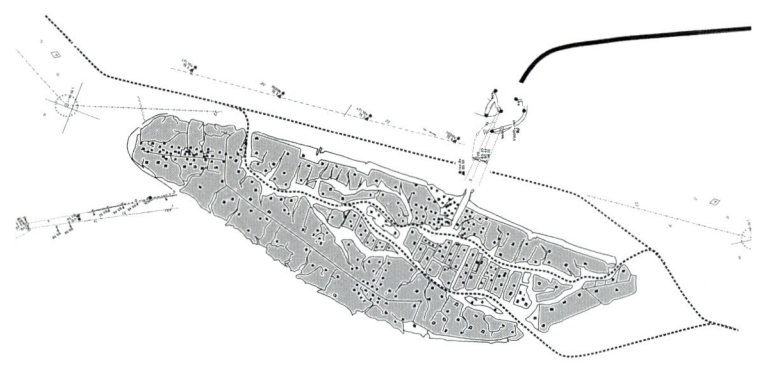

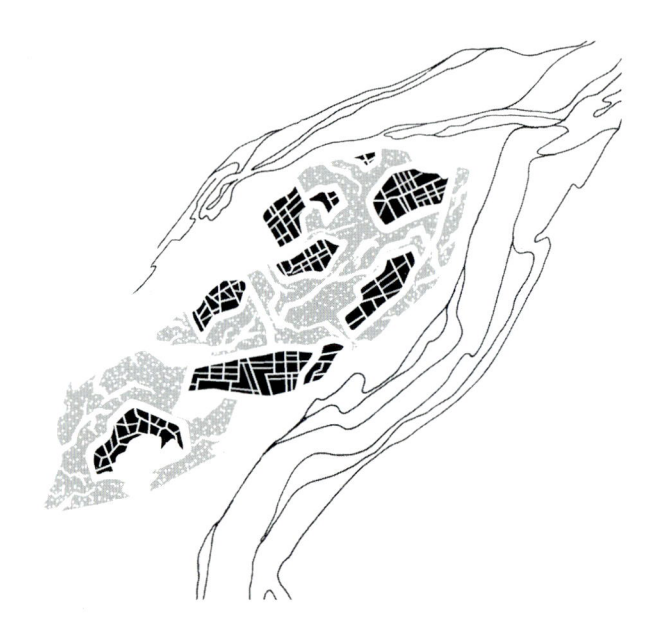

Zierikzees

Through its mediation, the development company will organize the various towns in the delta estuary into a 'league of twenty Zierikzees'. It will pursue a joint policy in order to develop all the little towns into a genuine 'state' based on the economic potential of the accommodation. An unbroken system of passenger harbours will be realized and a cook worthy of a Michelin star detached to each centre. The development company will develop 'subsidiary villages' in consultation with the existing settlements, and provide the residential needs for the growth of each. In these subsidiary villages the new generations of delta inhabitants will get the opportunity to give shape to their 'contemporary village life'.

Surfers' Dune

At Hellegatsplein the drinking-water company will develop a dune mass used for water infiltration. Parasitizing on this water supply will encourage an ecology of surfers, birds and 'parapenters'. A broad asphalt loop (Surfers' Boulevard) links up the dune with the N18 and A29; in summer electricity and tapping points at the roadside will turn the boulevard into a town of trailers, Volkswagen minibuses and caravans where German is the official language.

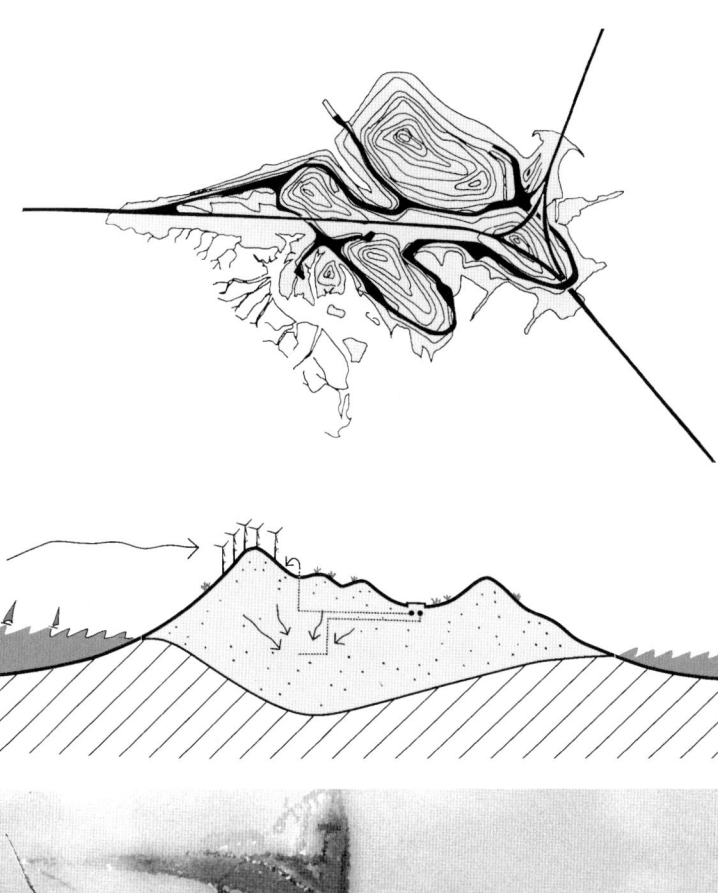

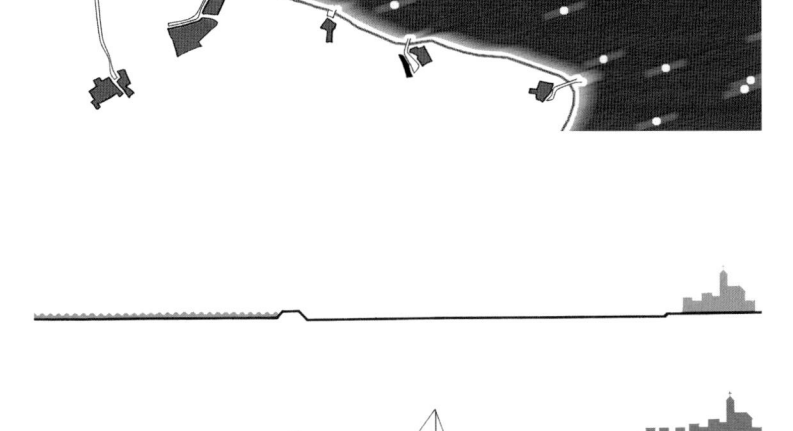

Rural landscape

The existing landscape is not taken seriously in physical planning in the Netherlands, in the opinion of Marieke Timmermans and her team. It is regarded as space for urban ideas on new housing development, recreation and new 'nature', or as precious cultural heritage in need of protection. It does not play an independent role. Unfortunately, they think, for there are plenty of possibilities. For centuries our way of life and work determined the appearance of the landscape. This matter-of-courseness may return when we start living and working in the landscape again. A precondition is that it must be possible to build in the landscape, and that cultivation is environment-friendly. Boggy Friesland should become even wetter and the dry landscape of Brabant even more wooded. As far as ecological agriculture is concerned, each rural region has its own ideal sort of farming. In Hoeksche Waard this is the mixed farm covering an area of 100 hectares with the farmhouse in the middle, surrounded by cows, sheep and chickens. What is grown and when, depends on the groundwater level, the degree of brackishness, the quality of the soil and the inconvenience caused by wind. All the farms in the Netherlands are capable of incorporating a building volume of approximately 6000 m^3 without the landscape losing its rural character. A house with a garden will then be a house with a landscape. In Hoeksche Waard 1.6 million m^3 of house-building can easily be realized.

For God's sake what is landscape?

Landscape is probably the most convoluted word in the Dutch language. Formerly in the Netherlands, landscape stood for the regions beyond the cities, the countryside. Urban landscapes, industrial landscapes, parking landscapes, mental landscapes and data landscapes have seen to it that landscape as a noun has no meaning anymore. This account is about the landscape – the countryside – the rural landscape.

The most expensive icon in history

The cultural landscape has made the Netherlands world-famous. It is the country that God was unable to make, the polders, the dikes, the tulips, the cattle. This rural landscape is our logo, our export product, but oddly enough it does not play an independent role in spatial planning. All planning is in thrall to the task of building one million dwellings before 2015. Out of fear of the destructive effect of this large growth, politics have placed the landscape in the category of protected area. Spatial planning sees to it that the cursed city restricts itself in its urge for expansion, and focuses all design energy on finding urban compromises. The countryside is kept completely out of it. Red and green are used to distinguish the parties. The spatial translation of all 'urban' human activity has the dominant colour red. From a Calvinist sense of guilt each hectare of new red added at the expense of the landscape is compensated for with 9 hectares of new green in the form of recreation parks or something that we have come to call nature. Ironically, it is this very green comfort that is sweeping away large chunks of agrarian cultural heritage. A mock fight is taking place between red and green, which are actually two sides to the same coin: urbanization. Eventually, the landscape is the heavy loser. The Netherlands is becoming a quasi-urban nation, in which landscape is not much more than a gadget, an icon that has to be protected. Housing and agriculture, previously the driving forces behind the formation of cultural landscapes, are now seen as a threat and banned. Ethics and aesthetics have replaced logic and economy. Gradually but steadily the authentic production landscape is changing into a reserve where farmers perform sham agrarian movements; a fun landscape for the city-dweller, to be kept up artificially. It will be the most expensive icon the Netherlands has ever known.

'The New Map of the Netherlands' result of contemporary planning
Dispersion of red, green and blue fragments. Landscape is disappearing

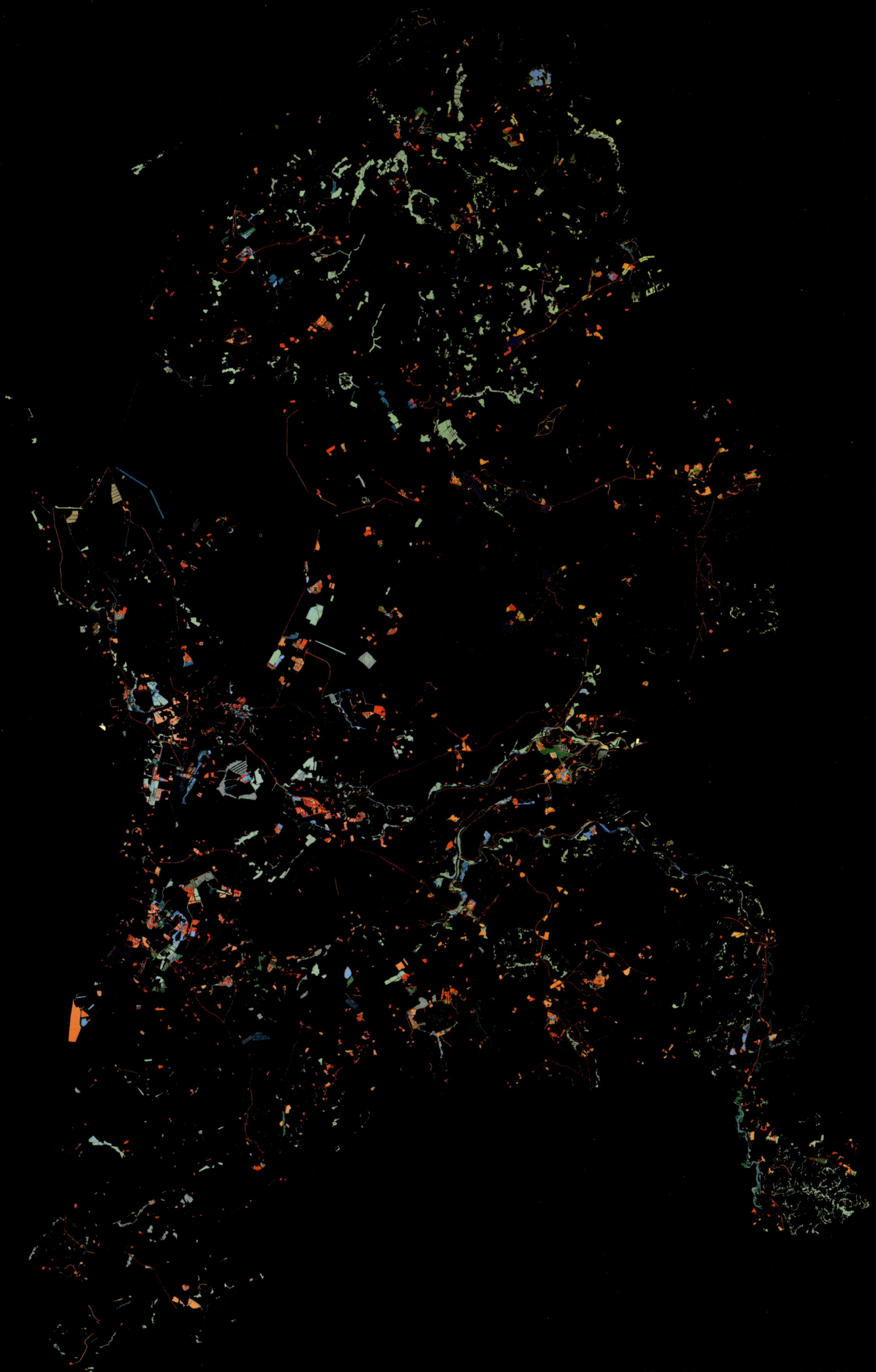

Green plans spread: 225,000 hectares

Green plans concentrated: 225,000 hectares

Blue plans spread: 35,000 hectares

Blue plans concentrated: 35,000 hectares

Red plans for the construction of 800,000 houses in town's outskirts: 25,000 hectares

800,000 country houses assimilated in the landscape, support the existing landscape

Rural landscape

AIR-Zuidwaarts/Southbound is not about Hoeksche Waard as an overspill area for urban functions from Rotterdam, nor about the strategic position of an economic corridor between two ports; this AIR is about the landscape as an active, vital player in spatial planning. Consequently, the task should not be approached from the point of view of urbanization, but from the landscape.

We are convinced that the countryside as a phenomenon is not outmoded. The rural landscape is a production landscape with enormous potential. It demands feeding, not protecting. All desires in the fields of living, production, recreation and mobility can be approached from this national potential.

In order to revive the countryside we propose a combination of four concepts that on the face of it are presently incompatible: nature, mobility, housing and agriculture. Ecological agriculture will become the norm for the entire Netherlands and will be detached from the cultural pessimism that appears to have a monopoly there. New housing will be relieved of its red stigma and be distributed across the landscape as an economic and spatial impulse. Nature will be actively included in agriculture and no longer be linked to the 'heart-lung machine' of Jac. P. Thijsse or abused as an antidote against urbanization. Mobility will be unhitched from the environment-polluting combustion engine and the road system put to better use.

New product

Thirty-eight per cent of Dutch farmers are living below the poverty line and current agriculture no longer has an attractive perspective to offer. On the one hand farmers are under financial pressure to produce cheaply and in great bulk, on the other hand the stricter environmental requirements present ever narrower limits. Once the product fails to comply, the operational management will have to be adjusted – a current method for depressed lines of business. There is a growing market for ecological products. Leading supermarket chains in the Netherlands have successfully taken advantage of this fact for some time now. With ecological agriculture, the landscape is purified of pesticides, fertilizers, hormones, antibiotics, animal stress, genetic manipulation, overproduction, loss of smell and taste, manure surpluses, stench nuisance, product inflation, quota policy, nonsensical EC subsidies, cut-throat competition and social insecurity. National productivity will decrease by 20 per cent on average as a result of an ecological production method. Paradoxically, this will mean the farmer's deliverance. It will put an end to the vicious circle of overproduction and price decreases by which farmers compete each other to death. The ever more expensive EC subsidy and quota policy can be abolished. Production is brought in line with the ecological possibilities of each country. Ecological agriculture is not the hobby of a handful of idealist farmers, but an economic condition for better product quality and a flourishing countryside.

125

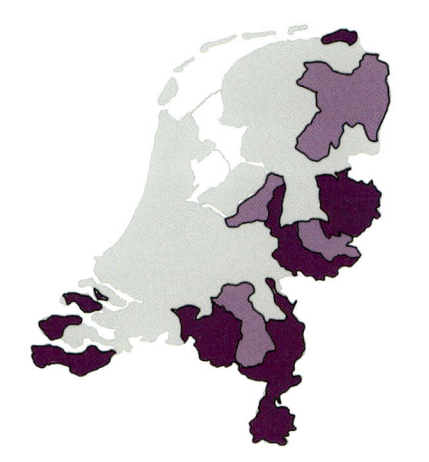

Soil dessication

Manure pollution

Soil silting

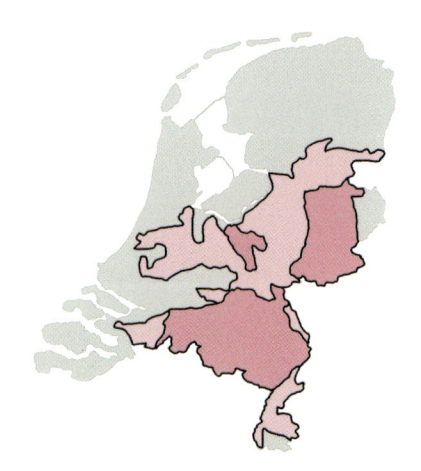

Animal distress

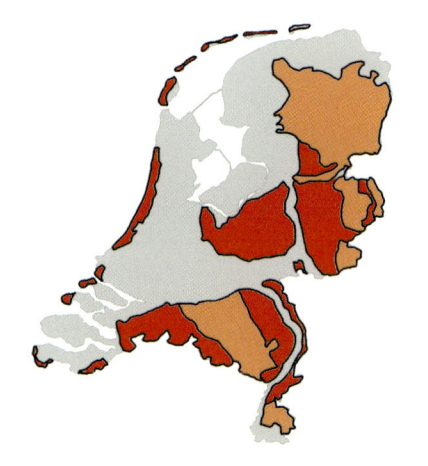

Soil acidification

Smell pollution

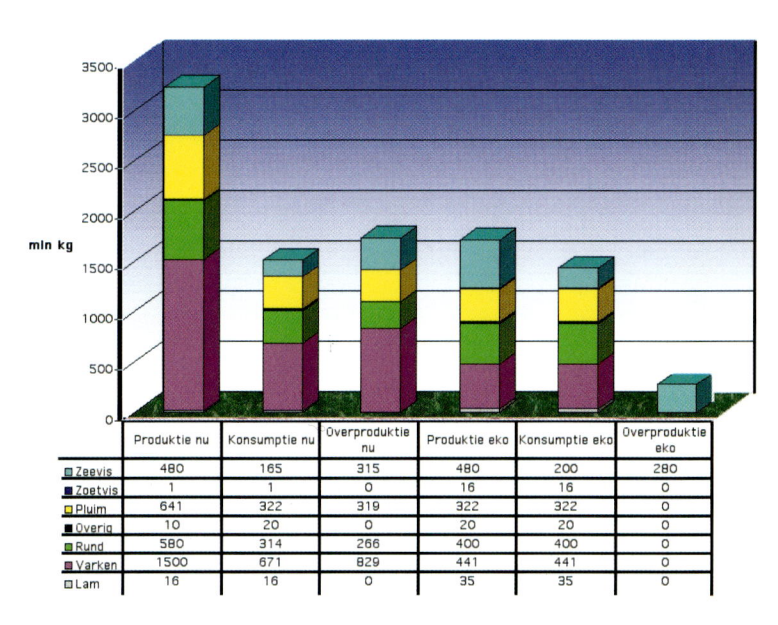

	Produktie nu	Konsumptie nu	Overproduktie nu	Produktie eko	Konsumptie eko	Overproduktie eko
Zeevis	480	165	315	480	200	280
Zoetvis	1	1	0	16	16	0
Pluim	641	322	319	322	322	0
Overig	10	20	0	20	20	0
Rund	580	314	266	400	400	0
Varken	1500	671	829	441	441	0
Lam	16	16	0	35	35	0

Production and consumption changes balance overproduction

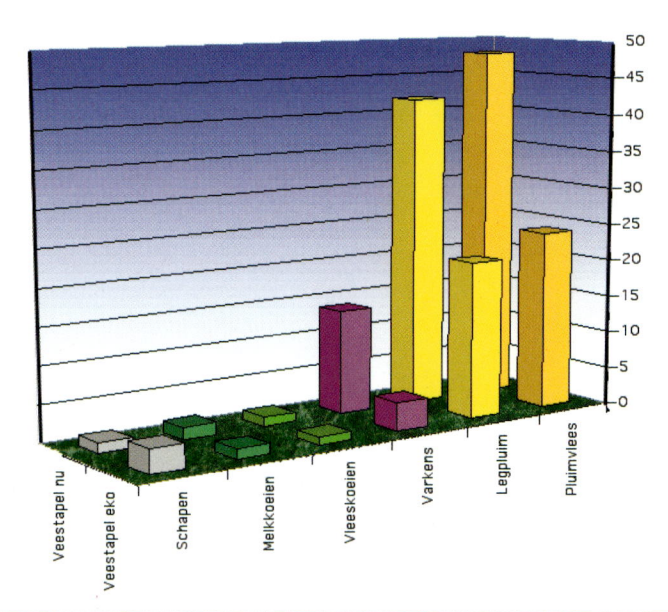

	Schapen	Melkkoeien	Vleeskoeien	Varkens	Legpluim	Pluimvlees
Veestapel eko	3,2	1,3	1	3,8	21	24
Veestapel nu	1,4	1,6	1,2	14	42	48

Livestock changes

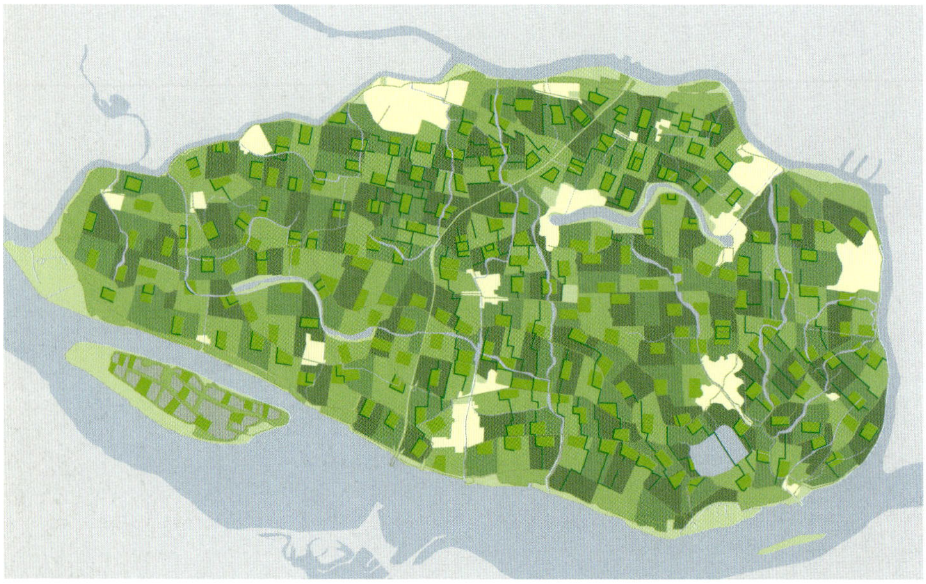

AIR-ZUIDWAARTS / SOUTHBOUND

DESIGN RESEARCH
FRITS PALMBOOM/JAAP VAN DEN BOUT
PETER CALTHORPE/MATTHEW TAECKER
STEFANO BOERI
FRANÇOIS ROCHE
DETTMAR/BEUTER/FRITZ/HASTENPFLUG
BINDELS/GIETEMA/HARTZEMA/KLOK
MARIEKE TIMMERMANS
DIRK SIJMONS/YTTJE FEDDES

Black-tailed godwits and geese

Crops will be mixed as much as possible, preferably within one farm. This will turn farms into closed systems which scarcely bring in foodstuffs from outside or dispose of waste matter externally. The entire countryside will turn into one large ecological field, where nature is to play a co-productive role. All the lots will get an optimum size of five till ten hectares and will be separated by zones of natural growth, flowers and trees as breeding places for insect-eating insects. This biodiversity will provide agriculture with a home-made pest control system. Nature no longer needs to be protected and hence is no longer at the mercy of the benevolence of a political whim. The opportunistically planned Ecological Main Structure with its nature-related types will fade in comparison with the vast expanses of 'real' nature. Using biopesticides and biofertilizers, ditch water will become clear and of drinking-water quality and the natural breeding of freshwater fish such as pike, perch, tench and particularly eel will be possible on a large scale again. The many new lakes, creeks and water parcels will also serve as places of water retention and an effective solution against the drying out of the Netherlands. Chickens will be released in the large clover meadows among the cows to produce pure free-range eggs. Sheep will graze along with them free of charge. Pigs will re-enter the woods, where they can eat truffles, acorns and chestnuts. Meat will make an unprecedented jump in quality.

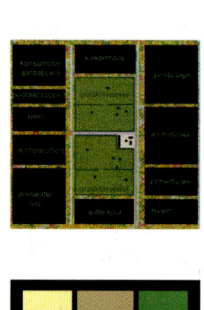

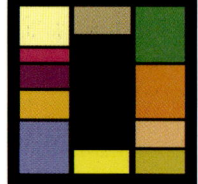

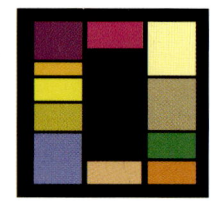

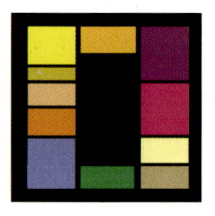

Creeks for natural freshwater-fish farming, use of hedges and flower beds to protect crops ecologically and 250 'residential sheds' to reform the Hoeksche Waard landscape

Ecological farmers select crops, depending on the spoil type and climate conditions, for their production cycles, which results in a landscape palette

Survey for ecological production
Mixed farm and production cycles on 90 hectares; year 1, year 2 and year 3

The new 'Netherlandscape' as a result of ecological production: 500,000 hectares of new forest for pig farming, 100,000 hectares new, natural freshwater for fish-farming, 100,000 hectares different land use for the production-consumption balance of meat, vegetables and fruit in the European Union

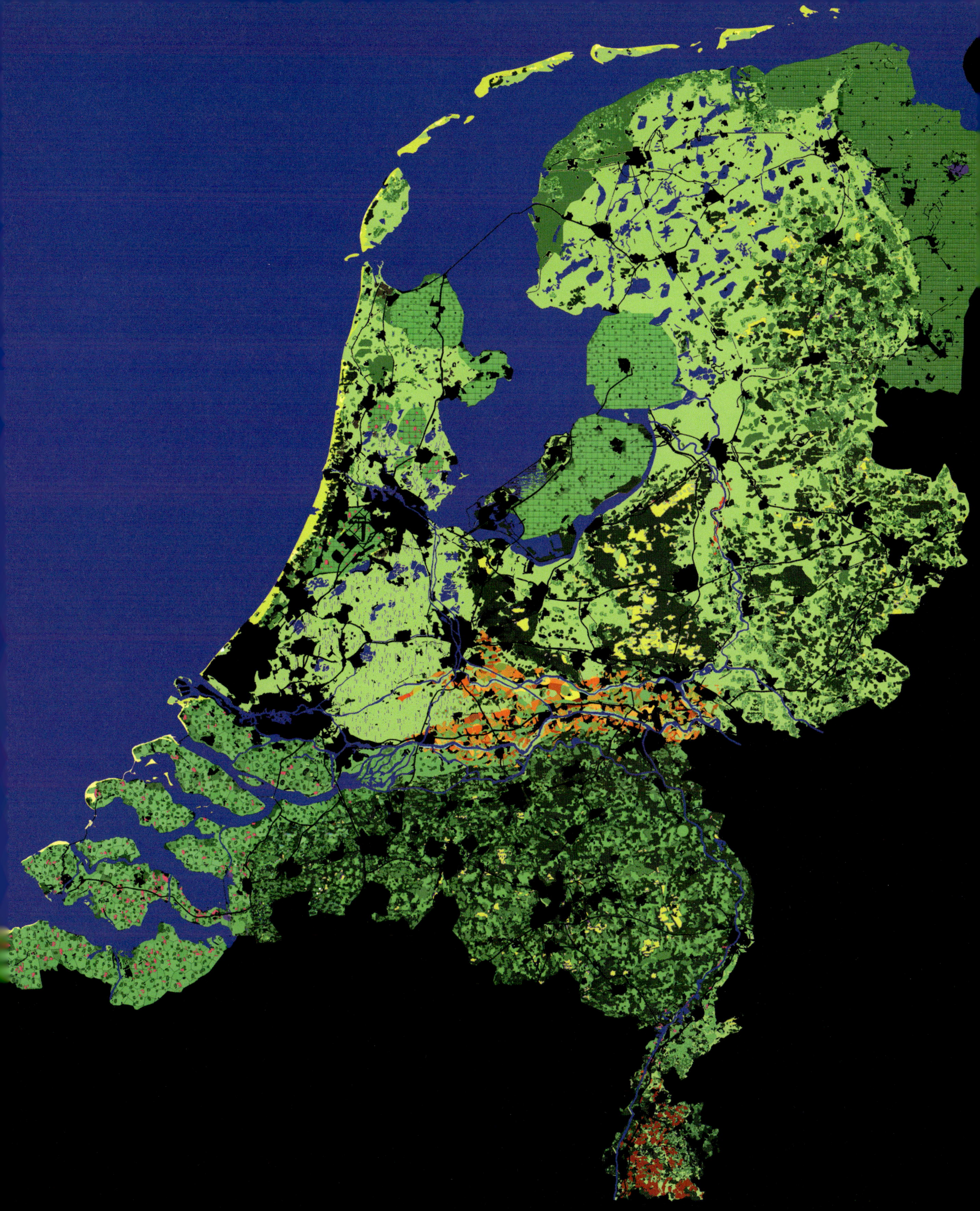

The density of the infrastructure and the amenities' network in the landscape is so substantial that even in the remotest areas all necessities are within easy reach. The proposed jet-foil transport system reduces travelling time between Rotterdam and Antwerp to 30 minutes at most. Water knows no traffic jams

A Dutch life of Riley

The economic capacity of the countryside is dwindling. Whereas housing is kept out in order to protect the landscape, municipalities attract large factories within their borders so as to generate extra income. The countryside is dying for new inhabitants. Moreover, according to the statistics, rural living is a gap in the market. The countryside is equipped for habitation. There is a well-maintained finely meshed road network with a large overcapacity. A ready-for-use underground infrastructure virtually covers the entire country. All day-to-day facilities are present in the existing villages. There is a service network which is heavily overdimensioned; fire brigades and ambulances cannot possibly arrive late these days. At present the economic capacity of all these facilities is not far removed from the critical minimum. Schools are closing, general practitioners are quitting, bus lines are being cancelled. Both in spatial and in economic respect, the landscape will profit from the building of rural dwellings. This need has always been ignored out of fear of corrupting the landscape and of the rising mobility. The Compact City and the Corridor were introduced to curb car use and save space.

Nevertheless car use continues to grow. Mobility has become an inalienable right. It offers freedom and pleasure. Associating mobility with pollution and thus with a negative image is based on a misunderstanding. It is not mobility that pollutes, but the combustion engine. By stimulating electric cars instead of limiting mobility and generating wind energy, building in the landscape will no longer entail environmental objections. The rural area can be opened up to the full by connecting each country road to the highway. A parallel acceleration lane can be added as an intermediary between highway and country road. The provincial roads, originally designed to deal with traffic flows in a flexible manner but nowadays chiefly congestion points, will be erased from the countryside. The traffic will be fully dispersed over the country roads and not come together until the highway. Driving will be recreation.

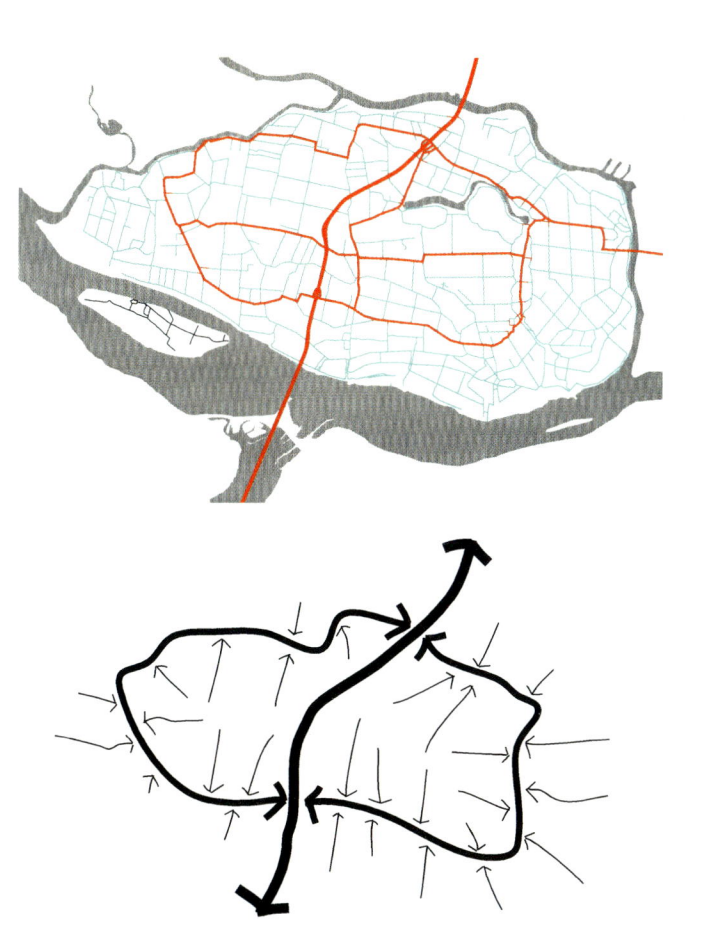

The traditional roads network of local roads connected with a collector, itself connected with a motorway, is easily congested if traffic increases as everybody uses the same roads. The collector and the motorway are always congested and the local roads are always empty

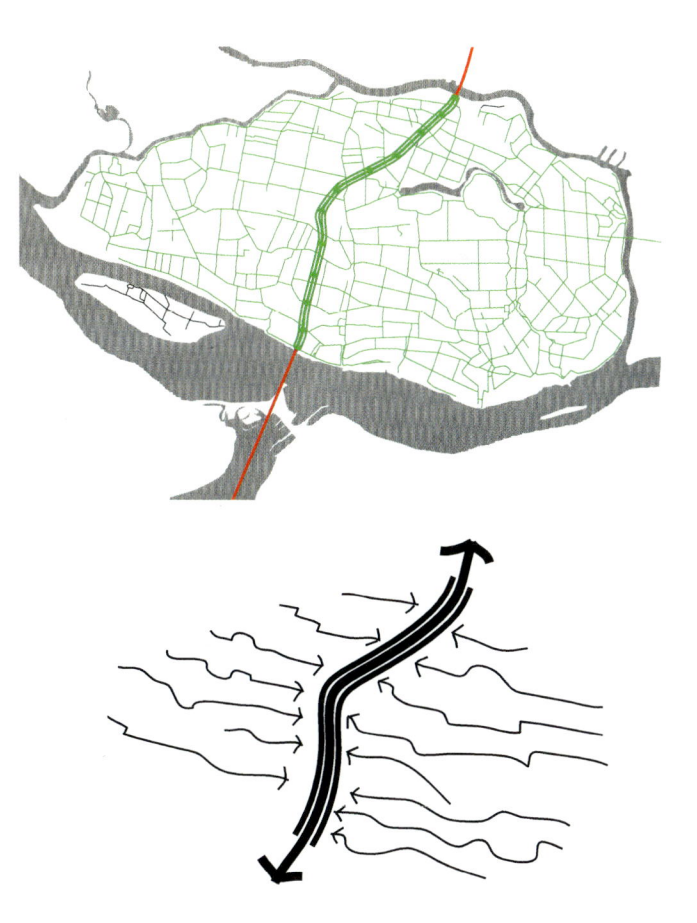

The proposal: to remove the collectors and connect the local roads direct to the motorways together with a parallel road. This will double the motorway's capacity and offer everybody the shortest way. Traffic spreads evenly and congestion becomes a thing of the past

AIR-ZUIDWAARTS / SOUTHBOUND

DESIGN RESEARCH

FRITS PALMBOOM/JAAP VAN DEN BOUT
PETER CALTHORPE/MATTHEW TAECKER
STEFANO BOERI
FRANÇOIS ROCHE
DETTMAR/BEUTER/FRITZ/HASTENPFLUG
BINDELS/GIETEMA/HARTZEMA/KLOK
MARIEKE TIMMERMANS
DIRK SIJMONS/YTTJE FEDDES

The synthesis of farm buildings and houses in a particular area produces a new typology, which varies as a result of the production type of that particular area

A house with a landscape

Suppose that 90 per cent of all farms in the Netherlands offer 6000 m^3 of residential accommodation in a concentrated form (8 dwellings of 750 m^3); the residential programme for the coming decade (about 800,000 dwellings) will be flawlessly integrated in its totality in the rural area. Capacious Zeeland province can easily accommodate the quota of its own municipalities and the South-West of the Randstad (15,3 million/m^3) in the landscape, while fully retaining its rural quality. The ecological farmer will thus be assured of a basic income and will have helping hands available in times of need.

Living in the rural area demands a new type. No fenced-in private paradises warding off the outside world and depriving the landscape of its character. He who lives rurally will have the countryside as his garden, possibly a small field or orchard at the farm. As a respite from a busy life, there is always the countryside. Instead of spending a fortune on a lawn and a waterscooter the rural inhabitant will help the farmer with haymaking and weeding. Recreation will be participation.

Current house-construction strategy: concentrated districts on the outskirts of existing towns and villages. The same quasi-urban environment everywhere

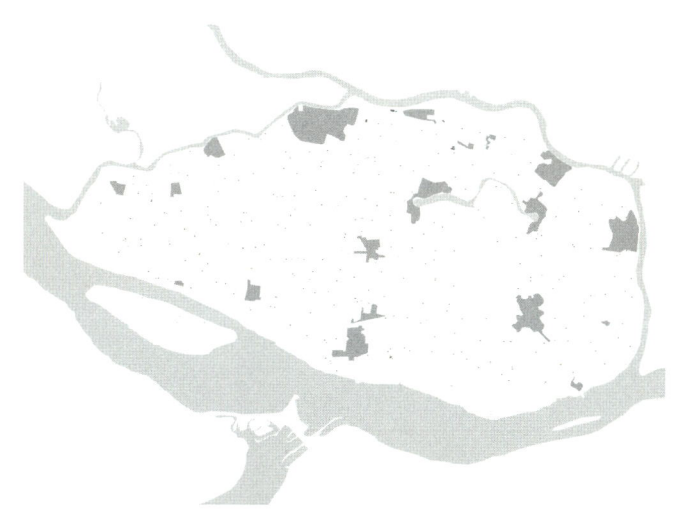

Proposal: to build a concentration of eight houses on each farm; identical number of houses but a thousand times as many different surroundings to live in

Dealing with water

As usual with the landscape architects Dirk Sijmons and Yttje Feddes the water management of a region is the basis for a plan serving many purposes. Apart from this, they think that changes in agricultural management and infrastructure are essential factors in Hoeksche Waard. When the planned extension of the A4 should be cancelled and agriculture acquires a stronger position in economic respect, it will be easier to keep undesired enterprises at a distance. Their proposal also presents new residential and business opportunities. Sijmons and Feddes also think that the Haringvliet sluices should be opened up a bit, so that the southern part of the island will become a tidal region again capable of absorbing overflow. As a result of this far-reaching measure the proportion between salt and fresh water will have to be regulated again. For this purpose the 'Oudeland van Strijen' operates as a water reservoir. Fresh water is further distributed over the island through a new system of six parallel high-water canals. These are favourable for agriculture and recreation, and moreover they form an attractive residential environment. For agriculture three operating models were investigated: ecological forms of agriculture, large-scale mixed farming and agro-refineries. Sijmons sees most perspectives for the latter, in which agriculture supplies the raw materials for e.g. the petrochemical complexes to the north of Hoeksche Waard. On the island of Ambachtsheerlijkheid a small town will be developed. Between the dikes and canals, in osier-beds and on the farmland in the country there will be room for second homes. Thus Hoeksche Waard is going to be a Rotterdam holiday region.

Meteorology in the Rijnmond–Scheldemond area

Hoeksche Waard lost its insularity in the slipstream of the execution of the Delta Works. The region was able to retain its own character because it always appeared to have been skipped in the hurry of reaching the blue heart of the delta or getting back to Rotterdam as soon as possible. Gradually, however, a cumulus cloud of – mainly urban – items of the programme are starting to build up over Hoeksche Waard. Possibilities of accommodating glasshouses and extensive areas for harbour-related activity are being explored. Besides, Hoeksche Waard seems to have been discovered for suburban living at twenty minutes' distance from Zuidplein in Rotterdam, as is evident from the rising prices of real estate. At the same time the present economic bearer of the region, arable farming, is faced with a difficult period. In the EU the conversion is being made from a product-oriented subsidy system to a system more directed at the world market with limited income support at most. Even now it is starting to dawn on the Dutch centres of arable farming how weak the competitive position is in view of the scale of the Dutch farms, the relatively high land prices, and in the light of expanding environmental legislation. In addition, there is the expected post-2003 expansion of the EU with inexpensively producing agricultural countries such as Hungary and Poland. In the Netherlands the perspective for products and crops which are dependent on price competition will soon deteriorate. The essence of the problem is to be deduced from this: urban high-pressure regions situated at a short distance from each other (Rijnmond and Scheldemond areas) and an agrarian low-pressure region (the sea-clay regions of the Zeeland and Zuid-Holland islands and West-Brabant).

Ambition

Drastic spatial and social processes of change will result from this field of tension. Our ambition in positive terms: guiding these processes in such a way that an attractive (urban) landscape arises for the people living and working there as well as a landscape whose spatial and social identity and possibilities of use are so evident that Hoeksche Waard will be etched on to the mental map of the city-dwellers. This psychological link is the only chance of there being an enduring and positive development. In order to achieve this it will be necessary to make the course of agricultural development the central theme of the design. If this is omitted, the result will almost certainly be a postmodern palette of farming styles and cluttered urbanization. Formulated in negative terms the ambition is 'never again to permit another IJsselmonde', where with the best intentions of all the sectors an impotent and fragmented non-landscape has arisen these past thirty years.

Territorial choice
Construction of A4 motorway under discussion, A29, the most beautiful parkway from town to seaside

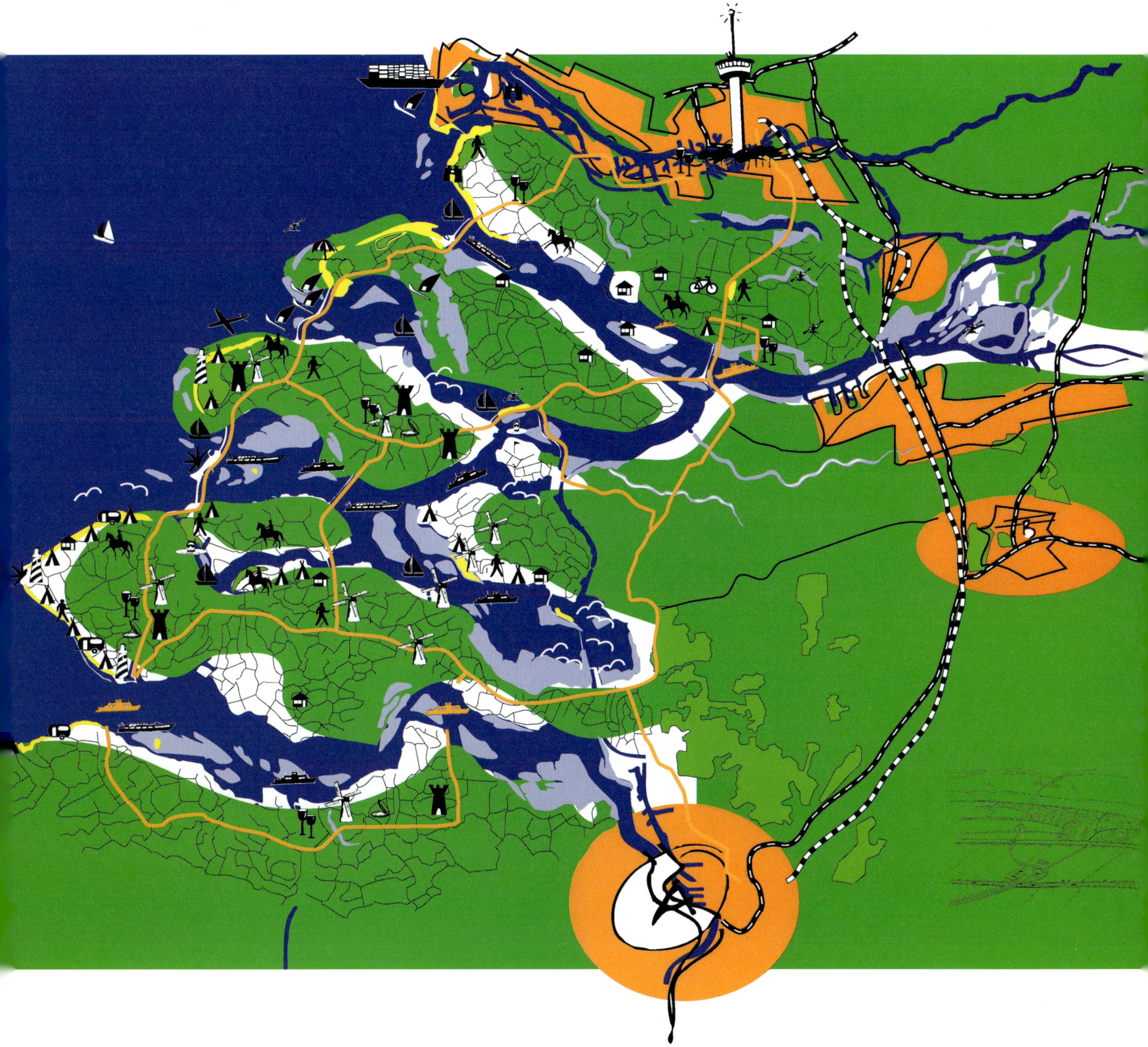

Territorial choice

On the scale of the 'Euregion' of Rijn-Scheldemond, there are a number of do's and don'ts involved in giving shape to such an ambition. In the first place it is important to bring up the construction of the A4 for discussion. Construction of this road does not only score badly from the point of view of capacity, the indirect spatial effects resulting from it will also largely obstruct the view of an attractive perspective for the future. A diagonal area the size of Rotterdam South will arise, attracting the sort of nondescript mixed industrial site that makes little use of the specific qualities of the region. Even more important is the cause and effect chain started by such a link with the A4 corridor. It is the extension of a ladder structure between Rotterdam and Antwerp, some kind of double 'cable chute' which will result in a sort of homeopathic dilution of the programme. This in its turn causes each municipality to launch its own little industrial site with the result that nothing will be quite successful anywhere, which implies the continuation of a wasteful use of space. Fragmentation and disintegration will advance on a broad front so that, all in all, the enormous opportunities available to make a clear territorial choice will be killed in the 'polder model' of consensus. We propose utilizing the combination A16 and HSL (High Speed Line) as the exclusive economic zone between Rotterdam and Antwerp. The 'twist' in it and the 15 minutes' loss of driving time this yields are our daily peace offering to diminishing the rush in the relieved blue heart of the Rhine-Scheldt delta. The A29 is to be geared to, and where necessary profiled for, utilization of its original quality: the most beautiful parkway of the Netherlands. Starting in the heart of Rotterdam it opens up all the great phenomena of the delta landscape. Industrial sites are kept at a dignified distance, the landscape itself is the high visibility location. Apart from being a halting place for ongoing motorists the so-called 'Aires' are direct links between the highway system and the finely-woven recreational networks for walking, cycling and sailing.

Water management

Water management forms the basic layer of spatial planning. Gradually different views are emerging on dealing with the hereditary enemy. An enduring strategy for coping with the consequences of the rising sea level consists of at least two parts: a vision on the development of the morphology of the coast, and on the way we drain off our river water. Both accounts have one common denominator: the insight that we should once again make natural processes, such as erosion and sedimentation, our allies. Under penalty of a struggle lost beforehand against harsh, inelegant civil-engineering methods. Natural engineering proves to be civil engineering for the advanced. The strategy of the past century – keeping the coastline taut and as short as possible – is supplemented with a revaluation of the significance of the permanent drainage of sediment by the rivers through the formation of a protective front delta. The great challenge is to restart a large-scale sediment transport. The designation of overflow areas and overflow polders throughout the entire Rhine branch from Switzerland up to the estuary plays a threefold role in this respect. Because of the retention capacity it will then be possible to drain off extremely high river water more gradually; more sediment will be carried along by the river in its flooding and this will yield an attractive river-related landscape. In the south-west of Hoeksche Waard a number of polders are acquired as overflow areas.

Salt-fresh gradient

In our planning area the Haringvliet sluices must be reopened – while retaining a flood barrier, of course. If it becomes a tidal region again, the sediment will also be removed. This is highly necessary, since the locked Haringvliet has literally become the sediment drain of half of Europe. An open connection between the Brielsche Maas and the sea will also be provided. The Spui will become a tidal region again. In the upper part of Hoeksche Waard some regions are 'de-poldered' so as to increase the basin-storage capacity of the system.
This restoration of the salt-fresh gradient, also due to the strongly improved quality of the water, may have quite a few surprises in store in the coming decades. Will the sturgeon, of which the last specimen was caught in 1955 in the Nieuwe Merwede, return to these waters?

Water for agriculture

There are problems, too. Since Hoeksche Waard will be surrounded by brackish water again, the supply of sufficient and high-quality fresh water for agriculture will have to be safeguarded. We propose leading the water surplus in Alblasserwaard by means of fresh-water pipes through Hoeksche Waard and Voorne-Putten to the users in the Westland. In a departure from the provincial plans, which provide central ongoing water pipes, we suggest having Hoeksche Waard, after the inlet at Puttershoek and the distribution point at Strijen, fan out into six imposed waterways which can then form the basis of a new agricultural high-water system. In east-west direction the Waard will be marked by wide and visible water. At present this is only the case at the Binnendijkse Maas. Furthermore, the retention of good, fresh rainwater in the region will be made possible by storing water in the peaty profile of Oudeland van Strijen. This sub-region operates as a water battery connected to a newly constructed high-water system. The greater part of the farms in the region will therefore get the possibility of hydrological precision control at farm level and hence a wider choice of crops. This flexibility is of vital importance since there is no definite answer to the present agricultural problems. A wide range of various farming styles should be made possible in the region: from farmers who see a future in an internationalizing market strategy to farms which are more aimed at a regionalizing strategy. All the intermediate forms of farming will also occur in the region. The new water system will enable farms to deal with these uncertainties.

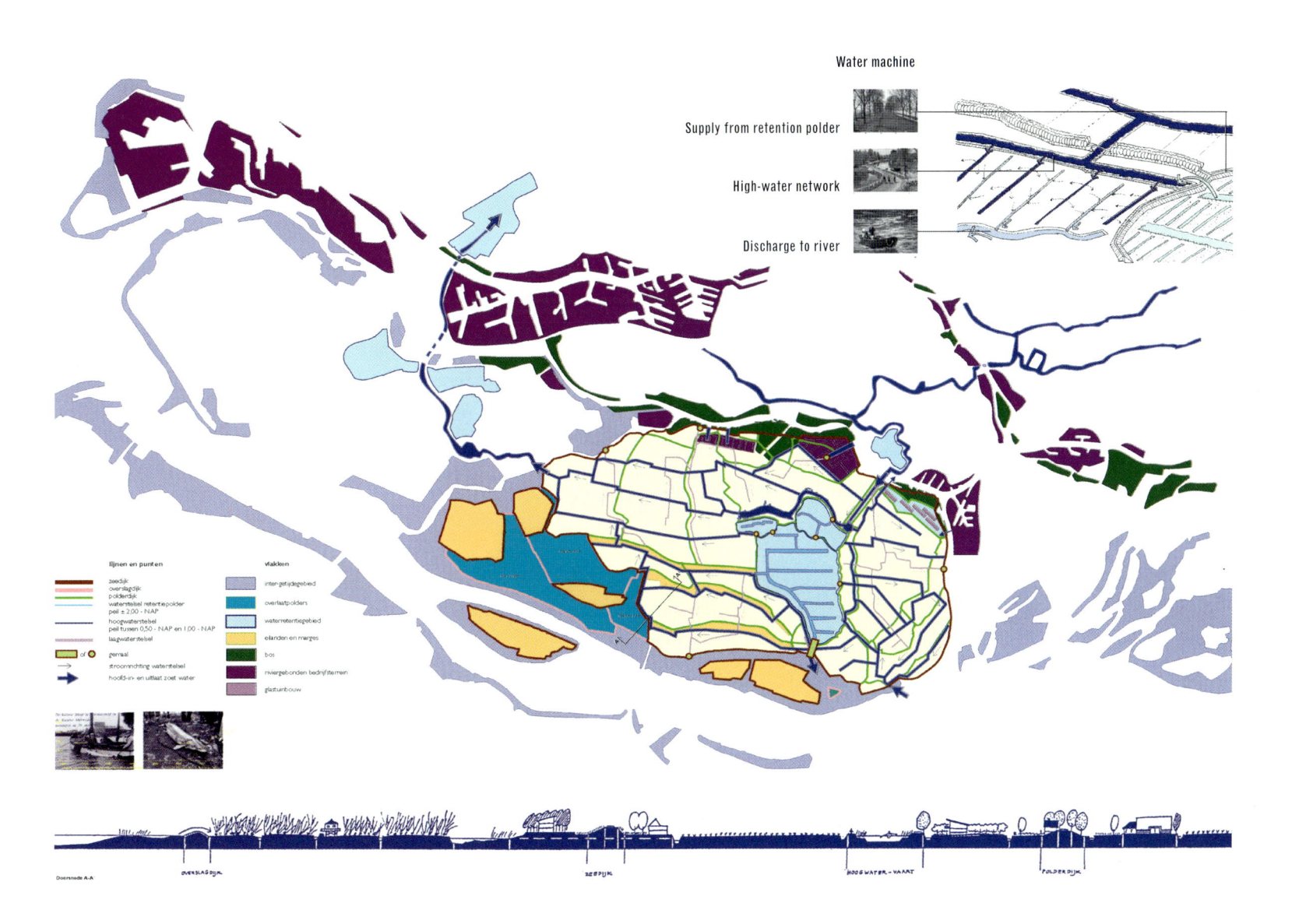

New margins

The interventions in the water system not only create new conditions for use. Locally they will also provide new margins, such as the zones between the high-water canals and the dikes. This will also benefit the public character of the landscape, and the imposed high-water canals and the accompanying viewing paths will provide a recreational route covering a considerable distance. Apart from their opening function, the water interventions will also create new isolated places, such as the Ambachtsheerlijkheden island in the Haringvliet. Besides, new contrasts will arise: the polder of Goudswaard surrounded by osier-beds is a good example. The plan has seized upon these new regional characteristics with both hands so as to create the differentiation the region sorely needs.

AIR-ZUIDWAARTS / SOUTHBOUND

DESIGN RESEARCH
FRITS PALMBOOM/JAAP VAN DEN BOUT
PETER CALTHORPE/MATTHEW TAECKER
STEFANO BOERI
FRANÇOIS ROCHE
DETTMAR/BEUTER/FRITZ/HASTENPFLUG
BINDELS/GIETEMA/HARTZEMA/KLOK
MARIEKE TIMMERMANS
DIRK SIJMONS/YTTJE FEDDES

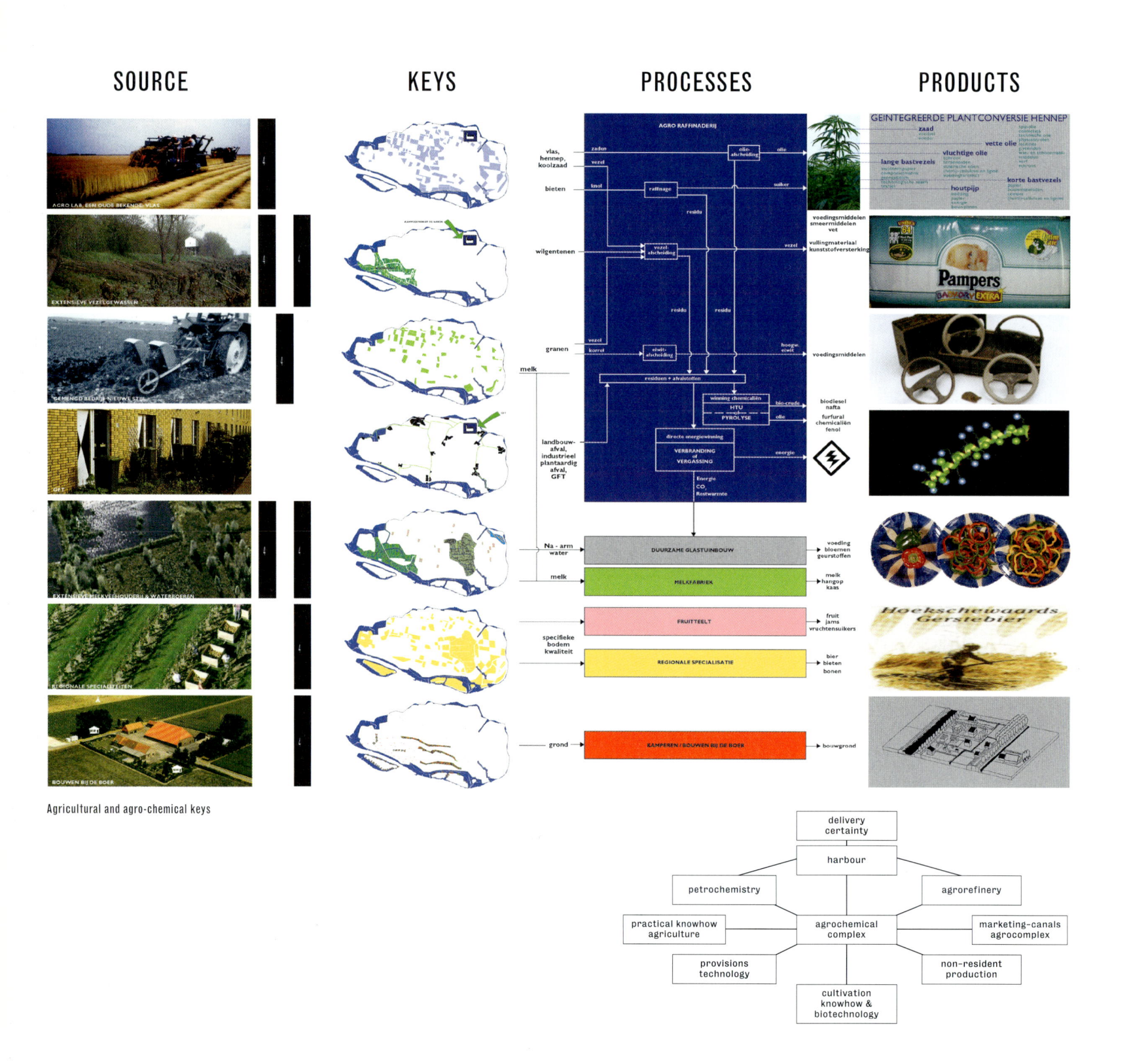

SOURCE | KEYS | PROCESSES | PRODUCTS

Agricultural and agro-chemical keys

Agrarian and agrochemical legend

We see three opportunities for agriculture in Hoeksche Waard. However odd this may seem, the first has to do with the proximity of the petrochemical complex and the port. The answer to the environmental problem should not only be formulated by agriculture. The petrochemical industry must also take a different course. It is expected that the environmental levies will see to it that fossil oil is only used for very high-grade applications. Biomass will increasingly be considered raw material for the processing industry, but not by converting an enormous bulk production of biomass into a raw material similar to oil. It can be done more cleverly and in a manner offering opportunities for the specific situation of the Netherlands. The new perspective more elegantly utilizes the organic structure already created by nature in the plants. All the parts of the plant can be used as raw material, residues can be converted into bio diesel or naphtha and the remaining parts converted into energy in the bio oil burner. This approach is called 'integrated plant conversion'. Research in Wageningen shows that hemp and flax offer opportunities in the Dutch situation. Everything is used, from the ethereal oil to the fibres which have likely applications as reinforcement material in synthetic products.

Agrochemistry: closing cycles at a regional level

It is proposed that farmers should be included who are interested in an agrarian experimental garden for these kinds of crops, an agrolab where a Rotterdam agro/petrochemical complex can experiment with the new raw materials at a practical level. What is new is that for integrated plant conversion the whole plant must be harvested. The transport costs may easily rise in the case of such bulk. In the region itself the primary processing has to be realized in an agrorefinery. Transport up to 50 km appears to be feasible from an economic point of view. In this refinery the plants (hemp, flax, coleseed, grain, willows) are divided into easily manageable (and transportable!) chunks for further processing in the processing industry. The residues are converted into energy, residual heat and CO_2 in the oil burner of the agrorefinery. Hoeksche Waard offers opportunities for this development, when synergism is developed from the unique combination of the petrochemical complex, the advanced food industry, a large port offering life security as well as scientific know-how in land development and genetic engineering, and last but not least the practical know-how of the farmers who were still growing flax until 25 years ago. An agrochemical complex in the making.

Mixed farming: closing cycles at farm level

The second course is the course of new-style mixed farming. Here, too, the cycles of energy and matter are cleverly closed. Not, as above, on an industrial scale, but within the farm. The renaissance of mixed farming is a reaction to the conclusion that the current specialized agricultural production systems are not enduring. They are characterized by narrow and one-sided cultivation plans, nutrient surpluses, a high input of fertilizers, crop-protection materials and fodder, and have to cope with (latent) unemployment due to the small scale of the farms. The mixed-farming system reduces the use of external input and produces more efficiently by the use of home-grown low-nitrogen and high-energy fodder, by using residues, by a more efficient use of the nutrients in manure, by including grass parcels in the rotation, by widening crop rotation in the cultivation plan and finally by an optimum input of papilionaceous flowers which bind nitrogen from the air and therefore operate as green fertilizers. This will also result in a better employment situation and more effective spread of the income risks.

Broadening the countryside economy

For a farm innovation is also possible by orientating more towards the regional market. The proximity of the city is an advantage. There are opportunities for milk products, biodynamic or eco vegetables, fruit and fruit products, special applications of grain (Hoeksche Waard beer!) etc. These market segments are growing steadily and are expected to serve between 10-20 per cent of the consumers, whether or not through direct market sale or subscriptions. Besides, we also propose having farmers profit from the rise in the value of land for residential purposes. The traditional 'camping at the farm' can be locally extended to 'building at the farm'.

AIR-ZUIDWAARTS / SOUTHBOUND

138

DESIGN RESEARCH
FRITS PALMBOOM/JAAP VAN DEN BOUT
PETER CALTHORPE/MATTHEW TAECKER
STEFANO BOERI
FRANÇOIS ROCHE
DETTMAR/BEUTER/FRITZ/HASTENPFLUG
BINDELS/GIETEMA/HARTZEMA/KLOK
MARIEKE TIMMERMANS
DIRK SIJMONS/YTTJE FEDDES

The jump southward

The agrarian entrepreneurs who opt for a transition to 'new-style mixed farming' have the best perspectives in the north of the Waard (5), since these lowest-lying parts are suitable for including a grassland phase in the rotation. There will also be perspectives for other areas, for that matter, because of the high-water system. This will concern large farms of between 80 and 150 hectares. Besides beetroots, new crops such as hemp and familiar ones such as flax will determine the image of arable farming. The flowering flax will colour parts of Hoeksche Waard blue (7). The high-water and low-water system offers opportunities to perform an experimental-garden function for other crops as well (for instance, perennials such as Miscanthus, Switch-grass). The Agrorefinery could be sited at a number of places. A maximum operation area can be achieved by locating it at the southern side of Hoeksche Waard or on the Moerdijk. As yet, we assume a direct link with the large harbour complex: a northerly position close to the other 'agrorefinery', the present sugar factory (8). A large glasshouse complex close to the refinery will profit from the energy, CO_2 and residual heat released in the production and biogasification of the residue. The new glasshouse complex will also be situated at the inlet of the water system, so that water low in sodium will be guaranteed in sufficient quantities (9). The farms targeted at the regional market segments can take advantage of the marketing possibilities offered by the 'new islands', such as Goudswaard for the sale of biologically grown arable-farming products and firstlings from pure-soil vegetable cultivation (10). Of course, this strategy is also an obvious option in the little accretion polders which are too small for the new farming development. The development could possibly start with partnerships between cattle farming and arable farming. By further expansion in Oudeland van Strijen (water farmers) the milk quota will be attained. A combination of extensive dairy farming with income support from a 'water-farmers' regulation and the already existing geese subsidy is a plausible development for Oudeland van Strijen (6). Finally, a matching agricultural use has been opted for in the overflow polders. After purchasing the right to water management, the land is to be leased out for osier-bed cultivation (energy and fibre crops supplying the agrorefinery) and extensive pasturing. Building, exploitation and management of the datsja's for city-dwellers are part of the management and are structurally included in the employment picture (3).

Just building-on in Hoeksche Waard is probably the gloomiest perspective conceivable. 'Another IJsselmonde' will almost certainly be the consequence. What we want to aim at is making an urban Bob Beamon-jump from Rotterdam to Haringvliet. A jump southward. The south coast of Hoeksche Waard where an introverted new urban

1. New town

2. New margins: double ribbon

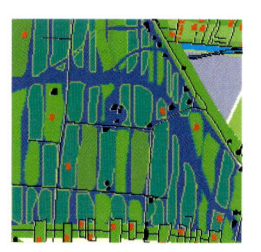

3. Osiers and datsja's

4. Hoeksche Waard 'Aire'

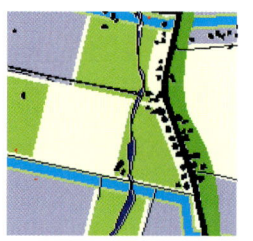

5. New-style mixed farm

6. Extensive cattle farm and water farmers

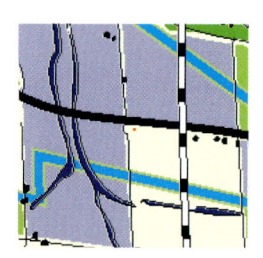

7. Agro-laboratory

8. Agro-refinery in industrial park

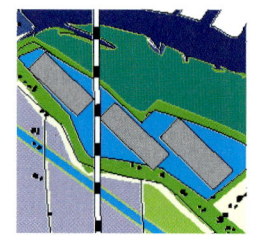

9. Glasshouse project

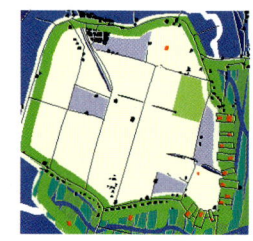

10. Geographical marketing

The southbound leap

residential environment contrasts with the restored vastness of the tidal region: the cleared island of Ambachtsheerlijkeid (1), equally interesting for the Zuid-Holland and West-Brabant housing markets. The south, where in the margin between the taut framework of the dikes and the new high-water system a new informal occupation produces a double ribbon (2). The southern overflow polders, where like a kind of 'Rotterdam holiday land' simple but high-water-free cottages are concealed among the osier-beds along the opened-up edges (3). The urban programme makes the jump southward and elegantly lands in the glue joints created by the transformations in hydrology and agriculture. The latter will profit financially from 'building at the farm' and will thus increase the possibilities for housing as well as recreation.

Rotterdam holiday land

The recreational programme is of vital importance to have Hoeksche Waard take up a more prominent position in the emotional experience of the city-dweller. A second condition is the public character (the landscape of Hoeksche Waard is shut away at present). From the existing church and viewing paths along the new high-water system a covering network is woven for recreational cycling and walking. Connection with the car network is found at the A27 parkway where you can directly transfer from your car at the Aire of 'Hoeksche Waard' (4) to canoe (high-water system) or bicycle (Danserweg). The plan aims at a clear hierarchy for the road system. The number of turnings on the A27 is limited to two. The southern turning opens up both the island of Ambachtsheerlijkheden and the willow plantation. The northern turning links up with the provincial road, which is to be connected with a system of north-south secondary roads. The dike roads make the network complete. Utilitarian farm roads and the recreational network form the capillaries of the system.

AIR-ZUIDWAARTS / SOUTHBOUND

AIR-Zuidwaarts/Southbound studied the specific culture of Hoeksche Waard in order to get a grip on the dynamics and resistance of the island in the changing urban field. Besides, it was a design research resulting in eight different concepts and strategies for the regional design. These three afterthoughts deal with the research done by visual artists, photographers and anthropologists, the design research and the effect and significance of the regional design.

AFTERTHOUGHTS

ARNOLD REIJNDORP
BROESI/JANNINK/VELDHUIS
ERIC LUITEN

AIR-ZUIDWAARTS / SOUTHBOUND	INTRODUCTION	PROGRAMME	RESEARCH	DESIGN TASK	DESIGN RESEARCH	AFTERTHOUGHTS	APPENDIX

WYTZE PATIJN
ADRIAAN VAN DER STAAY
MIRJAM SALET

ANNE-MIE DEVOLDER

VISUAL RESEARCH
JOHN DAVIES
HET OBSERVATORIUM
MARK PIMLOTT
SCHIE 2.0
HENRIK HÅKANSSON
AD VAN DENDEREN
WIJNANDA DEROO
BERTIEN VAN MANEN
HANS VAN HOUWELINGEN
BIRTHE LEEMEIJER
JOOST GROOTENS
JAN KONINGS/ESTER VAN DE WIEL
HONORÉ δ'O
ANTHROPOLOGICAL RESEARCH
HENK DE HAAN
PHYSICAL PLANNING RESEARCH
SJOERD CUSVELLER

SJOERD CUSVELLER/
ANNE-MIE DEVOLDER

FRITS PALMBOOM/JAAP VAN DEN BOUT
PETER CALTHORPE/MATTHEW TAECKER
STEFANO BOERI
FRANÇOIS ROCHE
DETTMAR/BEUTER/FRITZ/HASTENPFLUG
BINDELS/GIETEMA/HARTZEMA/KLOK
MARIEKE TIMMERMANS
DIRK SIJMONS/YTTJE FEDDES

ARNOLD REIJNDORP
BROESI/JANNINK/VELDHUIS
ERIC LUITEN

CHRONICLE
PERSONAL PARTICULARS
PERSONS INVOLVED
COLOPHON

Pleasure and purpose in the Dutch Landscape

AIR-Zuidwaarts/Southbound was not about Hoeksche Waard. But AIR-Kop van Zuid (1982) wasn't about the Kop van Zuid either. Neither was AIR-Spoortunneltracé (1988) about the railway tunnel site, nor AIR-Alexander (1993) about the Alexander polder. The areas which AIR (Architecture International Rotterdam) addresses are examples of topical architectural and urban planning issues. AIR-Kop van Zuid was about the redevelopment of superseded docklands and its contribution to revitalizing the city. It was also about the culture of ports, and how city and port grow apart. The AIR railway tunnel event focused on the city's 'collective memory' and the significance of architectural and planning structures in that context. AIR-Alexander spotlighted the outskirts of the city, or rather the in-between areas, in which the city runs on, and on. However, it was based on a debate on the changing ideas about city and urbanity. That event enabled, for the first time, artists, photographers, authors and journalists to comment on the culture and rapidly altering face of the post-war expansion areas. Such a comprehensive study into a specific culture would seem to contradict the theory that AIR-events do not relate directly to the areas they address. Yet that is not the case. The survey that every AIR-event in fact amounts to, is much more an attempt to understand a certain spatial 'condition'; to pin down the dynamics and resistance at a specific place in the changing urban scene.

European region

AIR-Zuidwaarts/Southbound focused primarily on the entire delta between Rotterdam and Antwerp. Rotterdam-Rijnmond was no longer taken as the Randstad's southern flank, but as the northern flank of one of the most highly urbanized regions of Europe. The event took the line that there is scope to link up with the economic field opening up between London, the Ruhr and Milan. In a more localized context, it highlighted competition with the port of Antwerp and the exodus of businesses and inhabitants to West Brabant. The original project 'AIR-Port' underlined the design of developments in a southerly direction. It was to have focused on the one hand on designing the infrastructure of motorways and public transport, and the connections with ports and airports. On the other hand, the idea was to pay more attention to the unplanned, small-scale economic, social or cultural activities which arise in the strangest of places and ostensibly out of nowhere, and add importance to certain areas. These are dubbed 'stims' and include such facilities as transport cafes, Michelin-star restaurants, hotels, art galleries, theme parks and discotheques.

Elaboration of the project added emphasis to the quality of the region as a setting for European habitation. The most attractive regions are characterized by a special combination of metropolitan and scenic elements. In south-east England the rapidly suburbanized countryside of Kent and Sussex presents itself as the 'garden' of London, and in northern Italy, much of Milan's appeal lies in the proximity of the Alps and the lakes. In the present context it was relevant to question how the 'blue heart', the delta area of Zuid-Holland and Zeeland with its expanses of water, islands and beaches combined with continuing urbanization between Rotterdam and Antwerp, might supply an area with similar appeal at a European level.

Blank spot

Given the region thus established, attention inevitably focuses on that one large blank spot on the map: Hoeksche Waard. Many people are unfamiliar with the area. They leapfrog across it on their way to Brabant or further afield, or from the south to the Randstad. Various authorities have had an eye on Hoeksche Waard for years, for housing, leisure and distribution centres for the port of Rotterdam. Urbanization of the area along the usual lines seemed imminent. But an opportunity would have been missed, of stepping up residential quality in the already highly urbanized Rijnmond region and thus achieving the level of other, scenically attractive urbanized regions in Europe. AIR-Zuidwaarts/Southbound pursued another option: Hoeksche Waard might become the garden of Rotterdam, instead of a glory-hole like the island of IJsselmonde. Homes and work could be combined with enhanced scenic qualities and environmental values. It would not only be a matter of the qualities of Hoeksche Waard itself, but also of the contribution to increasing the delta's attraction as a region on a European scale.

The project, when formulated in this way, is no longer an urban planning exercise. It is not enough to replace the requirements of housing programmes and industrial floor area with those of open countryside, nature or leisure amenities. The development of the possibilities of Hoeksche Waard is a cultural exercise. So the area would no longer be seen as an empty space to be filled with all manner of programmes, but as a collection of places overlaid with meanings engendered by social processes. The meanings are not predetermined, but are the subjects of discussion and conflict.

This kind of cultural approach entails a different working method, in which the tension between the area's local dynamics and the forces affecting it have a more important part to play. That is why AIR always takes a specific area as its design exercise. A design study of that specific collection of places is, after all, the only way to discover what is involved in the spatial transformation, to which abstract terms like network city, urban field or urban landscape are applied. The aim is not to establish the area's 'cultural' identity, but to explore the different worlds to which the area belongs. Those worlds operate at different speeds, and so the area itself is not only situated in different worlds but also in different times. The desire to know about the cultural identity of places is also a desire to know about the time with which they are linked. To quote Kevin Lynch: 'What time is this place?'. The changing perspective, from urban planning to cultural exercise and from abstract space to concrete place, has consequences for the terms within which the discussion on the possible future of a region like Hoeksche Waard is conducted.

Rurality

Terms like town, country, nature and landscape are no longer sufficient, at least not as designations of spatial entities. Nevertheless, they play an important part in a cultural debate on the quality of our society and the part played by the planning of space there. All four are linked to social, political and cultural values: civilization, tradition, responsibility and beauty. These values can no longer be attached to clearly demarcated spatial units. Consequently they become more fluid and now take the form of urbanity, rurality, nature-ness and landscape-ness. Sometimes they solidify, and, for instance, a 'museum of rurality' is set up somewhere. Rather like a garden centre, where they sell all manner of planters, buckets and other country curiosities rather than plants. Rurality, nature-ness and landscape-ness would seem to be part of one single argumentation relating to urbanity. It is a distinctly urban view of the countryside, landscape or nature. That view proves to be of far greater influence than institutional urban planning in changing the look of the countryside, in the same way as landscape adapts to the tourist's expectations (see Dietvorst, Urry).[1] Dietvorst shows how that process has taken place in Mediterranean areas. In south-west England one can clearly see how the idea of rurality has been transformed into a suburban idyll.

Four distinct themes have been chosen to provide greater clarity on the social, cultural and spatial developments determining the city-country-nature-landscape relationship. Two have been pinpointed as spatial developments: upscaling alongside downscaling, and the coincidence of anonymization and commodification. The others relate to developments in time: differences in speed – dynamics and resistance, and social mobility – identity and involvement.

Upscaling and downscaling

Upscaling exists, both in towns and in the countryside. Production and consumption are part of world-wide systems. To use Manuel Castells's words, they form a 'space of flows', i.e. of transport and communication movements. At the same time, a 'space of places' is coming about: the importance of the place with its own identity is again on the increase. However, such places are not only being defended, but are being produced in growing numbers as well. The pursuit of places with their own identity would seem everywhere to be producing places with the same character instead.

Spot your spot: anonymization and commodification

The nature of the organizations concerned with designing town and country has changed. Associations of farmers, retailers, residents, employers and employees, leisure-seekers and nature-lovers present themselves as organizations with a social objective: to improve the countryside, the economy, housing, accessibility, landscape. An organization of that type may, apart from being a pressure group (like the ANWB – Royal Dutch Touring Club), also be a landowner (like Natuurmonumenten – Nature Preservation Society). Their activities make intervention in town and country planning more anonymous and the concomitant discussions more abstract. The farmer's or resident's interests are not what count, but more elevated aims like responsible management of our scarce space. At the same time, such organizations see space from their own specific objectives, as a consumer commodity – housing environment, recreation area, nature. In this way town and country are increasingly becoming 'spot your spot' items, a landscape full of signposts telling you exactly what you can find where.

Dynamics and resistance: differences in speed

Generally speaking, stone and brick are felt to signify a dynamic presence. It is there that changes and innovations are born, and life lived at a pace. Whereas the country is felt to be the place of resistance to change. Consequently, the city is synonymous with modernity, the country with tradition. This stereotype no longer applies (and hasn't for some time). In town and country alike different times and speeds occur concurrently and conjointly. In some respects the country would seem to be far more dynamic than the town; towns appear to be straitjacketed in history and cultural values, whilst in the country there is room for innovation.

Social mobility: identity and involvement

The country is still associated with farms and villages, inhabited by one generation after another. This is a situation that has been rapidly changing in the past decades. Yet there are great differences between rural areas based on differences in land ownership and succession. Hoeksche Waard has always been a highly dynamic region, socially speaking, with tenant farmers. So one wonders how the arrival of new residents has influenced these dynamics. The suburbanite forms the landscape according to his expectations and 'freezes' it.

The artists participating in the event spotlighted these different aspects of the area's dynamics. Some would seem to embrace unashamedly the principle of 'spot your spot' (Jan Konings and Ester van de Wiel, for instance), whilst others literally map out the resolution of the differences between town and country (Schie 2.0). Some indicate the tremendous urge for change with which the original landscape is transformed (John Davies, Ad van Denderen), but the small changes with which nature and landscape are appropriated are also pinpointed (Wijnanda Deroo, Birthe Leemeijer). 'Resistance' is reflected in Hans van Houwelingen's film and Mark Pimlott's film, and Bertien van Manen's photographs present the different 'times'. The designers are less clear about the role played by the themes in question. Sijmons and Feddes provide a framework in which agriculture continues to be the mainstay of the area, but with new dynamics, seeking to tie in with the scale of the entire world as well as that of the new regional market. Dettmar and company strive towards a sustainable relationship between city and surroundings with their 'suburban' ecotopia. Palmboom and Van den Bout allocate different spaces to the different speeds in the area. Calthorpe and Taecker seek to circumscribe the city once and for all, but sketches pictures of a suburban reality. Bindels and colleagues create a spatial and organizational frame in which town and country can evolve further into a differentiated urban field. Timmermans opts for fragmentation as a means of achieving greater diversity between landscapes. In her set-up, the city-dweller is the farmer's guest. Boeri sees urbanization of the countryside as a connected network of villages, differentiated according to amenities. And lastly Roche envisages the transformation of the landscape as a 'mutation', in which the landscape is literally cut open in order to absorb urbanization.

Purpose and pleasure

Regardless of all the differences, the Dutch contributions in turn differ distinctly from the non-Dutch. That is due to a difference in attitude towards the landscape, apparent in the terms in which the proposals are presented. François Roche uses metaphors familiar to all French intellectuals. You can choose between two complexes – one linked with war and the other with the body and eroticism. One complex entails manoeuvres, strategies and tactics, the other implies seduction, sensuality and ecstasy. Many French texts about cities refer to the city's erogenous zones, merely meaning squares and parks, the meeting-places of the city. In fact, on reflection, that urban eroticism could be worse (or better, if you like) and the same applies for the militant language in the war metaphor. Still, there is a pronounced difference in the terms in which the Dutch, and then the German, Italian, French and American proposals are couched. The foreigners touch on a stratum which Dutch landscape architects and urbanists do not dare to address. François Roche uses the comparison with war and with sexuality. He describes the town as evolving from a fortress (with the landscape as a field of battle or fire) to an open city and a landscape, like a body that 'transmutes'.

The landscape architect Alle Hosper, in an interview given shortly before his untimely death, explained to me that the Dutch landscape came about in three stages. First there was land-making and water control (get dry feet first); the next stage (that of purpose) focused on making the hard-won or hard-preserved land productive; the third stage is that of pleasure: when the other two have been settled, parts of the land can be allocated purely for pleasure, a farm becomes a pleasure garden, walks and parks are laid out. We have never really become familiar with that third stage in the Netherlands. The beauty of the countryside or town is usually subservient to something else. Leisure serves labour, nature serves education. Repose and inaction are not positive-sounding words in Dutch. Most topics, in keeping with this tradition, concentrate on the first two stages: water and infrastructure forming the framework for 'occupation' of the area. Then, the occasional hint of pleasure, of delight.

However, the landscape of the Dutch delta can no longer cope with competition from other regions in Europe purely at the 'useful' level. The scenic attractions of northern Italy or south-east England are important factors in settlement as such. Most plans for AIR-Zuidwaarts/Southbound also contain proposals of that tenor, but are modest and tend to relate to pleasure rather than delight. François Roche may augment the sensuality of the landscape with curves and openings, but Marieke Timmermans arranges it in a different way, admittedly as a garden, but a garden with a useful purpose. The pleasure experienced from the landscape is that of a day out at a farm, helping to till the land and care for the animals. Marieke Timmermans's landscape is decidedly pastoral, a landscape of restrained delight. True, there are sterner proposals from the Dutch contingent, while Calthorpe's idyll is one of the 'almost perfect small American town.' I recommend assessing the various proposals for their contributions towards shaping what is for Dutch designers (and administrators) the terra incognita of delight.

Effectiveness

The capacity to seduce might well be the most important force in the feasibility of the proposals. In fact, instead of constantly wondering whether something is feasible, it would be better to ask what effects the plans have. This wording is deliberately vague: more precise study is needed into the instruments advanced in the plan (how it works) and what it generates (its outcome) in the discussions on Hoeksche Waard, and in a wider context on how we deal with town and country, with urbanity, landscape and rurality.

1. See: Adri Dietvorst, 'De tijd-ruimtelijke onteigening van het toeristische landschap', in: 'Vrijetijdsstudies' no. 15 1997 and John Urry, 'Nature as Countryside', in: Phil Macnaghten and John Urry, 'Contested Natures', Sage Publications London 1998

Gallery with Nina Folkersma, recording the minutes, Manja Ellenbroek, Craigie Horsfield and Rutger Wolfson

Han Meyer, Mrs Sieverts, Thomas Sieverts. Willy Spaan is sitting behind Han Meyer

Observers: Eric Luiten, Sjoerd Cusveller, Michelle Provoost and Luuk Boelens (not in the photo). In the background: Bert van Meggelen

Paul Shephaerd

John Urry

Krijn Jan Provoost, Jo Kolf and Joop van Riet

Stefano Boeri

Edzo Bindels, Henk Hartzema and Peter Calthorpe

François Perrin and François Roche

Frits Palmboom and Yttje Feddes

Jörg Dettmar and Harald Fritz. In the back Lucas Verweij

Joost Grootens and Mark Pimlott

The International Conference, October 1998

AIR-ZUIDWAARTS / SOUTHBOUND	INTRODUCTION	PROGRAMME	RESEARCH	DESIGN TASK	DESIGN RESEARCH	AFTERTHOUGHTS	APPENDIX
	WYTZE PATIJN ADRIAAN VAN DER STAAY MIRJAM SALET	ANNE-MIE DEVOLDER	VISUAL RESEARCH JOHN DAVIES HET OBSERVATORIUM MARK PIMLOTT SCHIE 2.0 HENRIK HÅKANSSON AD VAN DENDEREN WIJNANDA DEROO BERTIEN VAN MANEN HANS VAN HOUWELINGEN BIRTHE LEEMEIJER JOOST GROOTENS JAN KONINGS/ESTER VAN DE WIEL HONORÉ δ'O ANTHROPOLOGICAL RESEARCH HENK DE HAAN PHYSICAL PLANNING RESEARCH SJOERD CUSVELLER	SJOERD CUSVELLER/ ANNE-MIE DEVOLDER	FRITS PALMBOOM/JAAP VAN DEN BOUT PETER CALTHORPE/MATTHEW TAECKER STEFANO BOERI FRANÇOIS ROCHE DETTMAR/BEUTER/FRITZ/HASTENPFLUG BINDELS/GIETEMA/HARTZEMA/KLOK MARIEKE TIMMERMANS DIRK SIJMONS/YTTJE FEDDES	ARNOLD REIJNDORP BROESI/JANNINK/VELDHUIS ERIC LUITEN	CHRONICLE PERSONAL PARTICULARS PERSONS INVOLVED COLOPHON

Snapshot or sequence?

A horrifying story is circulating among geologists. This story is based on developments beyond human control, developments deep in the earth. Every year the African continent is shifting a few centimetres to the north, pressing parts of Europe together and northwards. As a result of this pushing-up Europe will split into two parts. This cleft runs from Basel by way of the course of the Rhine towards Cologne and from there in a north-westerly direction clear across the Netherlands. Whatever happens, the message is clear enough: spatial planning is not determined by man alone. One day primal forces will assert themselves, as nature strikes back.

The tension between human influence on the one hand, and dealing with nature and landscape on the other is not just a subject for the distant future. The river floods in the nineties and the forecasts about the rise in sea-level once again confront us with nature's influence. Infected pigs, mad cows and diminishing subsidies for farmers will lead to major changes in agriculture and landscape. At the same time the influence of the city will increasingly spread over the Netherlands. This combination of developments has instigated a fundamental debate in the world of spatial planning, its key question being: how are we to deal with the way the Netherlands is physically changing and being used?

A number of specialists in spatial planning feel that the classical twin concept of 'city' and 'countryside' is inadequate and too simple to get a grip on the current planning transformation. They focused on this hypothesis at the international AIR conference in October 1998. Taking Hoeksche Waard as an example the discussion on the desired future relationship between city and countryside was fuelled from various vantage points and marked by divergent interests, processes and ways of thinking. The many isolated aspects introduced by the different participants made it clear that city and countryside have lost their univocal meaning: spatial planning can be unfolded in many ways.

Eight designs have been made for the occasion of AIR-Zuidwaarts/Southbound. They show, whether deliberately or not, five approaches to interpreting and tackling spatial planning. The different approaches are to be characterized in the form of film titles: 'The Good, the Bad and the Ugly', 'Speed', 'The Net', 'Gulliver's Travels' and 'Paris-Texas'. Each approach presents different choices, possibilities and issues. Together they reveal the layeredness of spatial planning in the Netherlands. But the proposals go further than that. With Hoeksche Waard as exemplar, they explicitly raise the issue fundamental to the Netherlands: in what sort of environment do we want to live? And expanding this, they ask almost casually: what (democratic) system do we wish to adopt to achieve it? An initial reconnaissance follows.

The good, the bad and the ugly

Suppose we define city and countryside as two clearly distinct areas, as built environment and open landscape. In that case physical patterns should be clearly separable, and boundaries easy to read as a result. In this approach the open space requires functions that can resist the city. New forms of recreation, new agriculture and new nature are some of the major ingredients with which to combat advancing urbanization. At the same time existing urban areas will have to be further intensified. This response can be identified in various of the proposals.

Peter Calthorpe brings up the contrast between new landscapes and cores of urbanization. In his proposal the island of IJsselmonde is further urbanized so that the city boundary will advance only to the Oude Maas River. In Hoeksche Waard expansions will take place on the outskirts of existing villages. Distinct village edges mark the boundary with the countryside. This countryside is made more efficient by having it perform a function in the storage of surplus river water. Other regions are used for cultivating high-quality foodstuffs. Stefano Boeri brings up the contrast between 'open' and 'closed' by the strategy of ribbon development. The expansion of the building programme takes place along the dikes. Each dike will get its own theme, for instance through a concentration of schools, retail trade or facilities. The space between the ribbons will remain open; the use of this space is not defined. Jörg Dettmar protects open spaces by designating them as taboo areas. Examples include the Green Heart, the Biesbos and the delta south of Haringvliet. Hoeksche Waard does not fall into this category. New, sustainable urbanization is permitted here, provided that it follows the characteristic linear structure of dikes, ditches and rows of trees.

'The good, the bad and the ugly' put the physical appearance first and foremost. In this approach the relationship between city and countryside is a relationship between 'the good' and 'the bad', where it is not quite clear which is which. But undoubtedly any intermediate form will be 'the ugly'. From this position there are only two options left for Hoeksche Waard: it will either become the urban expansion island of the city of Rotterdam or it can choose to be part of the rural Zeeland delta. From the designs it can be deduced that the present form of the island as a whole has little bearing on its physical characteristics. The dikes in particular are visually defining elements: the space in-between can be made either urban or rural.

Speed

Suppose that the relationship between city and countryside cannot be seen as separate from the physical networks connecting the various places. It could be very productive then to try and utilize these networks positively in order to create new planning conditions. According to some design proposals urban areas and rural areas are linked with various systems. The landscape in the Netherlands is largely dependent on the water management and the changes in it. The city for its part is inextricably linked with large-scale infrastructures, such as railways, highways and waterways.

Nearly all the proposals pick up on the assumed future problems in the water management of the delta. Frits Palmboom and Jaap van de Bout use the water system of the delta and the car infrastructure as the major instruments of control: in their approach interventions in water and infrastructure condition new landscapes and cities. Dirk Sijmons and Ietje Feddes have designed a water machine and so have created the conditions for new nature and innovative agricultural production. Edzo Bindels, Ruurd Gietema, Henk Hartzema and Arjan Klok propose among other things to instigate the project 'Delta 2.0': the freshwater and salt-water tidal system is revived, the Delta-works are brought up to date and the water management is reorganized. As an urban counterpart Bindels c.s. present their Diamond City project. There the large-scale infrastructure around Rotterdam is utilized for a huge compacting operation. Particularly transfer and distribution activities, offices and warehouses get a place in Diamond City. These designers propose a minimum of new infrastructure. Marieke Timmermans trebles the capacity of the A29 in Hoeksche Waard so that this road can start to function as a collector: a road into which the agrarian road network is directly linked.

'Speed' stresses the importance of larger systems that monopolize space. In fact the landscape imposes its will just as much as the city does and fights with the same calibre of weapon: large-scale systems. A major vision emerging here is that it is not only the physical appearance of city and countryside that is important, but most especially the underlying processes. Not the image but the conditions are of central interest.

It is striking that the car infrastructure in particular seems to present a more clever use of the existing network supplemented by the upgrading or addition of a regional road. Much more drastic is the impact of the water. The larger peak drainages of the rivers and the dynamics of the tides will demand an ever-expanding role in spatial planning. The dynamics of the delta are evident and inescapable for the future transformation of Hoeksche Waard. The designs comprise many like-minded proposals that vigorously capitalize on this fact.

The Net

If the spatial planning of the Netherlands is strongly influenced by the continuing developments of telecommunication and mobility, then we can assume that concepts like city and countryside will become less relevant. The world of the Internet links the private house to the entire world. Living, working and leisure come together in the individual plot. In fact only the scale of the private dwelling and its immediate environment matter, since the rest of the world can be simulated virtually. These simulations change the way in which we experience the world and use space. The fact is, though, that they remain limited to a projection on a screen or from a beamer.

In François Roche's proposal the merging of city and countryside gets a literal translation into the physical world. By folding the landscape upwards, houses can be tucked under it. Thus the sharp boundaries between city and countryside dissolve, at least this is what is suggested visually. Marieke Timmermans is another to construct a narrative in which the boundaries between urban and rural melt. According to her proposal it is possible to so dilute the housing task that it disappears from sight altogether. That is, on a map with a scale of 1:1,500,000.

In 'The Net' the polarization between city and countryside is removed and replaced by a hybrid of city and landscape. At first sight little has changed, but on closer examination city and landscape have melded into a new mutant. In this space housing density may vary from very high to extremely low. For those who prefer Hoeksche Waard as a residential environment it is important that its character is retained in spite of the large increase in the number of dwellings. From a visual point of view the strategies of both Roche and Timmermans comply with this. Both designs issue from a thinking based on the possibilities offered by telecommunication. This technology can be plugged in anywhere: in the city, in the countryside, in the car and in the train. Roche and Timmermans show that concepts such as accessibility and public character can be extended to a world that can no longer be grasped in purely physical terms. In proposals like these the use of space and the way in which we experience it are uppermost.

Gulliver's Travels

If our perception of the environment takes in ever-larger areas, then the definition of city and countryside largely depends on the scale adopted by the viewer. Do we take the district, the city, the region, the country or the world as a perspective? This perspective to a great extent determines the scale at which we wish to intervene, as well as where we look for the characteristics and what measurements we adopt for urban and landscape units. Consequently, balancing on the interface of city and countryside also implies balancing between different scales. On what scale should we aspire to large-scale, univocal planning? And on what scale should we pursue the maximum of variation and difference? The designs illustrate the various possibilities.

Stefano Boeri shows that Hoeksche Waard as one of the Gardens of Europe can be planned homogeneously and univocally. Thus it could acquire significance at a European level. Dettmar, on the other hand, argues that Hoeksche Waard as Garden of Rotterdam will need to offer a great diversity of recreational environments for the city. Bindels c.s. propose formulating the commission at the scale of the entire delta. Marieke Timmermans, on the other hand, firmly believes in the scale of the individual lot, and in Peter Calthorpe's opinion we can define a critical size for villages.

Each design explicitly opts for positioning Hoeksche Waard within a specific scale. At all events they place local identities in a force field that transcends Hoeksche Waard, the delta, or even the Netherlands. Jointly, the designs indicate that the relationship between city and countryside plays a role at every scale. Thus it has become clear that Hoeksche Waard will also have to make a choice. Is it an island, is it part of the Zeeland delta, is it an overspill area for Rotterdam, or is it the expansion tank of Zuid-Holland? At the same time the designs show that the future of Hoeksche Waard will be determined just as much by decisions at a local level as those made at the scale of the delta as a whole.

Paris-Texas

If urbanism has to do with multiplicity and if rurality could be defined as univocal, then we can make a distinction between urban and rural transformation strategies. Multiplicity means that a place is complex because it has many different meanings. It can be fed by confronting slow, natural systems (for instance, waterways and nature reserves) with fast, urban functions such as highways or forms of mass recreation. Convergence of the macro scale and the local scale at a given place contributes to its complexity. And when different times converge there, since it is anchored in the past as well as in the present, its ambiguity increases. Rurality is the opposite extreme. Rural places or regions are characterized by the presence of either exclusively natural systems or exclusively urban use forms. They appear to be either exclusively large-scale or exclusively small-scale. And their meaning is either very recent or only exists in the past. These definitions of rurality and urbanism imply that both may occur in the city as well as in the countryside. When the sun is shining, the beach of Zandvoort is one of the most urban of areas. And the VINEX housing developments are possibly the most rural areas in the Netherlands.

Most of the designs done for AIR-Zuidwaarts/Southbound can be characterized as strategies. They make a strict separation between regions that are part either of nature or of the city or the countryside. An exception is the 'aire' in the proposal of Sijmons and Feddes, where a direct link is made between the world of the highway and the world of the landscape. This is even more the case in the crossovers in the scheme of Bindels c.s. They deliberately insert these junctions between different worlds in the dynamic delta as departure-points for design interventions.

The plans make it clear that Hoeksche Waard encourages both rural and urban strategies. The large-scale, univocal tasks such as that of the water, require powerful and unequivocal government interventions. On the other hand, true multiple strategies can only be achieved by bringing together parties with divergent interests. A promising impulse to such a strategic coalition was given by Bindels c.s. with the Golden Delta consortium. Creating a development company like Golden Delta is not the obvious course to take. Our spatial planning system works in such a way that various layers and scales are separated from one another. At present, the responsibilities for the water system, infrastructure, agriculture and urbanization are neatly divided among the various departments. The government, the provinces and the municipalities each take care of a specific scale. Private parties are expected to keep to the execution phase.

In the Dutch context, creating the condition for urbanism requires a great effort in the form of complex negotiation proceedings between private initiators, the population and the authorities. And most of all this means being aware of the different durations that natural and urban systems have.

Snapshot or sequence?

At the close of the conference in October 1998, with the stating of the design brief, a number of designers made negative noises about the 'empty programme'. They thought they had not been given enough to go on. In spite of this the designs have yielded a wealth of results. Together they show how spatial planning is to be unravelled into a physical world, a world of nodes and networks, a virtual world, and into various scales. Each of these worlds presents its own task. The condition for urbanism arises at the moment when these worlds are made to converge.

Initiatives like AIR-Zuidwaarts/Southbound make it possible to develop such insights. They play an important part in cultivating our knowledge of spatial planning, because they offer the opportunity to reflect on topical commissions without one-sided interests prevailing. Initiatives like AIR-Zuidwaarts/Southbound thus adopt an essentially different attitude towards the role played by public and private developers in spatial planning. These clients are strongly oriented towards developing plans as part of a continuous design-and-build planning process.

The existence of initiatives contributing to the free development of knowledge on the one hand, and the formal clients on the other, raises the question of how these two relate. At the final symposium at the NAi Joost Schrijnen formulated this as follows: 'To whom are the proposals of AIR-Zuidwaarts/Southbound addressed? How can we convert the developed ideas into successful practice?' The answer to these questions will show whether AIR-Zuidwaarts/Southbound is a superb snapshot, or will develop into a challenging sequence.

AFTERTHOUGHTS
ARNOLD REIJNDORP
BROESI/JANNINK/VELDHUIS
ERIC LUITEN

Was signed: Hoeksche Waard
The region as a planning experiment

AIR-Zuidwaarts/Southbound was a well-organized and much enjoyed event, which primarily focused on the future of the isle of Hoeksche Waard in the Zuid-Holland part of the delta. Over a period of two years the area's qualities have been opened up along four lines, viz. the line of cultural anthropological research, the line of artistic interpretation, the line of historical planning and the line of regional planning. This essay deals with the results, effects and significance of the third line.

Eight design groups from in and out of the Netherlands went to Hoeksche Waard armed with the same design task, to outline the future the island should have. The brief made three demands on the designers. First, to demonstrate the as yet unexploited possibilities of the rural area as a place to live and work – the rural complement of such compact cities as Antwerp and Rotterdam. Second, to state their opinions on the compatibility and adjustability of supra-local needs and requirements in agriculture, natural development, water management, new companies, traffic and transport. Finally, they were challenged to try to operationalize the area's regional identity in the design. They were asked, while drawing and reasoning, not only to study the opportunities and limitations of Hoeksche Waard as an urban landscape, but also to trace the *genius regionis*.

The plans

An initial assessment of the eight designs shows that not all designers have complied with the instructions. It is no coincidence that the architects Boeri and Roche have done no more than present new construction types and suggest new residential patterns. Their designs do not answer the complex planning questions, but rather demonstrate in detail which residential and working provisions might be introduced in this lush, flat country with its dikes. The two explicitly enter into the landscape legitimacy of a spread urbanization. Boeri's specialized residential ribbons indicate that he wants to continue, what he calls, Hoeksche Waard's 'genetic code'. Roche designs semi-underground hamlets, which at most become manifest as clay folds. The designs by Calthorpe, Dettmar and Timmermans are much more integrated, but not very tolerant. For all three are based on professional concern for the macro-ecological and landscape effects of Western civilization. Their contributions to AIR-Zuidwaarts/Southbound all start with a strongly worded appeal for a new mode of town and country planning. All three advocate critical reflection on agricultural overproduction, consumption of natural resources and individual car use, all of which tax the environment. They also advocate a single ideal model for rural land-use and prescribe a single behavioural pattern that is to be optimal in socio-economical terms. Their spatial engineering thus contains a large amount of social engineering. Yet, this more or less universal concern for the sustainably disrupted residential environment of the Hoeksche topography has quite varying results. Calthorpe and Dettmar support one another in the introduction of the urban-regional mean scale, in which densely populated city and thinly populated rural area may complement one another. In that respect Dettmar proclaims Hoeksche Waard as the Garden of Rotterdam. Calthorpe draws a firm line between red and green along the Oude Maas river. He is in favour of implosion and differentiation north of that border and self-sufficient residential and working communities south of it.

Timmermans's design illustrates in particular the abundantly producing, self-explaining landscape, which she regards as ideal. One single agricultural idyll at the scale of the entire area is enough for a colourful patchwork at the scale of the farm. There is no mean scale in this design. It is a scale-less topographical prescription.

In contrast to this rural morality planning Sijmons and Feddes, Palmboom and Van den Bout and the Bindels, Gietema, Hartzema and Klok collective do not begrudge one another a place in the regional sun. Sijmons comes up with the most complete, mechanized and exact design. We learn to look at Hoeksche Waard as a machine that is currently not very well tuned and we get to know spatial planning as a series of inventions. The design strongly emphasizes improvement of regional water management as a prerequisite for agricultural development, nature and living. Three agricultural scenarios demonstrate how Hoeksche Waard farmers may escape their subsidized fate. Palmboom and Van den Bout break through the generic formulas of spatial plans and replace them with a region-specific planning matrix. The matrix classifications are the result of the sensitive abstraction and grouping of spatial processes that actually occur or are anticipated in the planning area. The design presents a key to 'spatial agogics' rather than a spatial design. It is less a matter of whether all forms of zoning, planning and management have been covered than of what the regional or supra-regional authorities want these agogics

AIR-ZUIDWAARTS / SOUTHBOUND

AFTERTHOUGHTS
ARNOLD REIJNDORP
BROESI/JANNINK/VELDHUIS
ERIC LUITEN

to be – that is to say, in whose name regulation and control will be exercised. Bindels, Gietema, Hartzema and Klok have managed to solve this problem. In their opinion the region will develop most progressively under the 'Golden Delta Development Society', a risk-bearing agglomerate of various authorities and private parties with investment obligations. They act against the prevailing 'do's and don'ts'-planning, against risk-avoiding behaviour and landscape alienation. The design outlines a polemic balance between what is necessary and what is possible. What is necessary is a planning revision of – again – water management. Reintroduction of hydraulic dynamics, typical of the delta, is the challenging basis for undirected colonization by adventurous Western Europeans with lots of leisure time. The only rule private parties have been given, is that they are to act in alliance with other, potentially affected, parties or individuals. Natural residency, which might be activated on the basis of these starting-points has, as it were, been catalogued instead of designed by the architects. They believe that in the 'Golden Delta' free state there is no such thing as a regional architect, a planning department or a building inspectorate.

Balance AIR-Zuidwaarts/Southbound

This rich range of planning reflections, proposals and recommendations has been received with some reserve by Hoeksche Waard population. There was scepticism from the word go. They thought AIR-Zuidwaarts/Southbound had been dreamed up by the Province of Zuid-Holland and the City of Rotterdam, who together, clad in cultural camouflage suits, were seeking to prepare the region for urbanization. After three AIR magazines, artistic activity, anthropological research and provisional design demonstrations and discussion meetings in the villages, opinion on the event gradually became more favourable. However, the leap across the Oude Maas river has never really been two-way in the past couple of years. Few islanders attended the public meetings of the designers or the discussions of their designs in the Netherlands Architecture Institute. So a group of Hoeksche Waard dwellers decided to enlist international expertise for free, inviting these experts to the island in autumn 1999 and getting them to discuss Hoeksche Waard's future with pressure groups in a number of sessions.

For one of the most important of AIR-Zuidwaarts/Southbound's effects is reflection on the island's potential as a geographical entity. This has made it clear once more that the island's municipalities can only make a planning stand against the regional plans of the Provincial Authorities and the City of Rotterdam's structure plans, if they succeed in planning space on the same scale as their opponents, that is to say, intermunicipally. The eight designers take up widely varying positions on spatial design as a planning instrument. There are designs with scenario features, with radical or poetical purport but also with concrete organization programmes. However, all designers implicitly point out that planning for Hoeksche Waard can only be derived from a design for the island as an entity. Landscape borders, on which all eight designs have been based, would for once have to coincide with administrative borders.

Such an exercise evokes tension in each region, for cooperation does not only mean putting together energy and resources, but also subordinating an area's ambitions to a greater collective goal. Attempts to use land more efficiently and differentially are usually at the expense of efforts to achieve a complete package of provisions on the individual, municipal level. Peter Calthorpe has probably best felt this tension when he launched his ideal model of a self-supporting Hoeksche Waard, but he immediately declared it applicable to every village community. The islanders will do well to carefully examine all designs and assess them on their balance between local sentiment and regional persuasion.

Conversely, the provincial and city planners might well ask themselves on what scale and with what instruments they will operate most effectively. Recent introduction of such policy concepts as police regions, transport regions and eco-regions has left reflection on regional spatial planning dangling. An as yet ill-founded preference has emerged for the region as an ideal planning scale, as the level at which any demand, possibility or complaint might receive harmonious consideration. This regional fascination may be partly explained by a landscape differentiation which our country demonstrates at exactly that scale. However, we must realize that this differentiation results from a series of factors that in the past determined the Netherlands' cultivation and became significant on the scale of the landscape regions (wind-borne sand areas, peat meadows, seapolders, peat cultivation, etc). These factors no longer apply today.

The region as an intermediary is, in the light of the current and future spatial efforts, a panacea. Some of the eight designers effectively illustrate this, other badly neglect it. Spatial planning and engineering has become the art of balancing between the virtual, the (inter)national and the local, especially in urbanized regions such as the Randstad's outer reaches. Confrontation becomes visible in the landscape. Agriculture, transport policy, river management have been based on multinational criteria and agreements. This is in stark contrast with the increasing individualization that is enveloping the desire for living comfort and recreation. Concern for nature is global, but in a country like the Netherlands it gradually threatens to disintegrate with so many different owners and/or professional managing organizations. It is no longer a matter of keeping up a regional unity of action which may bridge such breaks in scale, even if Palmboom and Van den Bout's contribution is a reconciliatory but predominantly rhetorical effort in that direction.

There is no regional authority that covers all relevant spatial processes. Rather than solve or harmonize the discrepancy between the various rationalities operative, it is more important to visualize the discrepancy, controversies and paradoxes in the cultivated landscape. As to the dimension of regional planning, the design by Bindels, Gietema, Hartzema and Klok will probably be the most significant for us.

AIR-Zuidwaarts/Southbound has more to say about spatial planning. The eight designers are predominantly critical of the usual coordination and coincidence of spatial targets. In Hoeksche Waard they have looked for a significant distinction between dominant and consequent spatial processes or they explicitly suggest the ideal sequence of policy-making and acting. Attention is drawn to a division between responsibilities for various priorities, competencies and terms. Sijmons and Feddes' design is the most consistent in this respect. They believe that sophisticated water management is a key condition for any rural renovation and that agriculture will be the first discipline to present its list of demands. Other conditions and spatial users are only slightly less important. Such preferential treatment is unheard of in Dutch spatial planning, which is there for everyone. However, it may well be asked whether the latter attitude gives the best results. History teaches that maximalization of a single objective has yielded the clearest, most powerful and best-known city tissues and landscape patterns. An unambiguous spatial basis allows for a variety of activities and applications without loss of character. Hoeksche Waard is no exception to this rule.

This fascination with the organization of surface water is also prominent in other designs, which hopefully indicates a revival of topography in spatial planning. For years we have had to be content with abstract collages of smudges, spheres and arrows, especially if the design concerned supra-local ambitions. For decades spatial planning has been dominated by programmes and surface claims, which, helped along by imploring formulas and cartographic tricks, had to be balanced against other claims. That approach left no space for local developments, attention to hidden qualities or to coincidence. Spatial planning considers urban expansion as a growing red spot, not as a collective heightening of urban culture or the cultivating of attractive countryside for residential purposes. The fact that spatial planning embraces water management is an important first step towards a situation in which the balance between the social space-demand and the landscape burden has been restored.

Restriction

This brings us to a final instructive signal that may be inferred from the eight designs. Practically all the designers have struggled with the degree in which the developments proposed by them needed submitting to rules and restrictions. Particularly the design by Bindels, Gietema, Hartzema and Klok, but also the architectural tactics of Boeri and Roche and, to a certain extent, Calthorpe's proposal indicate the need for some form of restriction. It all boils down to that fatal mechanism whereby practically every exploitation of a specific quality leads to its destruction. Spatial planning might benefit from the introduction of feedback systems, such as those that stabilize the hormone and energy supply of mankind and animals. We need spatial concepts that carry such self-correcting elements, especially at the regional scale. Just concepts based on reaching a dynamic balance between a spatial programme on the one hand and substrate qualities on the other. This may well be a new basis for a closer relationship between urban planning as a discipline with a design approach based more on programme criteria, and landscape architecture as a profession that concentrates more on the possibilities and limitations of substrate topography.

AIR-ZUIDWAARTS / SOUTHBOUND

APPENDIX

CHRONICLE
PERSONAL PARTICULARS
PERSONS INVOLVED
COLOPHON

A Chronicle of AIR

Architecture International Rotterdam (AIR) initiates the debate on the architectonic and urban-planning developments of the contemporary city, communicates visions of designers to administrators, commissioners and public, stimulates the quality of architecture and urban development, is critical, informs, polemizes and increases interest in architecture, urban development and landscape architecture. A chronicle of the manifestations so far.

1979: Keurmeestersproject
In 1979 the architecture section of the Rotterdam Arts Council took the initiative for the organization of an architecture and urban development manifestation on the theme 'The image of the city'. With the so-called Keurmeestersproject (Sampler Project) alliance was sought with the international architectonic debate and some major speakers in Dutch architectonic culture were involved. In the 'Keurmeestersproject' architecture critics Stanislaus von Moos from Switzerland, Kenneth Frampton from England and Francisco Dal Co from Italy were asked to select the three best and three worst Rotterdam buildings from a list of twenty. Their findings were presented in a public debate.

1982: The Kop van Zuid
Oswald Mattheus Ungers, Josef Kleihues, Derek Walker and Aldo Rossi were invited to make designs for the harbour and industrial district on the south bank, the so-called 'Kop van Zuid' (The Soutern Tip), which was passing into disuse. At the same time they were asked to investigate the significance of the district for the city as a whole. The urban design practice, which before this date had hardly looked beyond the projects themselves, considered this approach worth following. Furthermore, this manifestation was a forerunner with the explicit question of deliberately putting in the seductive quality of architecture – the image production – so as to open up new perspectives and bring architecture under the attention of a wider public. The outcome as well as the public discussion on this issue influenced the eventual planning for the region. Rotterdam abandoned the original layout in order to use this district as overspill area for the surrounding urban renewal districts.

Design for the Kop van Zuid, Aldo Rossi 1982

1984: Japan-Air
The work of e.g. Arata Isozaki, Itsuko Hasegawa, Shoei Yoh and Toyo Ito was first introduced in the Netherlands. During this manifestation with exhibitions, design workshops by Japanese architects, publications and lectures the municipality of Rotterdam made the old library available to the Dutch government for the establishment of the later Netherlands Architecture Institute.

1986: Iberia-Air
introduced the work of young Spanish architects who had realized innovating projects in the Netherlands after the Franco period. Among other things, there were an exhibition, lectures and publications on the projects realized by Jaume Bach and Gabriel, José Rafael Moneo, Josep Mateo. The manifestation stimulated the debate on the quality of the layout of public space in Rotterdam.

1988: Rail Tunnel Track, Nine Designs
AIR asked the nine architects Wiel Arets with Wim van den Bergh, Peter Wilson, Bernard Tschumi, Joan Busquets, Henri Ciriani, Andreas Brandt, Cecile Balmond, Rem Koolhaas (OMA) and Pirluigi Nicolin to make designs for the Rail tunnel track that was to fall vacant in 1994. They were asked to make statements on the coherence between the town districts along the three-kilometre-long ribbon extending from the inner city in North, across Noordereiland and Feijenoord to the so-called railway triangle in South. Once again the designs functioned as catalysts in the discussion on the urban development plan for the area along the Binnenrotte, the cross-river connections between North and South and last but not least for the railway bridge 'de Hef', threatened with demolition at that time.

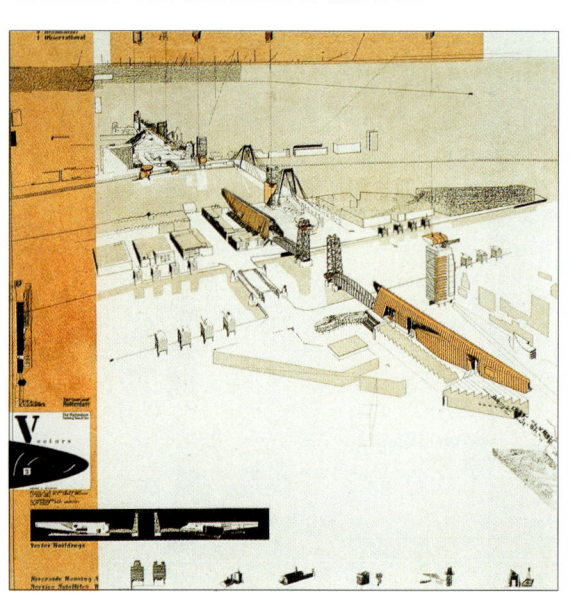

Design for Rail Tunnel Track, Peter Wilson 1988

1993: Air Alexander, New Urban Frontiers

The manifestation focused attention on the position and meaning taken up by the post-war residential districts in the city of Rotterdam and the social and cultural changes taking place there. Design commissions for the Alexanderpolder went to Rem Koolhaas (OMA), Robert Geddes, Manuel de Solà-Morales, Endry van Velzen, Adriaan Geuze, Wolfgang Engel with Klaus Zillich. The manifestation clarified the consequences of planning decisions for building projects crossing the municipal boundaries, in which the urban development plan on the central scale played an important part. New concepts were introduced for the urbanization commission as a response to the insidious pollution of the Green Heart. These views influenced the national debate. The culture of the districts was involved in that of the city.

In the course of time AIR as an independent outsider, unimpeded by practical obstacles, started off the discussion on the physical planning of Rotterdam and the region. AIR analyses spatial problems and new commissions. On the basis of this, commissions were given to architects, landscape architects and urban planners for concrete locations. The designs brought to light the spatial potential of these areas, as became apparent in the old harbour district, the public space and the periphery of the city. The adopted srategy proved to be applicable on the scale of the city and the region, and even resulted in views that were practicable on a national level. The manifestations introduced new ways and forms to visualize urban development plans, so that policymakers and public acquired more insight into them. Since 1993 the set-up of AIR has been interdisciplinary. The exchange of visions and ideas between various forms of art does not only make the designs more profound, but also interests a wider public for parts and results of the manifestation.

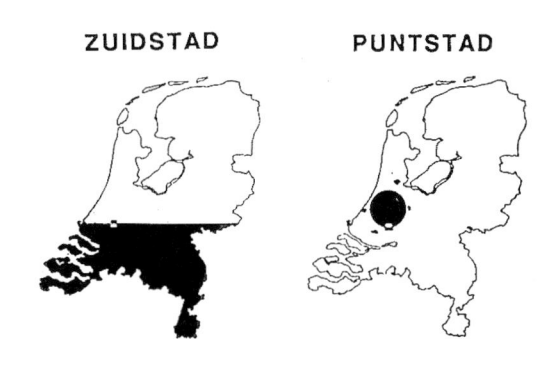

Study for AIR-Alexander, Rem Koolhaas 1993

1998-1999 AIR-Zuidwaarts/Southbound

In 1998 the Rotterdam Arts Council established AIR for the organization of manifestations in the field of architecture, urban development, landscape architecture and design, and notably the manifestation Architecture International Rotterdam several times a year. AIR-Zuidwaarts/Southbound has taken place from September 1998 through July 1999 on various locations in Rotterdam and Hoeksche Waard. The theme was the physical planning of the south wing of the Randstad and of the delta between Rotterdam and Antwerp. The manifestation particularly focused on the island of Hoeksche Waard, situated to the south of Rotterdam, a predominantly agrarian area where the pressure of urbanization is palpable. The island forms the link between the urbanized landscape of the island of IJsselmonde and the open landscape of the province of Zeeland consisting of large expanses of water, wide polders and low horizons. The investigation commission given to artists, photographers, designers and scientists, and the design commission within the framework of AIR-Zuidwaarts/Southbound was inspired by the current discussion on the steadily expanding city, the shrinking coun-try-side and the large-scale changes in the field of agriculture, recreation, nature conservation and water management, traffic and transport.

The urban planners and landscape architects invited were: Frits Palmboom and Jaap van den Bout with Stefano Boeri (Italy), Dirk Sijmons and Yttje Feddes with Jörg Dettmar, Ulrike Beuter and Harald Fritz (Germany), Marieke Timmermans with François Roche (France), Edo Bindels, Henk Hartzema, Ruud Gietema and Arjan Klok with Peter Calthorpe, Matthew Taecker and David Katz (USA). They developed visions, concepts and strategies for the physical planning of the area between Rotterdam and Antwerp, the south wing of the Randstad and in particular the island of Hoeksche Waard situated to the south of Rotterdam.

AIR-Zuidwaarts/Southbound presented a platform for research, design, debate and new concepts, in which attention was focused on a synthesis between new functions and the cultural-historical and scenic values of the rural area. AIR-Zuidwaarts/Southbound was seeking for international visions on the present European problem of city-countryside, which create a new synthesis between urbanization, mobility, agriculture, nature conservation and water management.

Personal particulars

STEFANO BOERI (I) has his practice 'Stefano Boeri Architetto' in Milan. He is interested in the issues of representation and interpretation of contemporary outlying regions. In particular he analyzes the spatial patterns and processes in the peripheries of European metropoles in cooperation with artists. Boeri works out concrete urban-planning and architectural proposals for the city centres and harbour districts of e.g. Genoa and Naples. Apart from that he is a teacher at the University of Milan, Genoa and the Berlage Institute in Amsterdam.

ROBERT BROESI, PIETER JANNINK AND WOUTER VELDHUIS (NL) studied architecture at the University of Delft and subsequently worked for the Physical Planning Office in Amsterdam. At the same time they operated their own practice: 'Must stedebouw-architectuurlabortorium' (urban development/architecture laboratory). Since one year they have been working fulltime for Must and work at various commissions in geared joint ventures, ranging from market place to European region.

PETER CALTHORPE AND MATTHEW TAECKER (USA) are from the firm 'Calthorpe Associates' in Berkeley near San Francisco. The firm is known for its innovative and pioneering work in redefining urban-planning models in the USA. Plans and advice for e.g. Sacramento and Salt Lake City elaborately examine the effects of light-rail systems in relation to building density, transport and environmental quality. Peter Calthorpe is co-founder of the Congress of New Urbanism, a group of architects and urban planners who wanted to react against the anonymous and anti-ecological way of building. He teaches at various international universities.

SJOERD CUSVELLER (NL) is an urban planner with his own practice: S@M Stedebouw-Architectuur-Management (Urban-architectural laboratory). He is also editor of the journal *De Blauwe Kamer*. He has numerous publications to his name, among which *Emmen revisited. Nieuw perspectief voor de naoorlogse wijken* (A new perspective for the post-war residential districts).

JOHN DAVIES (GB) is a landscape photographer. In black-and-white images he catches the vastness of the landscape, the changing lifestyles leaving traces in the landscape. In 1995 and 1996 in the series *Through fire and water: the river Taff* he followed the course of the river Taff which flows through Cardiff, where he lives.

AD VAN DENDEREN (NL) is a photographer and makes penetrating photojournalistic reports on, among other subjects, young people, asylum seekers and immigrants. Since 1973 his work is to be seen in photo exhibitions in the Netherlands and abroad. Reports by him regularly appear in the weekly paper *Vrij Nederland*.

WIJNANDA DEROO (NL) is a photographer and occasionally works under commission. From her interest in people and their environment she makes images of the natural as well as the artificial, of the intimate, personal as well as of anonymous worlds existing side by side. Her work is to be seen regularly in the Netherlands and abroad.

JÖRG DETTMAR, ULRIKE BEUTER, HARALD FRITZ AND SIMONE HASTENPFLUG (D) formed a special cooperation on the occasion of AIR-Zuidwaarts/Southbound. Until October 1999 Jörg Dettmar worked as a coordinator with the office of the 'International Bau-Ausstellung' (IBA) Emscher Park, which guided the transformation of the Ruhr region. On his invitation landscape architects Ulrike Beuter and Harald Fritz, of the practice Planergruppe Oberhausen, and Simone Hastenpflug, employee artists' projects at IBA, cooperated for the sixth AIR manifestation. Just as Dettmar, Fritz and Beuter are active in education, the judging of design contests and the realization of specialist publications.

ANNE-MIE DEVOLDER (B) was trained as an architect. She programmed the architecture debate at the Rotterdam Arts Council and among other things organized the AIR manifestations on the *Railway-tunnel line, nine concepts* and *Three Squares, six designs* in 1988 and *AIR-Alexander* in 1993. She has numerous publications on Rotterdam architecture and urban development to her name. At the moment she is director of the AIR Foundation and in that capacity organized *AIR-Zuidwaarts/Southbound*.

JOOST GROOTENS (NL) is a visual artist and (graphic) designer. He develops associative projects. Small observations can result in long stories. Places, objects or buildings are provided with their own, new layers of meaning. A (not realized) project of his was the project for the Albert Heijn supermarket in Kampen, where he proposed to print a line of poetry on each receipt.

HENK DE HAAN (NL) is a cultural anthropologist and attached to the Rural Sociology chair group at the WURC (Wageningen University Research Centre). A publication of his is *In the Shadow of the Tree, Kinship, Property and Inheritance among Farm Families*.

HENRIK HÅKANSSON (Z) is fascinated by specific phenomena in nature, which he imitates in a natural-artificial way. His contribution to the Biennale in Venice in 1997 consisted of a biotope for types of butterflies occurring in the city. At the moment he is doing research in the Amazon region.

HANS VAN HOUWELINGEN (NL) is especially interested in the public space of the city and its sociological aspects. In 1994 he realized a total design in the multicultural Utrecht district Amerhof for the layout of a square in the shape of a Persian carpet which ran on into the schoolyards of two primary schools. Along the edges of the carpet he placed 'western' lambs.

ARJAN KLOK, RUURD GIETEMA, EDZO BINDELS EN HENK HARTZEMA (NL) work for 'MAX.1 Architecture Urban Planning', 'Kees Christiaanse architects & planners' and 'West 8 landscape architects', respectively. Since their student years they form occasional collaborations for contests and study assignments. In their work all the themes of the physical planning of the Netherlands play a part. Notably, their design method consists of presenting a system of rules guaranteeing a strong, spatial organization and at the same time leaving room for great freedom. A number of projects are: *Weltevreden, Wadland* and *Grasstad*.

JAN KONINGS AND ESTER VAN DE WIEL (NL) are both designers and teamed up on the occasion of *AIR-Zuidwaarts/Southbound*. Konings, who is now one of the members of Schie 2.0, worked/participated in a lot of exhibitions and projects in the Netherlands and abroad, such as *Design, Art ou Industrie*, Le Carrousel de Louvre, Paris 1995, *Threshold: Design from the Netherlands*, Museum of Modern Art, New York 1996 and *Designprijs Rotterdam*, KunstHAL, Rotterdam 1997. Van de Wiel usually cooperates with other designers preferably active in a different discipline. Just as Konings she has worked/participated in a lot of projects, such as *Culture of the Dutch seaside resorts* IJmuiden 1997, *Visions & Tales* Eindhoven 1998, *Beach squares* Katwijk aan Zee 1998 and *Eindhoven 2000+* 1999. Apart from this, she contributed to a few recent publications: *FEC-City* (Vormgeversinstituut/Designers' Institute) 1998, *Stadsbeeld Eindhoven*, *Visions & Tales* (NAi Editors) 1999 and the publication and website *Coast on the Map* (Vormgeversinstituut)1999.

BIRTHE LEEMEIJER (NL) The aim of her work is to make the viewer look at the everyday environment in a different way and sometimes in a different light. For the project *Uitzicht* in Utrecht in 1997 she asked people about their favourite spots in the city. Her public could visit these places and listen to the stories belonging to them.

ERIC LUITEN (NL) is a landscape architect; for some years he had his own practice in Barcelona, where he also worked at projects in the Netherlands. At the moment he is education coordinator at the Academy of Architecture in Amsterdam and advises urban authorities on the structure of green spaces in the city.

BERTIEN VAN MANEN (NL) is a photographer and regularly spends longer periods abroad for her photoreports in order to build up a relationship with the subject of her photography. For instance, she lived and worked in Moscow and China for a few months, where she recorded everyday life in an almost anthropological manner.

FRITS PALMBOOM AND JAAP VAN DEN BOUT (NL) founded the practice 'Palmboom & Van den Bout, urban planners' in 1994. The practice gets its inspiration from the morphology of urban ensembles and landscape patterns. With the publication *Rotterdam, verstedelijkt landschap* in 1987 Frits Palmboom set his personal urban-planning course. Jaap van den Bout worked at the realization of the Rotterdam urban districts Zevenkamp, the Waterworks grounds and the Kop van Zuid.

MARK PIMLOTT (GB) was trained as an architect and collects stories and images of the changing public space. He writes about models of urbanization and spatial perception having a global validity. In 1997 he contributed to the project *De verborgen stad* in Middelburg, for which he made a description of a foreign square and asked people in Middelburg to find this square. They invariably managed to do so.

ARNOLD REIJNDORP (NL) studied architecture. He is an independent researcher and consultant in the field of urban planning and urban issues. Last year he published *Buitenwijk, stedelijkheid op afstand*. At the moment he is attached to the University of Berlin as a visiting professor.

FRANÇOIS ROCHE (F) has his own practice 'Roche, DSV & Sie.P.' in Paris. This practice does not exclusively consist of architects, but artists also contribute to the architecture. A much-discussed project is *House among Trees* in Compiégne, where the designers developed a sort of camouflage scenario. In the course of twenty years a transparent, sectional pile dwelling is gradually being wrapped up in trees. Growth and change of the seasons thus become integral parts of living.

SCHIE 2.0, TON MATTON AND LUCAS VERWEIJ (NL) investigate from the points of view of architecture, urban planning, town and country planning and industrial design how the world can be mapped differently over and over again so as to break out of set notions. In 1996 Lucas Verweij published *De nieuwe kaart van Nederland*, a map with an inventory of all the planned new construction and new green spaces in the Netherlands.

DIRK SIJMONS AND YTTJE FEDDES (NL) work for the practice 'H+N+S Landscape architects', founded in 1990 by Dirk Sijmons amongst others. It is a leading design and advisory firm which makes plans and executes research in the field of development and management of green spaces. The plans, focusing on the quality of the landscape, are marked by their austerity and unadorned character. Dirk Sijmons published his experiences and visions in the field of regional design in the book *(H+N+S)= Landschap* in 1998.

MARIEKE TIMMERMANS (NL) has worked for the practice 'B+B Stedebouw en Landschapsarchitectuur' since 1995. Her projects aim at executing landscape-architectural corrections in traditional urbanization schemes. Timmermans won awards with her plan for flexible housing on the IJ *(City Center Park)* and for her idea of dike improvement and house-building near Zaltbommel within the framework of the design manifestation *Waterwerk*.

HONORÉ δ'O (B) anticipates the existing space with his work and often literally fills it with objects and links. At the end of the exhibition *This is the show and the show is many things* in 1994 the visitors were allowed to take his work home. They became the owners of the work and were free to do with it as they pleased.

Persons involved

BOARD AIR FOUNDATION Adriaan van der Staay (chairman), Bert van Meggelen, Wytze Patijn, Nanny Peereboom (vice-chairman and secretary), Fred de Ruiter, Huub Wieleman (treasurer), Jaap Wolf.

BOARD OF SUPERVISION Robert de Haas (director Rotterdam Arts Council), Jan Laan (mayor of Nieuwegein), Joan Leemhuis-Stout (former Royal Commissioner for the Province of South Holland).

STAFF Anne-Mie Devolder (director), Andre Dekker (press and publicity), Willemien Ippel (project coordinator), Ilse Vandingenen (office manager), Mark van de Velde (general assistant) Chantal van der Zijl (assistant as regards content) and Henk Arnold (accounting), Myron Freeling (maintenance website), Aletta de Jong (artists' presentations), Iebèl Vlieg (press and publicity).

SECTION ARCHITECTURE ROTTERDAM ART FOUNDATION Ben van Berkel, Anne-Mie Devolder (policy assistant architecture), Willem Frijthoff (chairman), Maria Heiden, Bart Lootsma, Han Meyer, Maurice Nio, Frits Palmboom, Ed Taverne.

WORKING GROUP INITIAL MEMO Christine de Baan, Caroline Bos, Anne-Mie Devolder, Bart Lootsma (chairman), Maurice Nio, Arnold Reijndorp, Dirk Sijmons, Anna Vos, Enno Zuidema.

ADVISORY COMMISSION PROGRAMMING Christine de Baan (chairperson), Lex ter Braak, Jan Ilsink, Reyn van der Lugt, Eric Luiten, Arnold Reijndorp, Dingenus van de Vrie.

WORKING GROUP DESIGN COMMISSION Sjoerd Cusveller (final editing), Frank D'hondt, Ron Gast, Rob Groeneweg, Jan van 't Verlaat, San Verschuuren, Anne-Mie Devolder, Chantal van der Zijl

ADVISORS Frits Gierstbergen, Jeanne van Heeswijk, Arno van Roosmalen, Jayne Slot, Camiel van Winkel.

EDITORIAL COUNCIL DATAWOLK HOEKSCHE WAARD Christine de Baan, Suzanne Briegoos, Anne-Mie Devolder, Lara van Druten (chairperson), Jan Ilsink, Anne Nigten, Mathias Schwenck, Mark van de Velde, Piet Vollaard

EDITORIAL STAFF AIR-MAGAZINES Lex ter Braak, Anne-Mie Devolder (final editing), Willemien Ippel, Olof Koekebakker, Eric Luiten, Tracy Metz, Dieuwke van Ooij, Piet Vollaard, Chantal van der Zijl.

COMPOSITION ARCHITECTURE AND LANDSCAPE MAPS HOEKSCHE WAARD Ad Bogaerds, Mart Ros, Gert Vollaard, Chantal van der Zijl.

PROGRAMME COMMISSION DEBATES AND FINAL SYMPOSIUM Luuk Boelens, Anne-Mie Devolder(chairperson), Eric Luiten, Arnold Reijndorp, Tjerk Ruimschotel, Chantal van der Zijl.

EXHIBITION design: Kossman en De Jong; Production guidance: Roger Teunissen, Herman van Dongen (NAi); Composition: Xylos; Audiovisuals: Ineke Schwartz and Piet Oomes (direction), Kay Mastenbroek (producer Polderfilms), Jaap Verdenius (production leader), Vladas Naudzius (camera), Rogier Kappers (sound); Coordination artists' presentations: Aletta de Jong; Technique: Frank Pachen; Audiovisual technique: Kappelhof en Fermont.

DESIGNERS Edzo Bindels, Ruurd Gietema, Henk Hartzema, Arjan Klok (Benjamin Jacquemet, Erik Klok, Richard Lie, Hans Rattink,); Stefano Boeri (Gianandrea Barreca, Marijke Beek, Luca Bertolini, Angela Cortini, Maddalena De Ferrari, Isabella Inti, Marinus Kooiman, Giovanni La Varra, John Lonsdale, John Palmesino); Peter Calthorpe, Matthew Taecker (Harry Bidwell, Roger Hodges, David Katz, John Monynahan); Jörg Dettmar, Ulrike Beuter, Harald Fritz, Simone Hastenpflug; Frits Palmboom, Jaap van den Bout (Hans van Bommel, Michiel Bosman, Pieter de Koning, Monique Mooij, Machiel de Vries, Franz Ziegler, scale model: Made by Mistake); François Roche (Alexandre Boulin, Gilles Desévedavy, Stephanie Lavaux, François Perrin); Dirk Sijmons, Yttje Feddes (Lodewijk van Nieuwenhuijze, Ruut van Paridon); Marieke Timmermans (Jan Adegeest, Bureau B+B, Pepijn Godefroy, Paul de Graaf, Sanda Lenzholzer, Harmen van de Wal).

ANTHROPOLOGICAL RESEARCH Henk de Haan, Bertien Bos, Rens Huisman, Jenneke Juffer, Petra Klein, Bart van der Mark, Natasja Veen.

PHOTOGRAPHERS John Davies, Ad van Denderen, Wijnanda Deroo, Bertien van Manen.

VISUAL ARTISTS Honoré δ'O, Joost Grootens, Henrik Håkansson, Hans van Houwelingen, Birthe Leemeijer, Mark Pimlott, Het Observatorium (Geert van de Camp, Andre Dekker, Ruud Reutelingsperger) and Graigie Horschfield, Annabel Howland, Theo van Meerendonk, Arjo Roosendaal, Gerco de Ruiter, Els Snijder, Kees Touw, Eveline Visser.

GRAPHIC DESIGNERS Jan Konings/Ester van de Wiel, Schie 2.0 (Ton Matton/Lucas Verweij).

FILMERS Nathalie Alonso Casale, Jan Willem van Dam, Mart Dominicus, Jeroen Eisinga, Floris Paalman, Jos de Putter, Harm Smit, Froukje Tan invited by Albert Wulffers.

HOEKSCHE WAARD INITIATORS' GROUP Jo Kolf, Krijn Jan Provoost, Jan Robbemond, Mart Ros, Willy Spaan.

COMMENTATORS, OBSERVERS, SPEAKERS AND MODERATORS INTERNATIONAL CONFERENCE Cees Jan Asselbergs, Christine de Baan (moderator), Luuk Boelens, Stefano Boeri, Ineke Booden-Stoffelsen, Gerty Both, Rudolf van Broekhuizen, Robert Broesi, Henk de Bruijn, Hieke Compier, Sjoerd Cusveller, Adri Dietvorst, Heleen Grimberg, Adrie Groenenboom, Harry Groeneveld, Henk de Haan, Willem Koerse, Jo Kolf, Paul Kuypers, Gerard Litjens, Eric Luiten, Bert van Meggelen (moderator), Anne Nigten, Peter Overwater, Krijn Jan Provoost, Michelle Provoost, Mart Ros, Ruut Roth, Bernard Santen, Paul Shephaerd, Thomas Sieverts, John Urry, Yvonne Verhorst, San Verschuuren, Piet Vollaard, Vera Wijnker.

COMMENTATORS, OBSERVERS, PEOPLE INTERVIEWED AND MODERATORS DEBATES AND FINAL SYMPOSIUM René Boomkens, Roos Bosua, Hans van der Cammen, Jos Dekkers, Adriaan Geuze, Bert de Graaf, Jan de Graaf, Peter van der Gugten, Maarten Hajer, Carol Hol, Jan Ilsink, Taeke de Jong, Joost de Jong, Klaas Kerkstra, Jo Kolf, Eric Luiten, Winy Maas, Bert van Meggelen, Han Meyer, Jaap Modder, Jan Douwe van der Ploeg, Nico van der Pool, Krijn Jan Provoost, Rudy Rabbinge, Arnold Reijndorp, Gé Rooimans, Vincent van Rossem, Tjerk Ruimschotel, Mirjam Salet, Gert van der Slikke, Joost Schrijnen, Henk Wijnsma.

COOPERATING INSTITUTIONS Academy of Fine Arts, Rotterdam; Academy of Architecture, Rotterdam; Ad Ballonvaarten B.V., Breda; ANWB/VVV, Oud-Beijerland; ArchiCenter Rotterdam; ArchiNed, Rotterdam; AZ Kunstprojecten, Nieuw-Beijerland; CBK, Rotterdam; Citysafari, Rotterdam; gallery Delta, Rotterdam; gallery Cokkie Snoei, Rotterdam; gallery Liesbeth Lips, Rotterdam; Hoekschewaards Landschap, Oud-Beijerland; Nederlands Architectuurinstituut, Rotterdam; Nederlands Fotoinstituut, Rotterdam; Project Drecht towns, Dordrecht; Project Drecht riverbanks, Dordrecht; KUNSTGEBOUW, Rijswijk; MK Expositieruimte, Rotterdam; Museum Bijmans Van Beuningen, Rotterdam; Project Drechtsteden, Dordrecht; Project Drechtoevers, Dordrecht; Ram Foundation, Rotterdam; Rotterdamse Schouwburg, Salle de Bains, Rotterdam; Foundation Kunstzinnige Vorming, Rotterdam; Foundation DE STAD, Dordrecht;Technical University, faculty of Architecture, Delft; V2_Organisatie, Rotterdam; Witte de With, Rotterdam; WURC, Wageningen.

AIR-ZUIDWAARTS/SOUTHWARD WAS FINANCIALLY SUPPORTED BY Anjerfonds, Rotterdam; **The Architecture platform VROM (Ministry of Housing, Physical Planning and Environment, OC&W (Ministry of Education, Science and Cultural Affairs), V&W (Ministry of Health, Welfare and Sports), The Hague; Bouwfonds Cultuurfonds, Hoevelaken**; Cultural fund of the Bank Nederlandse Gemeenten, Den Haag; DURA Bouw BV, Rotterdam; ECT (Europe Combined Terminals), Rotterdam; EFL foundation, The Hague; **Fortis Investments, Utrecht; Municipality of Rotterdam**; Municipality of Binnenmaas; Municipality of Cromstrijen; Municipality of 's-Gravendeel; Municipality of Korendijk; Municipality of Oud-Beijerland; Municipality of Strijen; Harbourshed, Rotterdam; Port Authority Moerdijk; Kolpron, Rotterdam; Vereniging Natuurmonumenten, 's-Gravenland; Ministry of VROM, The Hague; **Mondriaan Foundation, Amsterdam**; Ontwikkelingsbedrijf Rotterdam; **Prins Bernard Fund, Amsterdam**; Project Drechtsteden, Dordrecht; Projectbureau Kop van Zuid, Rotterdam; **Proper Stok Woningen BV, Rotterdam; Province of South Holland, The Hague; Rotterdam Arts Council**; City region, Rotterdam; Stichting Volkskracht, Rotterdam; **Stimulation Fund for Architecture, Rotterdam; TRS Ontwikkelingsgroep BV, Rotterdam; VSB Fund, Utrecht.**

colophon

AIR-ZUIDWAARTS / SOUTHBOUND

PUBLICATION
© 2000 AIR FOUNDATION
POSTHOORNSTRAAT 12A
3011 WE ROTTERDAM
& THOTH PUBLISHERS
PRINS HENDRIKLAAN 13
1404 AS BUSSUM
THE NETHERLANDS

COMMISSION
THIS PUBLICATION IS
MADE IN COMMISSION
OF THE GOVERNMENT
ARCHITECT

EDITORS
ANNE-MIE DEVOLDER
WILLEMIEN IPPEL
CHANTAL VAN DER ZIJL

TRANSLATION
JOHN KIRKPATRICK
WENDY VAN OS
PHILIP PETERS
ELLA PLOEGER
ULRICA VRIJMAN

DESIGN
LIJN 5
CONCEPT DESIGN MANAGEMENT
ROTTERDAM

PRINT
DRUKKERIJ MART.SPRUIJT
AMSTERDAM

BINDING
EPPING
WOERDEN

All rights reserved. No part of this publication may be reproduced or transmitted in any form or by any means, electronic or mechanical, including photocopying, recording or any information storage and retrieval system, without permission in writing from the AIR Foundation, Posthoornstraat 12a, 3011 WE Rotterdam and THOTH Publishers, Prins Hendriklaan 13, 1404 AS Bussum, the Netherlands.

ISBN 90 6868 241 5

Three Architecture and Landscape maps with bicycle and walkingroutes are available with the AIR Foundation (0031 (0)10- 2809700)